The Cycle of the Year:
Traditional Predictive Astrology

by

Charles Obert

Foreword by

Dr. Benjamin N. Dykes, Ph. D

Almuten Press

2018

Published and printed in the United States of America

By Almuten Press

3507 Taylor Street NE, Minneapolis, MN 55418

http://studentofastrology.com

©2018 by Charles Obert

All rights reserved. No part of this publication may be reproduced, stored in or introduced into a retrieval system, or transmitted, in any form or by any means (electronic, mechanical, photocopying, recording or otherwise), without the prior written permission of both the copyright owner and the above publisher of this book.

The scanning, uploading, and distribution of this book via the Internet or via any other means without the permission of the publisher is illegal and punishable by law. Please purchase only authorized electronic editions and do not participate in or encourage electronic piracy of copyrighted materials. Your support of the author's rights is appreciated.

ISBN-13: 978-0-9864187-2-3

A PDF version of this book is available for purchase at the author's website,

https://studentofastrology.com

Also by Charles Obert

Introduction to Traditional Natal Astrology: A Complete Working Guide for Modern Astrologers (2015)

Using Dignities in Astrology (2018)

(Both of these books are available in print through standard retail outlets, and in PDF form at the website, https://studentofastrology.com)

This book is dedicated to my students at Kepler College, with a special thank you to Rebecca Bihr and Denise Menton for taking the time to thoroughly read and review previous versions of this book.

Table of Contents

Foreword..9

Introduction..11

    Using this Book with Morinus..12

    A Note on House Systems..12

Symbolic Directions and Time Lords..13

    Symbolic Directions..13

    Returns..14

    Time Lords..15

General Interpretive Principles..16

    Evaluating Dignity and Debility..18

The Cycle of the Year - Overview...21

Profections..23

Solar Returns..29

    Solar Return with Profection - Charles Obert....................................32

Primary Directions...36

    Primary Directions - The Basics..36

    Directing Other Points..38

    Directing Through the Bounds...39

    How Directing Through the Bounds Works.......................................43

    Significant Points to Direct...45

    How to Read the Directions Listings..46

    Start with the Ascendant..47

    Jimi Hendrix...50

    Anita Bryant...53

    Herman Melville...56

    Harry Belafonte..59

Transits..62

    LOY and Transits - Charles Obert..63

Yearly Solar Return Directions..**67**

    Franklin D Roosevelt..71

    Margaret Thatcher..80

Preparing for a Client Reading..**89**

Tying it All Together - Examples..**95**

    Marilyn Monroe..96

    The Las Vegas Shooting, October 1, 2017..100

    Napoleon Bonaparte..109

    The Gods Smile on Me - Charles Obert..119

    Maya Angelou..124

Conclusions and Questions..**137**

Where to Go from Here..**143**

Table of Essential Dignities..**145**

Using the Morinus Astrology Program..**147**

Foreword

Although the traditional revival in astrology has been underway for many years, it takes time for people to properly digest, understand, and practice new techniques. This is especially so when new vocabulary and concepts are combined in new ways. Most people have heard of "directions," but what about profections or distributions? Likewise, we learn about things like "exaltation," but what does it really mean? We need solid, clear training to help us navigate the old texts, which can be unfamiliar.

In *The Cycle of the Year*, my friend and colleague Charlie Obert is doing a great service to students of astrology and the traditional revival in particular. The traditional approach to prediction not only included a number of techniques not widely known today, but combined them in special ways to include both symbolic and real-time motions. The "cycle" or "revolution" of the year refers not just to solar revolutions (solar returns), but all of these techniques taken together and revisited on an annual basis.

Charlie begins by providing a solid but easy overview of key interpretive concepts, especially the idea of "time lords," and explaining that these techniques combine both symbolic time and motion, with real-time motion (such as transits); we could even say that solar revolutions bridge the gap between them, because a solar revolution is a set of transits at a symbolically important time (a year). Further chapters use numerous natal charts to explain and illustrate transits, profections, primary directions, the fuller technique for directions called "distributions," solar revolutions, and then directions of the solar revolution Ascendant.

Charlie's book is also valuable because a number of nativities are addressed more than once, with multiple techniques. And happily for the student, he explains how to program and use the free *Morinus* astrology program. Finally, he includes advice on what to prepare for client consultations when you use these techniques.

I know that you will appreciate Charlie's straightforward approach to training people in these powerful techniques, and your astrology will improve as a result!

Benjamin Dykes

June, 2018

Introduction

This book is the third in a series, designed to introduce the concepts and techniques of traditional Western astrology to a wider audience, including practicing modern astrologers.

This volume covers a suite of predictive techniques known as the Cycle or Turning of the Year. It is the most common combination of predictive techniques that was developed and widely carried forward throughout the traditional astrology period.

My work with these techniques started with a study group on traditional astrology that I led here in Minneapolis for around 3 years. The regular members included my friend and teacher, Dr. Benjamin Dykes, Ph. D., the fine traditional astrologer Estelle Daniels, and the (mostly) modern astrologers, Shawn Nygaard and Madeline Youngstrom. I learned a great deal from all of them.

Further material on directions came from a series of sessions I did with Ben Dykes, working with him on some concepts he was developing. The subject of these sessions was the best method of primary directions to use in moving through the minor dignity known as bounds or terms.

Prior to this work, I had not found primary directions to be all that terribly useful. Centering directions on moving through the bounds, and combining them with profections and solar returns, is what made the technique light up for me. Building on the work of Ben Dykes I have found enough fruitful results in my own research that I want to share them with the astrology community, so that this neglected timing technique can get the attention and use that it deserves.

I will be assuming a basic knowledge of astrology throughout this book. If you have a general background in modern astrology you should be able to follow along, and I will be explaining terms and concepts as I present them.

In an appendix at the back of the book there are suggestions for good sources of information on traditional astrology in general, and on the specific techniques covered in this book.

My purpose in this book is not to be comprehensive, but to lay out a usable working framework of techniques combined with general interpretive principles. Given this framework and background, the wealth of further details in the many traditional texts available can be fruitfully studied and integrated. The book will focus very heavily on examples showing how the predictive techniques manifest in actual events.

Along with covering the entire cycle of the year, the second major purpose of this book is to recover the forgotten principle that primary directions is intended to be a time lord system, one that deals with spans of time rather than primarily pinpointing specific event times.

The core techniques I am using here are useful to both traditional and modern astrologers. Hopefully this will help to inspire more work with these techniques by a variety of schools.

Using this Book with Morinus

There is a very good free astrology program available named Morinus, which can be used to generate the necessary charts and listings to work with the full cycle of the year. The program includes the natal chart, profections and solar returns. It also includes the primary directions to use with the bounds, and the yearly direction of the solar return ascendant around the wheel in one year.

The program runs on all main computer operating systems - Windows, Mac and Linux.

I have full instructions for downloading and using Morinus in a separate chapter at the end of this book.

As you read through the book I encourage you to draw up the charts and listings and apply them to your own life. That will give you a very good feel for how the techniques work, as you watch them come alive in context.

A Note on House Systems

The predictive techniques covered in this book can be used with any house system. With the possible exception of profections, the techniques apply equally well. I discuss issues with profections and quadrant house systems in the chapter on that topic.

All chart examples in this book use whole sign houses, which is my preferred system.

Symbolic Directions and Time Lords

Throughout the history of astrology there have developed many different ways of moving a chart forward in time for predictive purposes. The most obvious one, transits, works with the actual location of the planets during a given time period or moment in time.

Transits work for prediction - but they don't always work consistently. Working with transits by themselves there is no good, reliable way of figuring out which transits will be important, and which will come and go without any particularly significant event. (I have seen modern astrologers argue that every transit has a significant effect or event, but that sometimes the effect is internal so that we can't visibly see it. For me this begs the question. To say that all transits are significant, but sometimes we don't perceive what that significance is, renders the concept of significance meaningless.)

For astrology to be really useful there needs to be some way of figuring out when significant events are likely to happen. There are many different ways of doing this, and this book will be using a combination of them that is the most commonly found throughout the tradition.

Before we look at the specific systems, we need to consider the concept of symbolic directions.

Symbolic Directions

Directions are based on taking a defined symbolic way of moving a chart forward, and equating it to a period of time.

Let x = y. Let this particular movement in the chart equate to this particular period of time.

There are many, many different systems for doing this.

The most basic system, the grand-daddy of them all, is called primary directions, and is based on the daily movement of the circle of the zodiac as it rises up above the horizon at the Ascendant. Using the Ascendant, primary directions takes the distance that the zodiac moves past the Ascendant in 1/360th of a day, which is 4 minutes of clock time, and lets that movement symbolically equal one year of life.

Another very common system, secondary directions, takes the distance that a planet moves through the zodiac in one day, and defines that as equal to one year of life. Planets all move through the zodiac at different rates, so each planet has its own rate of secondary direction.

Solar arc, which is a derivative of secondary directions, moves all of the planets and points in the chart the same distance that the Sun moves. In solar arc the distance the Sun moves in 1 day equates to one year of life. In secondary directions each planet has its own unique motion, and in solar arc every planet is moved the same distance as the Sun.

The system of profections, which is very widely used in traditional astrology, works by defining a movement of one zodiac sign as equal to one year of life. It is very simple, and very effective, and is a central part of the predictive system we will be using in this book.

The important point to realize is that every one of these systems is based on a strictly symbolic equation. There is absolutely nothing which says that four minutes of movement of the Ascendant relative to the zodiac should equal a year, or that movement of one sign should equal a year. For this reason I do not think you can argue that primary directions are in any way more "real" than secondary directions, or that either of those are any less symbolic or arbitrary than the equation of one sign per year in profections.

There are many, many more systems of symbolic direction that have been used throughout the history of astrology. The British astrologer Charles E O Carter has a very fine book on the subject that is well worth reading and pondering. The fact that so many different systems of symbolic direction work so very well is one of the amazing and mind-boggling things about astrology. It is very well worth meditating on what the fact of symbolic directions working might tell us about the nature of the universe. This is far beyond any sort of correlations that can be explained by a simple scientific cause and effect model.

Strictly speaking the only non-symbolic way of moving a chart forward is using transits, which is mapping the actual position of the planets at a given moment in time, sometimes stand-alone, sometimes combined with another chart like a natal chart. All other systems - primary directions, secondary directions, solar arc directions, minor and tertiary progressions, profections, and so on - are symbolic, and no one of them can claim to be any more or less "real" than any other.

Returns

Astrology also gives great significance to the moment in time when a planet or angle returns to exactly the same point that it occupies in the natal chart. These are called returns.

The most basic, and most important, is the solar return or birthday chart. The return is calculated for the time each year when the Sun returns to exactly its natal position. The position of the planets at the time of the solar return determine how the events of the coming year will go. Since solar returns happen once a year, the return chart is in effect for a year. Solar returns have been a cornerstone of predictive astrology since its beginning, and it is a core technique in the system we are using.

Every planet has its own cycle of return charts, and all can be used for predictive purposes. The Saturn return is probably the most important of the other planetary returns, but all of them are used.

Both return charts, and the many different systems of symbolic direction, are designed to work with a concept that goes back to our Hellenistic Western roots - the concept of time lords.

Time Lords

In traditional astrology the different ways of dividing up time mark periods where different planets become active and take charge of the person's life. These are called time lord systems.

In time lord systems the planets take turns running things in a particular area of a person's life for a particular period.

There is an important concept here that is quite a bit different from how modern astrologers ordinarily think about transits.

The time lord direction systems are not about individual points in time, they are about extended periods of time. This is the key to using primary directions, profections, solar returns, and other time lord systems.

Primary directions, also known as distribution or circumambulation through the bounds, is one of the most important and widely used throughout the tradition until modern times. It works with the minor dignity of term or bound. The ruler of the bound is the time lord responsible for that period, and we look at the position and condition of that planet to see how that period will work out. We will be going into this system in great detail. Again, remember - these directions are about periods of time, not individual events.

There are also other time lord systems in traditional astrology. The system of aphesis, also known as zodiacal releasing, is another time lord system which has recently been re-discovered, and which has become more widely known from the teaching work of the modern Hellenistic astrologer Chris Brennan.

Profections are another time lord system that takes the symbolic movement of one zodiac sign to equal one year. The ruler of the zodiac sign the profection comes to is the Lord of the Year, and we look to that planet's position and condition. Yearly profections are one of the major techniques in the cycle of the year we are using in this book.

In a traditional context, solar returns can also be understood as a time lord technique, since they are activated and in authority for that year of the person's life.

The cycle of the year, the predictive group of techniques we are using in this book, take a nested group of these time lord systems to determine how a period of time will work out.

Before we look at those systems we need to review the general interpretive principles that are used with all of them.

General Interpretive Principles

There are a lot of very specific rules and examples found throughout the astrology tradition on using the prediction systems. What I want to cover here are some basic principles that provide a framework for understanding and organizing the details of the tradition. Given these principles you have a way to approach and study the wealth of detailed rules and examples in the traditional source material.

These are the main organizing principles for working with predictive systems.

1) **Evaluating condition** of the planets and points in the chart is at the very heart of traditional astrology. Each of the planets is weighed in terms of how balanced or unbalanced, how helpful or harmful, how strong or weak, how prominent or hidden its expression is likely to be. Learning the various rules for evaluating condition is the core of learning traditional astrology. I will be using basic evaluative principles in the examples, and explaining them as I go along.

2) **Fulfilling the promise of the natal.** All predictive techniques start with, refer to and end with the natal chart. The expression of a planet in a timed technique like directions or a solar return will always be shaped by its location and condition in the natal chart. If the potential is not in the natal it will not be fulfilled in the direction. If you have a very strong Jupiter in a return chart, and Jupiter in the natal chart is weak and debilitated, then the expression in the return will be middling at best. If you have a debilitated planet in a return chart that is very strong and balanced in the natal, its expression will be hindered that year, but it will not be as harmful as it could be if it were also in bad shape in the natal. By contrast, a planet that is very strong in both the natal and return charts will likely be very strong and positive in expression that year. *Any planet which is activated in any of the predictive systems will express in terms of its natal condition and potential*.

3) **Predicting backward to predict forward** - To evaluate how a planet will express as a time lord, check if there are any previous periods in the person's life where that same planet was active. If you get a sense of what happened in the previous period, and what kind of feel it had, it is likely that the current period with that same planet as time lord will have the same qualities. This applies to all time lord techniques including directions, solar returns, and profections, as well as repeated transits.

As an example of predicting backward, I usually draw up a solar return for the previous year for a client, and then have some dialog on how the previous year has been for the client based on that return chart. This helps me to discuss the current year, and I builds credibility with the client. I discuss predicting backward further in the chapter on preparing for a client reading.

4) **Congruence or Alignment** - For a significant event, you are looking for having the different systems line up. When the potential of the natal is matched by the other levels then you have the potential for powerful action for good or ill. The more the different levels line up, the more significant the event. **Correlation** is another good word for the same principle - the more correlations there are pointing to the same kind of event, the more likely there will be a significant event. You will see this at work in the examples later in the book. This principle is actually an extension of the second principle, fulfilling the promise of the natal. Another, simple way to say it - when the stars all line up, big things happen. (*When the Moon is in the seventh house, and Jupiter aligns with Mars...*)

5) **Questions providing focus** - This is a general principle for any interpretation in astrology, and it is particularly important when dealing with the overwhelming amount of data involved in coordinating multiple timing and prediction techniques. ***Astrology is designed to answer questions***. Clients come to a consultation with an agenda, a need, a question that needs answering. That question provides the focus and frame for interpreting the timing data.

The language of astrology is symbolic and multi-valent, having a wealth of different meanings. Astrology charts do not mean anything in general; they only take on meaning within the context of a question.

The question provides the frame and filter telling you what to look for in the chart data. It helps you pick out what is important. Given that frame, my experience is that the astrology data organizes itself around that question, and provides a coherent answer.

I discuss this principle in much greater length in the chapter on preparing for a client session.

Evaluating Dignity and Debility

The heart of traditional astrology is this process of evaluating strength and weakness, dignity and debility. This is a brief summary of the main conditions and vocabulary used. (Please see my book, *Using Dignities In Astrology*, for an extended treatment of these concepts.)

Dignity - A planet having a dignity has an assigned role and responsibility. Dignity strengthens a planet, gives it more influence and makes it more at home.

Debility - The opposite of dignity. A debilitated planet is weakened in some way. It can be off balance, not at home or in an uncongenial environment.

Benefic - Helpful. Jupiter and Venus are called benefic because their action is usually moderate, comfortable and helpful. We usually enjoy benefics, and they feel good.

Malefic - Harmful. Mars and Saturn are called malefic because their action is usually immoderate and extreme. The malefics can limit, injure, oppose or destroy. Malefics are usually not considered to be enjoyable. A Saturn return may end up being a useful and positive time, but not that many people would describe it as fun.

Sect - This divides chart and planets into day and night, or diurnal and nocturnal. A day chart has the Sun above the horizon, and with night it is below. The day planets are Sun, Jupiter and Saturn. The night planets are Moon, Venus and Mars. Mercury varies - when rising before the Sun at an earlier degree he is diurnal, and after the Sun at a later degree is nocturnal. Planets are more at home if the sect of the chart matches their sect. The Sun and Jupiter are happier and more helpful in day charts, while the Moon and Venus are more at home and effective in night charts. Similarly, the day planet Saturn is more crabby and harmful at night, and the night planet Mars is more irritable and hurtful during the day.

Essential Dignities are based on zodiac position, so they are the same for everyone on the planet at a given point in time. There are five essential dignities, two considered major and three considered minor. There is a table of essential dignities at end of book.

Each of the major dignities has a corresponding detriment at the sign opposite.

The Major Dignities are as follows:

Rulership is the strongest dignity. The ruler of a sign is its controller, manager, owner. The ruler is the main planet responsible for the affairs of a sign.

Detriment happens when a planet is in the sign opposite to one it rules. A planet in detriment is out of its home in an unfriendly environment. It is off balanced, uncomfortable and stressed. A planet in detriment can be a loner or an outsider working for change, so detriment can be turned to advantage.

Exaltation is the other major dignity. An exalted planet is valued, honored, listened to and given respect. I could also connote arrogance or a high opinion of oneself.

Fall is the opposite of exaltation. A planet in fall is not valued, not honored, ignored and not given respect. Often planets in fall work extra hard to over-compensate for this lack of respect and attention.

The minor Dignities are as follows:

Triplicity is a group or tribe dignity. There are three planets that have triplicity in each of the four elements. a planet in triplicity is at home in its group and has general support and good fortune from its tribe or extended family.

Term or Bound is featured in the traditional use of primary directions. A planet with dignity by term is competent and functional, and it is in charge of how things are implemented. That is why the technique of directing through the bounds is so important.

Face is a very minor dignity, with very little power and no authority. Face usually concerns appearance, ornament, the image or mask that a planet presents to the world.

In terms of their strength the dignities are additive. A planet with two minor dignities is considered equal in strength to having one major dignity.

Peregrine is the condition of a planet with no essential dignity. The word means homeless or wanderer, someone out on the street with no accepted place. Peregrine planets rely heavily on the condition of their rulers, the planets having dignity over it, for how well they function. A peregrine planet with rulers in good condition is greatly supported, and a peregrine planet with weak or harmful rulers gets no support from its environment.

The remaining concepts have to do with how the planets interact with each other and with their position relative to the angles and houses.

Reception is a very important principle. It concerns how the planets interact and relate to each other in terms of their dignity with each other.

Reception is the relationship of ruler to ruled. Venus in Aries is received by Mars in its rulership - Mars manages or rules Venus, and is also responsible for treating Venus as well as it can given its own condition. Reception also applies to the other dignities. That same Venus in Aries is received by the Sun in its exaltation, and by its three triplicity rulers, Sun, Jupiter and Saturn.

Mutual Reception is the beneficial condition where each of two planets receives the other into one of its dignities. Venus in Aquarius and Saturn in Libra are each in the sign the other rules. Mixed reception, where the planets are received in different dignities, are also valid. For instance Saturn in Aries and the Sun in Capricorn have a mixed mutual reception from exaltation to rulership, and this greatly enhances their relationship.

Reception in a minor dignity is not as strong, but is definitely preferable to no reception. Two planets having mutual reception in two minor dignities is considered equivalent to major mutual reception.

Planets with reception are more inclined to work with each other, and planets without reception lack good will and responsibility towards each other.

Aversion concerns relationship and communication. The main Ptolemaic aspects are the conjunction, sextile, square, trine, opposition, in which planets can see each other and have communication. Aspects are by whole sign in the earliest Western astrology - a planet anywhere in Aries is considered trine to a planet anywhere in Leo. Planets which do not have a whole sign aspect to each other are called averse which means "turned away". Planets in aversion can't see each other. They are out of touch, and there is a lack of control and communication.

Combustion is a debility. Being too close to the Sun is the worst thing that can happen to a planet. Any planet within roughly 8 degrees of the Sun or less is called combust, meaning burnt up. A combust planet loses all its strength. There is a transition condition - planet that is between 8 and 17 degrees from the Sun is under the rays, also called under the beams, which weakens, inhibits and hides its action. Combustion or under the rays is considered much worse when a planet is approaching conjunction than when it is separating. The effect of combustion is strongly influenced by the dignities of the Sun and the other planet, and by any reception between them.

Cazimi is a special case where a planet is within 17 minutes of the Sun, at the heart of the Sun. Instead of being weakened, a planet cazimi is greatly strengthened. It is the king's favorite and sitting right on the king's lap on his throne. (17 minutes is the most commonly used orb for a planet being cazimi, but there are some traditional texts that use an orb as large as one degree.)

Angularity is the measure of the strength of a planet relative to its proximity to one of the four angles. Planets close to an angle are angular and considered very strong and prominent, visible and active in the world. The next house over is called succedent and is not as strong. The weakest condition is called cadent which means "falling away". A cadent planet is furthest from the angle and is very weak. Cadency can also indicate action turned inward.

Retrograde describes a planet moving backwards in the zodiac. Retrograde is moving against the grain and is generally considered a debility. It weakens, delays and impedes action. A retrograde planet can be stubborn or ornery, or it can be rebellious. Like all of the other conditions here, a retrograde condition is greatly influenced by how it combines with the other dignities and debilities. A retrograde planet that is otherwise dignified can be quite strong.

The Cycle of the Year - Overview

The group of time lord systems that I am presenting in this book is by far the most commonly used in the history of traditional Western astrology.

This system has its roots at the core of our Western astrology. It is found in Dorotheus in his landmark work, *Carmen Astrologicum*, which is arguably the single most influential text in the later development of astrology. The core principles are also found in Ptolemy's *Tetrabiblos,* in Vettius Valens and other influential Hellenistic astrologers.

The system was carried forward and developed further throughout the Persian and Arabic periods of astrology, and its fullest development is probably in the work of the Arabic Astrologers, notably Masha'Allah and Abu Mashar. In that setting it is known as the Cycle or Turning of the Year, referring to the time of the solar return that marks the start of a cycle, and is a suite of predictive techniques to be done annually.

The system is also found in Bonatti, and in William Lilly. Book three of Lilly's *Christian Astrology* is based on this system and includes an extensive series of chart examples showing how it plays out through the years in a single person's life.

The system forms an interlocking series of predictive techniques covering different periods of time. The following pyramid diagram gives a schematic idea of the basic techniques and how they build on each other, with the lower levels providing a context for the higher.

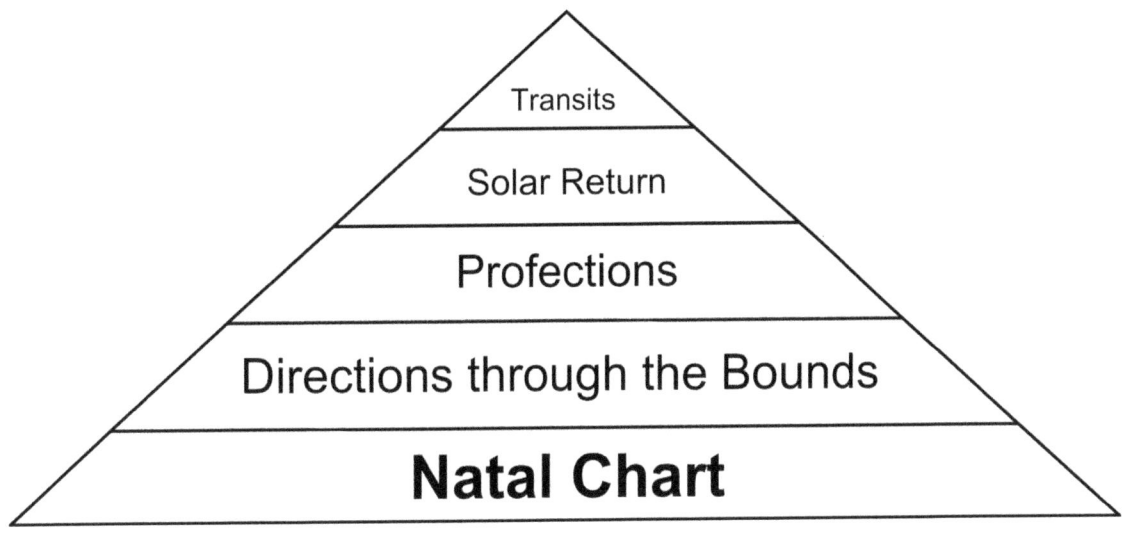

Starting at the bottom of the pyramid, the most important chart is the natal, the radix or root chart in effect for entire lifetime. You can think of it as a time lord chart where the span of jurisdiction of the time lords covers the entire life.

Next is the system of primary directions through the dignity of bounds. This divides the life into periods of different length, that can span months or years. The time lords here work in the context of the natal chart.

Next comes profections, an annual form of direction that is primarily used to determine the Lord of the Year who is featured in all of the charts for that year.

Within that context comes solar returns, abbreviated as SR throughout this book. This is also an annual system, where the configuration at the time of the Sun's exact return to its natal position sets the theme for the coming year.

Transits are last in importance, and they function within the context of all of the other systems combined.

We will now examine each of the predictive levels in turn. When you are learning time techniques, it is easiest to start with profections, and look at how they interact with the solar return.

Profections

Profections are a simple symbolic technique for moving a chart forward in time. With profections the equation is that one zodiac sign equals one year of life. For instance, if at birth an Ascendant is at 17 Sagittarius, on the first birthday the profected Ascendant moves to 17 Capricorn. On the second birthday it is at 17 Aquarius, and so on through the signs, until at age 12 the profected Ascendant returns again to its birth location at 17 Sagittarius and the cycle begins again.

In Hellenistic astrology, which works with houses primarily by whole sign, the profected movement is one sign at a time, and the entire sign is activated. In later traditional astrology, where quadrant houses are used, you will often see profection as taking place in 30 degree increments, which means that the profected sign can change in the middle of a solar year. Lilly describes the system in this form, but in his examples he effectively takes the location of the profected Ascendant as applying to the whole year and does not break it down further than that.

I primarily use whole sign houses in my work, and profections as a system are primarily designed to be used with whole sign houses.

If you think of the cycle going around the chart in multiples of 12, profections are quite easy to figure out. The profected cycle returns to the first house for all numbers divisible by 12 - 0 or birth, 12, 24, 36, 48 and so on. The second house gets numbers divisible by 12 plus one - 13, 25, 35 etc. The 7th house years are divisible by 6, and the 4th and 10th house years (in whole sign) are divisible by 3.

Take a person's age, divide by 12, take the remainder and add one to it, and that will give you the profected house of the year. For example, age 42 is 6 more than 36 so the profected house of the year is the seventh. Alternately, you could take the number of the house and subtract one from it. First house gets the birth year, second house gets first birthday, house 3 gets birthday 2. Age 12 (or zero) gets the first house again.

On the next page we have some chart illustrations that demonstrate the yearly movement.

Here is the birth chart of Jimi Hendrix, followed by the profected charts for his first, second and third birthday.

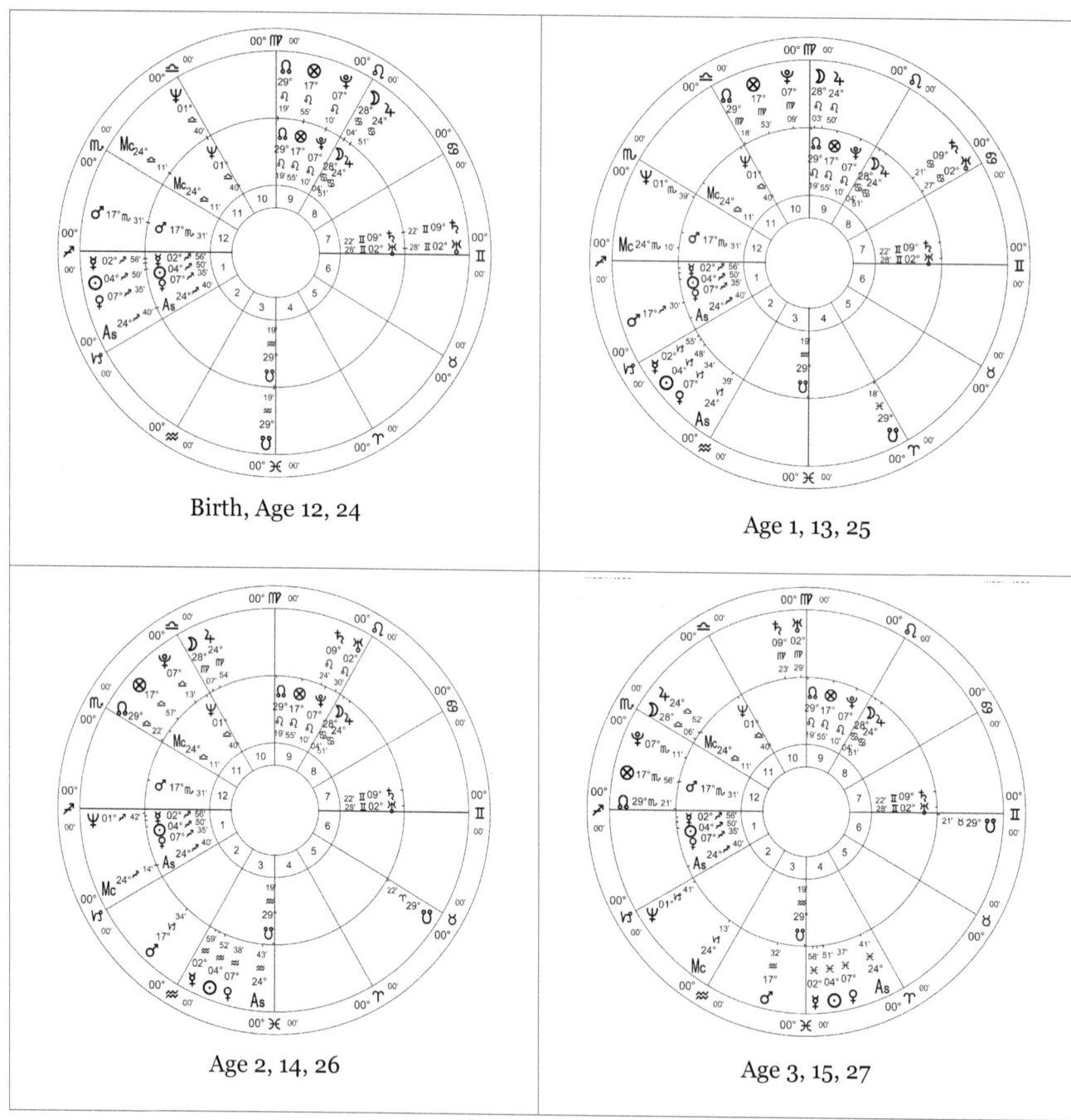

You can watch the chart rotate. When you put the profected chart in a bi-wheel with the natal you will watch the profected Ascendant and other planets move forward relative to the natal chart one sign at a time per year. At age one the Ascendant is in house two, at age two in house three, and so on.

Using Profections

The simplest way to use this technique, and by far the most common and basic, is to profect just the one point, the Ascendant, moving it forward one sign or 30 degrees in a year. The ruler of the sign of the profected Ascendant would be considered the profected Lord Of the Year, which I will refer to as LOY. That planet is particularly important for that year relative to its natal house and condition, and to its location and condition in the solar return for that year.

The profected chart is usually used in conjunction with the solar return, and the profected LOY is considered the most important planet in the SR. The profected sign and its house location in the SR also takes on increased importance. This profected sign is featured in a technique for directing the SR Ascendant all the way around the chart in a single year for finding peak times of activity, a technique we will explore in a later chapter.

On the next page is the natal chart of Napoleon Bonaparte with the profected chart for the year he was appointed consul for life.

Napoleon was born in 1769 and this is the profected chart for age 33, which moves the profection to the natal tenth house. That sign (Leo) is activated, the ruler of the sign (Sun) is Lord of the year, and the other planets in that house (Sun, Mercury) are also activated.

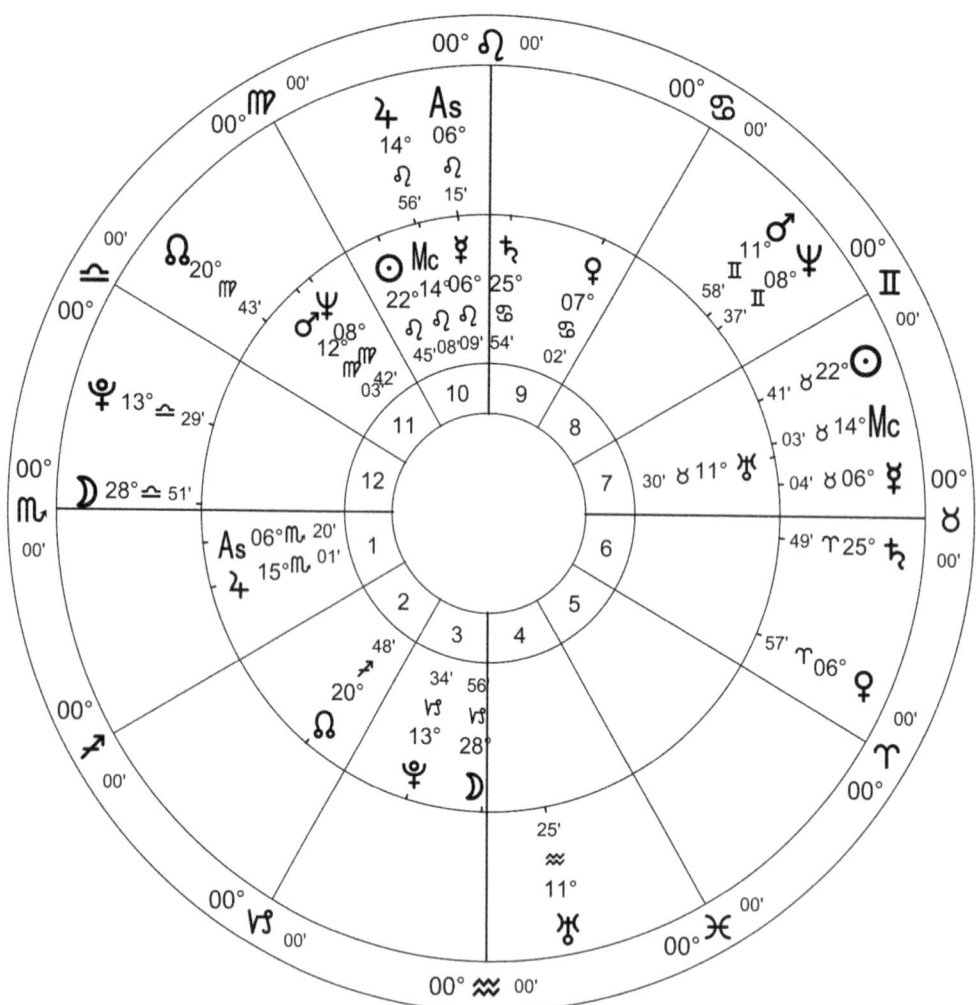

What is Important - What is Activated

Along with the Lord of the Year or LOY, there are other areas to consider being activated by the profected movement of the Ascendant to a new sign

The sign of profection itself is activated in both the natal chart and the solar return (SR). The house location of that sign in natal and SR are important, and transits or directions through that sign are worth noting.

In a supplementary way the signs are activated in what are called the stakes to profected sign. These are the signs in opposition or square. These are the signs of the same mode as the profected sign - so, for instance, when the fixed sign Leo is active, all of the other fixed signs are also activated. These are not primary, but they are worth paying attention to.

We mentioned that the Lord or ruler of the profected sign is primary in importance.

In addition, any planets in the profected sign in the natal chart are also activated. There is some difference in emphasis in traditional texts as to which planet(s) are more important, the sign ruler or planets in the sign. I find both to be important I usually start with the sign ruler, as that is always important since there will often be cases where there is no planet residing in the sign.

Very important - **note that only the traditional seven planets are eligible to be activated as time lords in this system**. While I do pay attention to any outer planets that reside in the profected sign, I do not give them the same emphasis or the same importance.

Along with the time lord, any other signs and houses that are ruled by that time lord are worth paying attention to.

Profections and Angles

The angularity of the house profected to in the natal has significance. In general, profections that fall on one of the angular houses - one, four, seven and ten - have more strength and sometimes more importance since they activate the natal angles. Profections to cadent houses can connote a relative lack of force or of activity in the world since cadent houses are considered weak. This does not seem to be as important or powerful as the condition of the LOY sign ruler, or of any planets in this house.

Angularity also makes a difference relative to the solar return chart. Having the profected sign of the year fall on one of the SR angles, especially the Ascendant or Midheaven, definitely increases its importance.

Profections with Quadrant House Systems

The system of profections is designed to work with whole sign houses, where movement of one sign equals movement of one house per year. Using profections with quadrant houses, where the houses are not all the same size and some signs span multiple house cusps, can create some problems.

The most common way to do profections with quadrant houses in the traditional literature is to move the profected Ascendant 30 degrees per year. Depending on the particular chart, this could mean that the profection falls in the same house two years running, and some houses will be completely skipped. To get around that problem, if you take the profected movement as applying to one house per year, then some signs and rulers can be completely skipped, and other rulers can stay LOY two years running.

Some traditional sources describe moving the Ascendant degree-wise through the year, so that it changes signs in the middle of the year. Theoretically this means that the profected Lord of the Year changes at that point. From what I have seen, even those sources that describe this changing of signs mid year still talk about the planet ruling the sign location at the birthday as Lord of the Year, and do not go into the interpretive meaning of changing signs. Effectively the system is usually described as the single sign and its Lord(s) applying for the whole year, which is the same as with whole sign houses.

There are enough anomalies with profections and quadrant houses that I use the system only with whole sign houses.

Profecting the Entire Chart

There is a fuller version of profection that I will also be exploring in some of the examples. The technique is to profect the entire chart, turning every point in the chart one sign per year. In the profected chart all of the planets stay in the same position relative to each other but they are in different signs, so they move to different houses relative to the natal chart.

The practice of profecting multiple points in the chart as they change signs and houses can be found in texts from the Arabic period of traditional astrology, including Abu Mashar. Vettius Valens also profects multiple points for different topics. Profecting the entire chart is found in book 3 of William Lilly's *Christian Astrology,* and Lilly's interpretations take into account new sign and house position, changes of dignity, and aspects from the profected chart to the natal. He effectively treats it as a stand-alone chart in its own right and as an entire chart in relation to the natal.

When you move the chart as a whole, the planets in the profected chart can line up with different planets in the natal chart, and the interaction affects how they are interpreted. I pay most attention to where the profected planets form near conjunctions with natal points and planets. This is in harmony with the general principle of profections that a point entering a sign activates that entire sign. It makes sense that planets occupying the same sign affect each other.

I also pay attention to how the shift of signs affects the planetary dignity, going from dignified to debilitated or vice-versa. These factors can be important when they concur with the directions and return for the year - as with all of the techniques, congruence between the systems is one of the key principles of interpretation.

Profections and Transits

Profections determine the main context for what transits are most important. Note all of the following transits as having special emphasis.

1) transits to LOY in natal or SR
2) transits of LOY to natal and to SR
3) transits through the profected sign of the year
4) retrogrades and stations by LOY
5) if the Sun or Moon is LOY, the full and new Moons can be important, and eclipses are especially important. Note where lunations occur that tightly trigger natal or SR planets or angles, especially hard aspects (conjunction, square, opposition).

Solar Returns

Most astrologers are familiar with the solar return chart, which is cast for the moment in time that the Sun returns to the exact location that it was in the natal chart. It sets the tone for the entire year.

In most traditional texts the solar return is cast for the natal location. Casting a return for the location the person is at the time of the return originated with the French astrologer Morin in the 16th century. I follow the tradition of using the natal location.

Relocated solar return charts do work, and they seem to be valid in the same way that relocated natal charts are valid. The birth location chart is still primary, and the relocated chart is a kind of overlay. I find that to be the same with the solar return chart - the return chart for time of birth is primary.

Solar returns were traditionally cast non-precessed, and that is what I will use.

How to Interpret Solar Returns - General Rules

Here are some guidelines for I how use solar returns when doing client work.

I always start with asking the client what particular themes or areas of their life are of concern in the reading. I use those themes as the primary frame of reference for making sense of the solar return and of all the techniques. I find that frame to be of primary importance in any kind of astrology work.

I know I have an important and valid reading when I can see the client's areas of concern showing up as the main areas of focus in the solar return and in the other predictive techniques, and that happens far more often than not. Their main concerns should make sense of the SR chart and other directions, and vice versa. Sometimes they may show that events will go in a direction they want, sometimes it appears that things will go contrary to their wishes, but the data is almost always relevant to their concerns.

I like to start with drawing up at least two, and sometimes three solar return charts - for at least half of the previous year, and for most of the year coming up. I find that helps to give a sense for a direction that things are going.

As another benefit, I find that talking about the past year and "predicting" it accurately builds confidence in what we will say about coming year. This is an example of predicting backwards to predict forwards. The information about the year just past often helps to flesh out the interpretation of the upcoming year.

As with all predictive techniques, for important planets you always evaluate and compare their condition in the natal chart to their condition in the SR. Do they reinforce, or contradict? Interpretation always starts with, and returns to, the natal chart.

There are some main places to look for determining which planets are likely to be important in the return, and they are exactly the same places you would look when evaluating a natal chart.

Start with the sign and house of the solar return Ascendant. That house, and natal planets in that house, are activated for the year. That is the rising sign, so it shows what is *coming up* this year.

The ruler of the SR Ascendant is activated in both the SR and the natal.

Any planets in SR angles, especially in the Ascendant, are also activated.

Along with its connection to the natal chart, it is important to remember that the SR chart is valid as a stand-alone chart, so it tells the story of the year by itself. I often find that the SR house placement is as or more important than natal house location in terms of the events of the year.

As with any other chart, check the solar return for dignity and debility of planets, and any close aspects or aspect configuration.

Signs of a Significant Year

There are some general signs that a given solar return is likely to be a significant year.

The single most important pointer of a big year is to see the solar return Ascendant on or near a natal angle, especially the natal Ascendant or Midheaven. Having the SR Ascendant within about 10 degrees of the natal Ascendant in the same sign is a very strong indicator of a big year.

Having the strong natal planets also strong and prominent in the solar return is another significant indicator. Those strong planets are likely to fulfill their natal promise.

It is also important when the planets active in the primary directions, especially for the Ascendant and Midheaven, are also strong in the solar return.

The main principle is congruence - you have a big year when the natal chart, directed time lords, profected chart and solar return all line up in the sense of all featuring or activating the same planets. Whenever a planet that is strong in the natal is also active and strong in the other levels of the system you have a particularly significant influence to pay attention to. We will be noting such redundant planets repeatedly in the examples.

Charts to Look At

These are the charts I look at when analyzing a solar return for a particular year.

1) The stand alone solar return as a chart in its own right.
2) A bi-wheel with the natal chart in the center and the SR around it.
3) A bi-wheel with the SR in the center and the natal around it.

Since the solar return chart is so important in its own right I find myself placing increased emphasis on its house positions. The bi-wheel with the natal around SR is often the most meaningful for houses.

Looking at the two charts together, check where significant planets from the two charts trigger each other, or where planets trigger angles. Planets that are angular in either chart are important.

Solar Returns Plus Profections

Analyzing the solar return chart I almost always start with the profected LOY. This is primarily the ruler of the sign of the year, but I also note the SR position of planets that are in the natal chart in the profected sign of the year.

Note the solar return house placement of the profected sign of year, and any planets in that house in the SR. The SR house and planet are at least as important as the natal location of the profected house, if not more important.

This next example shows how solar returns and profections work together with the natal. It is taken from my own life history for the year 2009, which marked some very important events in my life. In this example the profected lord of the year, its condition and house location are all of central importance.

Solar Return with Profection - Charles Obert

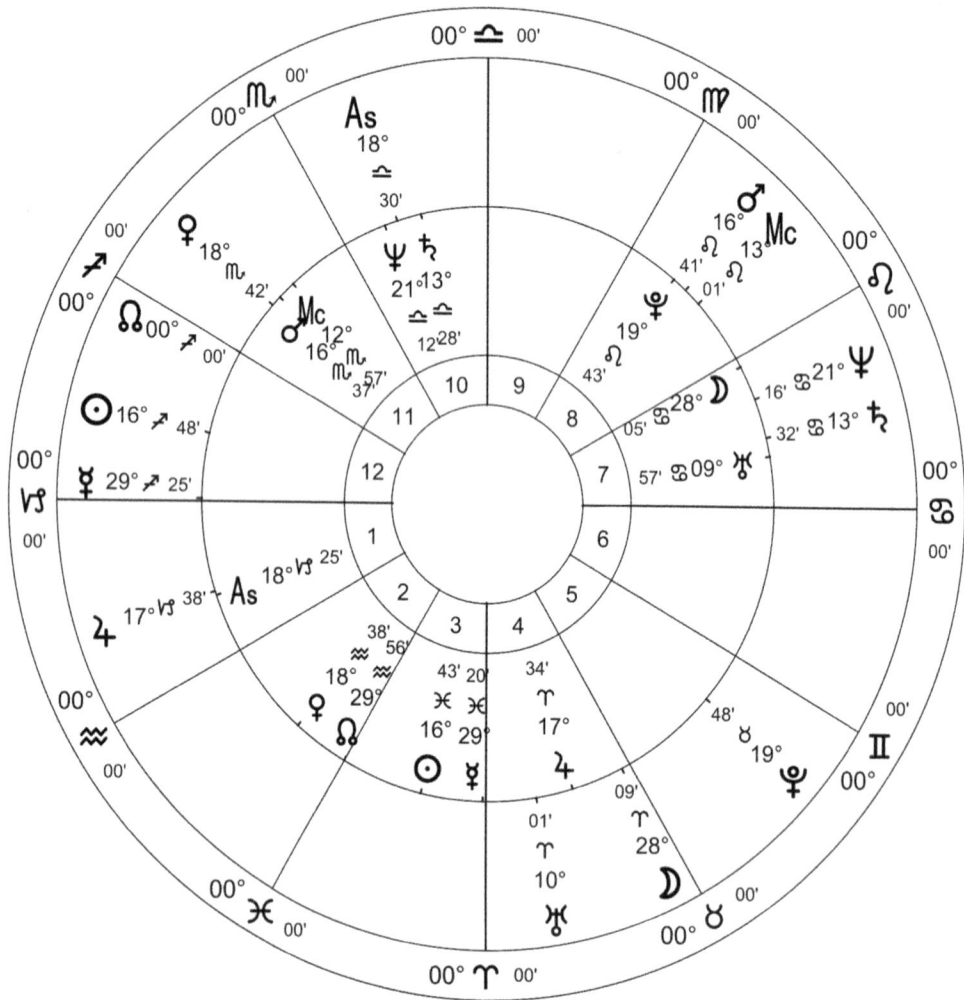

Charles Obert, March 7, 1952, 3:38 am, Queens, New York City. Rodden Rating A.

There were two major events in my life in 2009. By far the most important is that my wife Cindy died of cancer, after spending the last months of her life in home hospice. It was a very public death - we opened the house for our friends to visit, and before she died we held a memorial service for her that was attended by hundreds of our friends. That same year I accepted permanent employment at the Science Museum of Minnesota, a training position that I held for over ten years.

The chart above shows my natal chart surrounded by the profected chart for 2009. Note the profected Ascendant is in the 10th house of career, which speaks to my new job. The sign of the year is Libra, and the LOY Venus is in bad shape in the profected chart, in detriment, in Scorpio in the 11th house of friends and communities, right on my Midheaven - this speaks to the public hospice period and the memorial. The planet Saturn is in the profected sign Libra, and profected Saturn is in bad shape, in detriment in Cancer in the 7th house of my marriage partner.

In the next few chart illustrations I want to look at my solar return for that year, noting especially the house position of Venus.

This is my solar return for 2009.

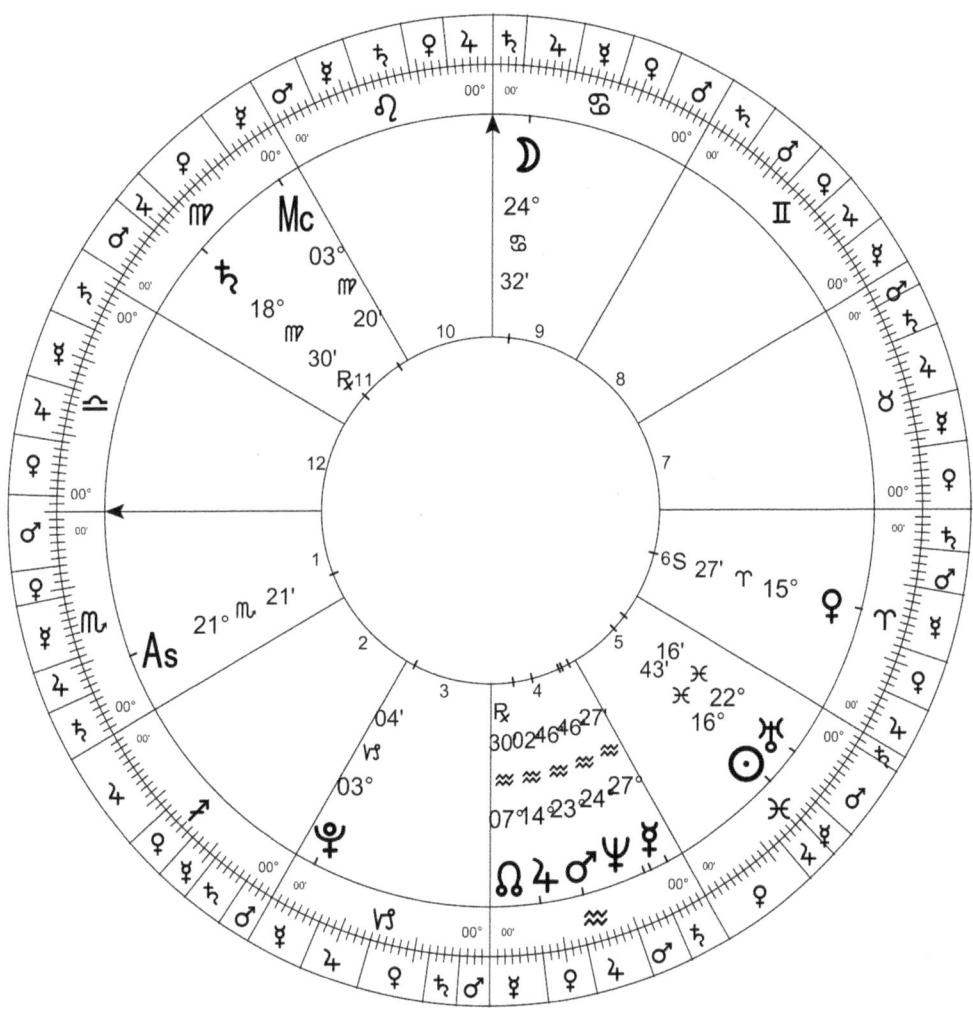

Note that LOY Venus is in detriment in this chart also, in the sixth house of illness. Venus rules the SR seventh house of marriage partner, and the SR twelfth house of illness, nursing and confinement. Mars, the lord of the SR Ascendant is in the fourth house, in a sign ruled by Saturn. Fourth house is concerned with endings, and with home, household - I spent much of the year home with Cindy in the period leading up to her death. The fourth house is also emphasized by a major stellium of four planets, plus the North Node, which magnifies whatever it is near.

Also note that Saturn, activated from the profection, is in a tight opposition with a Sun/Uranus conjunction, and Sun is applying, first to oppose Saturn, then to conjunct Uranus. Oppositions to the Sun can connote major relationships, and a Sun/Saturn opposition can connote the end of a relationship or death of a partner. Note that Uranus is in my natal seventh house in Cancer.

This bi-wheel shows my natal chart in the inner ring, and the solar return in the outer.

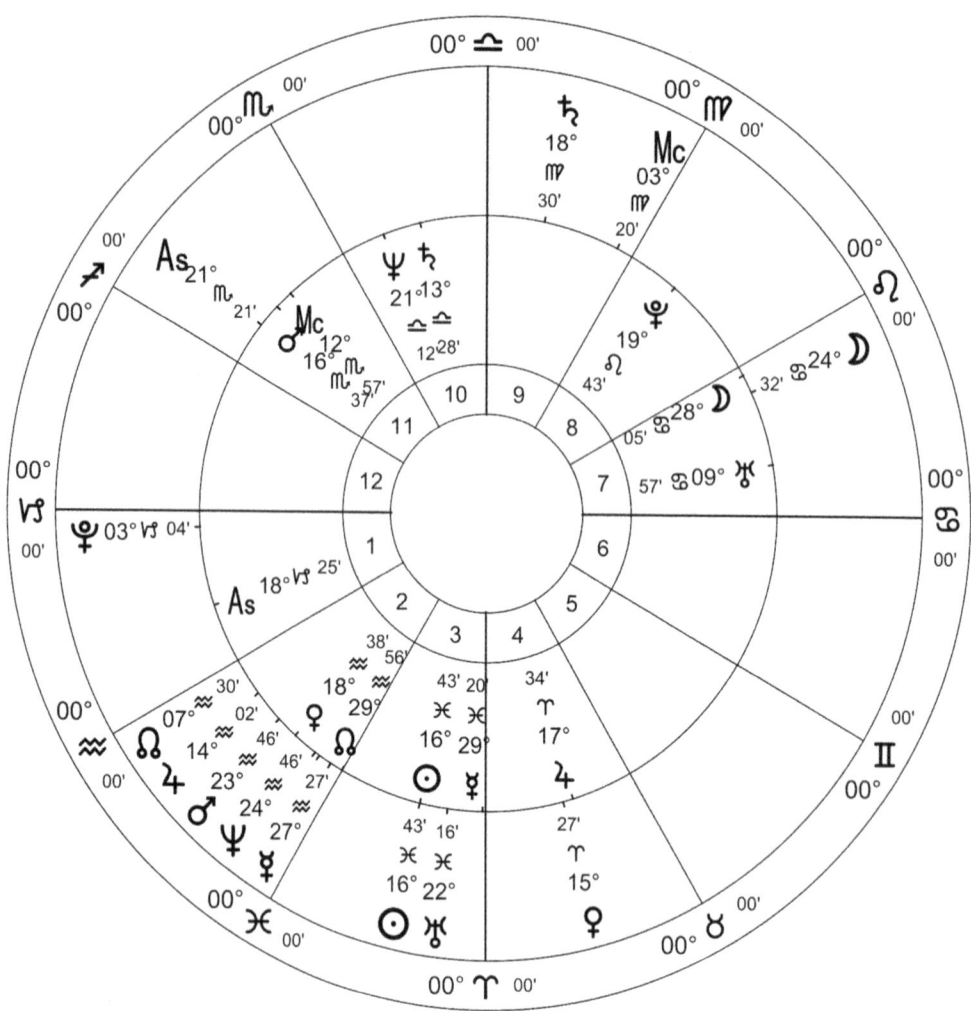

LOY Venus, in detriment in Aries, falls in my natal fourth house - Cindy spent the latter part of the year in home hospice, and she died at home. Fourth house and sixth house meanings are combined in home hospice. It is worth noting that SR Venus is conjunct natal Jupiter, and SR Jupiter is conjunct natal Venus. This could be related to the open and supportive community we had helping us in her last months.

In this chart the large stellium is in the second house, which is where natal Venus is located.

In this bi-wheel I reverse the two charts, with the SR in the center and the natal chart around it.

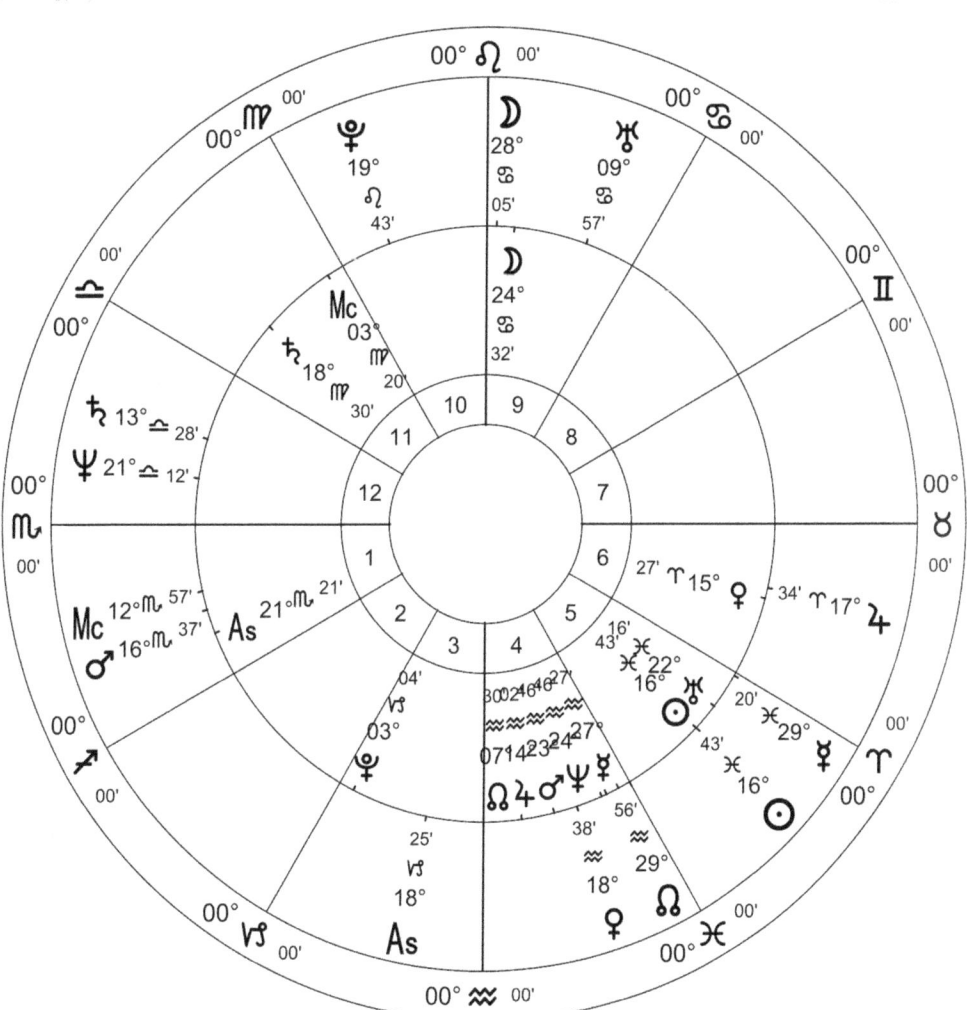

The connection between the fourth house (home hospice, dying at home) and sixth house (nursing, illness) shows up twice. In the inner ring SR Venus is in the sixth house, and in the outer natal ring Venus ends up in the fourth house.

Note also that SR Venus in the sixth is opposite natal Saturn in the twelfth house, associated with confinement, hospitals and nursing, and natal Venus in the outer ring is ruled by that same Saturn.

There are several repeated themes here: Venus being in detriment, the connections linking fourth and sixth house themes, and the connections to Saturn.

Later in the book I will be analyzing charts and events from 1985, which was the year Cindy and I first connected. Note that is 24 years prior to 2009, the year of her death. The relationship began and ended with the same profected chart, which shows an overlap of theme or life area - but you will see that the other charts are very different, just as the events were very different.

Primary Directions

A Little Bit of History

The use of primary directions, including directing through the bounds, goes back to our earliest Hellenistic sources that are the basis of Western astrology.

They are featured and used in the book *Carmen Astrologicum* by Dorotheus of Sidon, which is probably the single most influential surviving document in the history of Western astrology. (Some would say that all of Western astrology since then is a series of footnotes to Dorotheus...) The technique was passed down through the Persian and Arabic periods, and translated into Latin in the Middle Ages. Primary directions are also found in the work of Vettius Valens, and other Greek and Roman writers.

Direction through the bounds is a central part of the suite of predictive techniques that developed in the West. You will see them used in many of the books that Ben Dykes has translated. They are in *The Book of Aristotle* (thought by some to be by Masha'allah, but perhaps by al-Andarzaghar). These techniques are the core of the fully developed system in Abu Mashar. Those of you who find this technique interesting are encouraged to research the original sources.

Direction through the bounds also survives intact in the work of the English astrologer William Lilly. It is one of the main timing techniques he presents in Book 3 of *Christian Astrology*, the volume devoted to natal interpretation.

By the time of the very influential French astrologer Jean-Baptiste Morin in the 16th century, use of the bounds was lost until the late 20th century. Primary directions have fallen out of general use since the calculations can get quite complicated. We are currently seeing a revival of the use of primary directions, and I hope that this study contributes to that revival.

Primary Directions - The Basics

Before we look at specifics of directing through the bounds, we need to look at what primary directions are.

The system of primary directions is a symbolic way of moving a chart forward in time. Start with the astronomical fact that the wheel of the zodiac rotates all the way around the earth in 24 hours, which is 360 degrees of motion equaling 24 hours clock time. If you take each of those degrees and have its motion symbolically correspond to one year of the person's life, that one degree takes 4 minutes of clock time.

That is the symbolic equation - one degree of the earth's rotation equals one year of life.

If you consider what happens during the course of a day, the Ascendant and Midheaven axes stand still while the wheel of the zodiac revolves in a clockwise direction up over the Ascendant, so that all 12 signs cross the Ascendant point in the course of a day.

The different zodiac signs rise at different rates past the Ascendant because of the slant of the ecliptic relative to the equator and the earth's rotation. The rate that any zodiac sign rises past the Ascendant is called oblique ascension, oblique because of the slant of the zodiac relative to the earth's rotation.

Note: Because of the different rates of movement, one degree of oblique ascension may be either more or less than one zodiac degree. The exact rate varies by latitude and by zodiac sign because of the slant of the ecliptic relative to the earth's rotation.

Four minutes of clock time = 1 degree oblique ascension = 1 year of symbolic direction.

The earliest version of directions are sometimes referred to as distribution through the bounds, or circumambulation through the bounds. I picture the Ascendant going for a bit of a stroll through the zodiac as the day goes on. The two terms are synonyms for direction.

Consider the following chart.

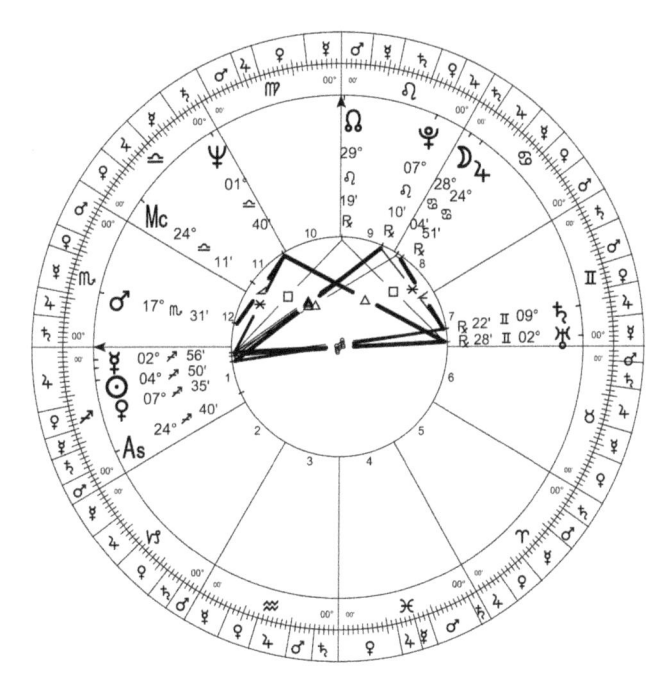

This is the birth chart of the musician Jimi Hendrix. Notice that the Ascendant is at 24 degrees 40 minutes of Sagittarius. If you could watch the zodiac in the hours after his birth, you would see the different zodiac signs coming up over the horizon, one after another, in what would be a clockwise direction in the above chart. This is primary directions, and this clockwise revolution of the zodiac in the course of a day is considered the primary motion of the zodiac.

Remember that the Ascendant is not moving through the signs. The Ascendant is standing still, and the wheel of the zodiac rotates past it. We speak of directing the Ascendant through the signs in a counter-clockwise direction, but actually the zodiac signs are moving in a clockwise direction past the Ascendant. If this is the Ascendant going for a stroll, then the road of the zodiac is coming to meet the Ascendant while it walks in place, like a kind of ultimate zodiac exercise treadmill.

The Ascendant was the earliest and most important point to be directed in this way. It is the most natural point to measure, and the easiest to observe.

Directing Other Points

The earliest method of directing other points in the chart involves treating every point as if it were at the Ascendant. Each point is moved at the rate of its oblique ascension, which is the rate it would move if it were coming up over the horizon. This method of directing the Midheaven and planets is still used by some traditional astrologers, especially those with a Hellenistic emphasis. If you use the astrology program Delphic Oracle, this is the method the program uses in the calculations it calls circumambulation through the bounds, treating each point as if it were an Ascendant in terms of the speed of its movement.

This doesn't match the rotation of the sky through the day. Thanks to the slant of the ecliptic, points move at different rates depending where they are in the wheel. This is most obvious with the Midheaven, which moves at the rate called Right Ascension. While oblique ascension varies according to latitude, right ascension is independent of latitude. Right ascension and oblique ascension move at different rates, so it makes sense to use right ascension with the Midheaven, and astrologers who use primary directions are agreed on how to calculate it.

During the course of the day the four angles remain stationary while the wheel of the zodiac moves past them. As we said, even though we speak of directing a point through the bounds it is actually the bounds that move and come to meet the point.

With directing the planets it is a different story. They do not stand still, but revolve around the earth in the course of a day along with the zodiac.

To direct the planets, picture them getting pinned to their particular position in the sky while the wheel of the zodiac moves past them. This is a strictly symbolic situation that has no correspondence to their actual daily movement. It is treating a planet as if it were an angle.

Since this doesn't actually happen astrologers have had to devise symbolic techniques for directing the planets, and the different forms of calculating primary directions are the answers to that theoretical dilemma.

One of the earliest of the solutions, the one I will be using here, is known as directing by proportional semi-arc. Basically this divides the daily wheel up into 4 quarters between the angles called semi-arcs, measures how long it takes the planet to move from one angle to another within that quadrant or semi-arc, and calculate what proportion of that quadrant the point has traveled.

The technical geometrical and mathematical details of these calculations are beyond the scope of this little book. See the appendix for sources of further information.

Fortunately we have the free astrology program Morinus, which does an excellent job with the calculations. In an appendix I give instructions how to use Morinus to calculate directions. The astrology program Delphic Oracle also does an excellent job of calculating primary directions in this manner.

Now that we have a sense of what primary directions are, we need to look at using directions through the bounds.

Directing Through the Bounds

These are the key concepts to keep in mind to interpret directions through the bounds.

Primary directions have to do with periods of time rather than specific points or dates. The bound lord is the most important ruler to consider how a given time period in directions plays out.

Bounds or Terms

The words bound and term are two different English translations for the same dignity. It means a circumscribed area like a plot of land, an area that has boundaries. "Bound" is the word used in the translations of Ben Dykes and of the Project Hindsight people, and "Term" is the word used by William Lilly and most English speaking astrologers since his time.

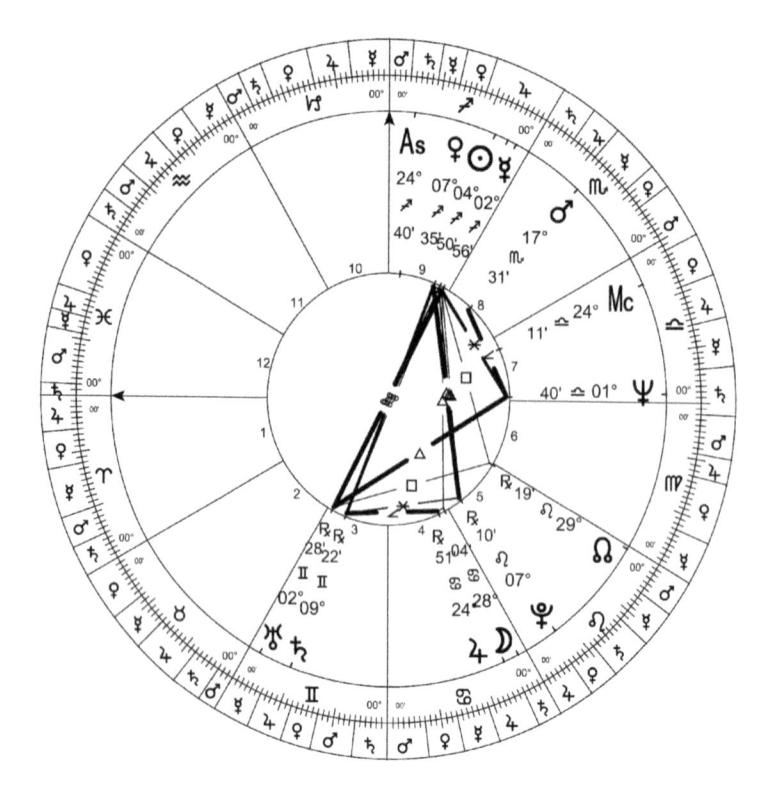

The small divisions around the outside of this chart show the dignity of bounds.

The division into bounds is one of the three minor dignities in the full system of 5 essential dignities in mature traditional astrology. The dignity of bounds divides up each sign into five unequal sections, one for each of the planets other than Sun and Moon. The version I am using here is known as the Egyptian bounds. It is found in Dorotheus of Sidon's enormously influential book, *Carmen Astrologicum*, and it is the oldest version of the bounds that we have. There is another version called the Ptolemaic bounds from Ptolemy's *Tetrabiblos*, which was the most widely used version in later Western astrology because of Ptolemy's influence. They were used by Lilly and other Renaissance astrologers.

In the chart above we see the twelve zodiac signs with Aries starting over on the left. The irregular division around the outside of the wheel shows the bounds. The first 6 degrees of Aries, from 0 to 5 degrees 59 minutes, is under the bound rulership of Jupiter. The next 6 degrees are the bounds of Venus, the next 8 degrees after that are the bounds of Mercury, and so on.

♈	0	♃	6	♀	12	☿	20	♂	25	♄
♉	0	♀	8	☿	14	♃	22	♄	27	♂
♊	0	☿	6	♃	12	♀	17	♂	24	♄
♋	0	♂	7	♀	13	☿	18	♃	26	♄
♌	0	♃	6	♀	11	♄	18	☿	24	♂
♍	0	☿	7	♀	17	♃	21	♂	28	♄
♎	0	♄	6	☿	14	♃	21	♀	28	♂
♏	0	♂	7	♀	11	☿	19	♃	24	♄
♐	0	♃	12	♀	17	☿	21	♄	26	♂
♑	0	☿	7	♃	14	♀	22	♄	26	♂
♒	0	☿	7	♀	13	♃	20	♂	25	♄
♓	0	♀	12	♃	16	☿	19	♂	28	♄

This is the same information on the bounds put in the form of a table. The number shown is the starting degrees of the bounds ruled by that planet.

Significance of Bounds

The meaning of the dignity of bound has to do with specific implementation, how something gets carried out. It is a lower level functional dignity. It doesn't have the high level of control of the sign ruler, but the sign ruler has to work through the bound ruler to get things done. If the sign ruler is CEO of a company then the bound ruler is the lower level manager who implements the directives from the CEO. If the sign ruler is the manager of a large farm, then the bound lord is in charge of implementing actions on a specific plot of land on the farm.

The main use of the bounds in traditional astrology is with the primary direction technique we are covering here.

These four charts are snapshots in time to illustrate directing the Ascendant through the bounds. The first chart is for Hendrix at his birth time, and the Ascendant is late Sagittarius, in the bounds of Saturn. Next chart 40 minutes later the Ascendant is early Capricorn in the bounds of Mercury. This corresponds to the directed Ascendant for Hendrix for age 10. The third chart is another 40 minutes later, and the Ascendant is mid Capricorn, very early in the bounds of Venus. This show the directed Ascendant for Age 20. In the fourth chart, another 40 minutes later, the Ascendant is late Capricorn in the bounds of Saturn, and corresponds to the directed Ascendant for age 30. These show the valid directed positions for the Ascendant and Midheaven. Directed positions for the planets need to be calculated symbolically.

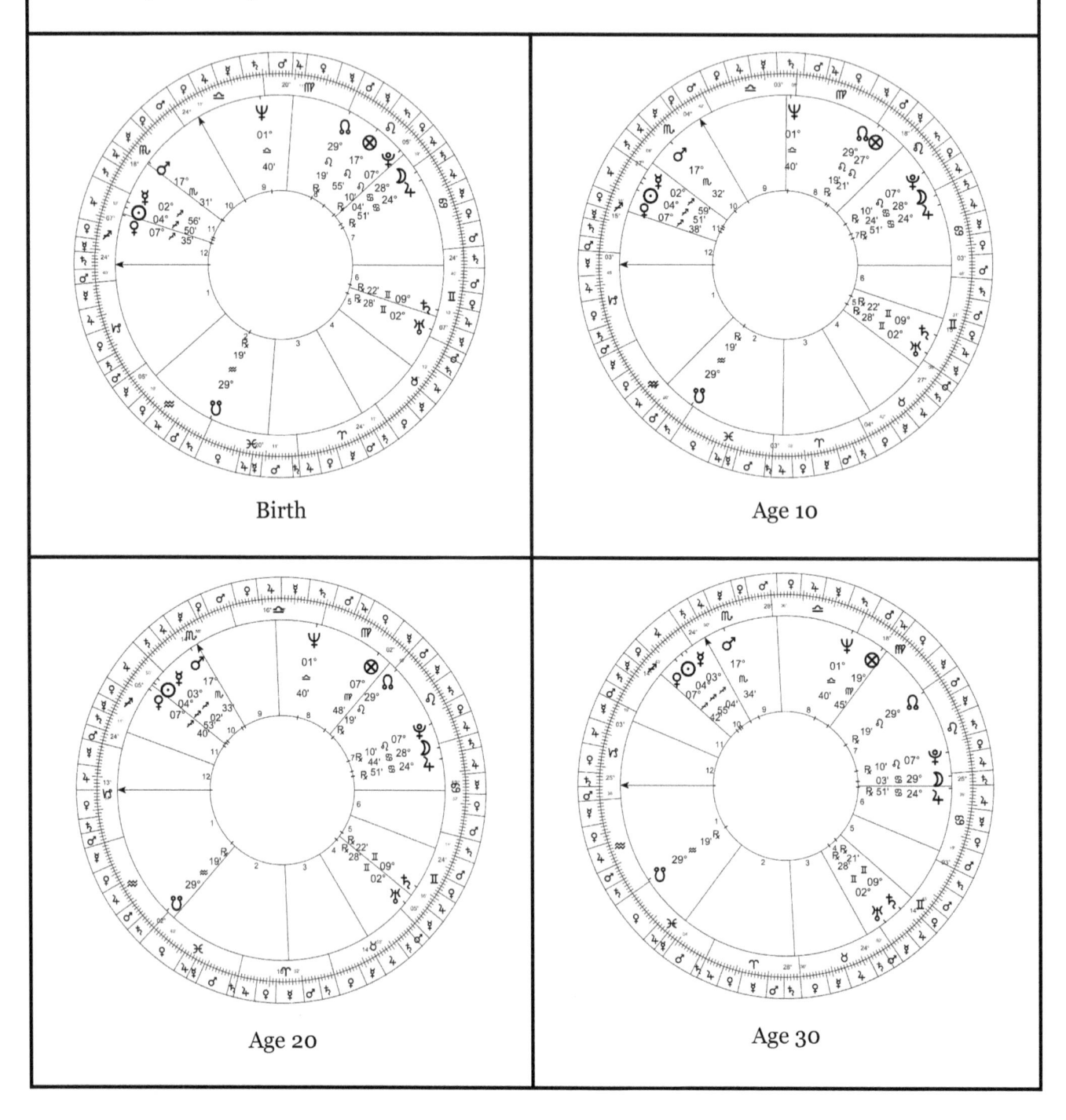

Birth

Age 10

Age 20

Age 30

42

How Directing Through the Bounds Works

This is a close up of a portion of the chart of Jimi Hendrix to illustrate how direction through the bounds works.

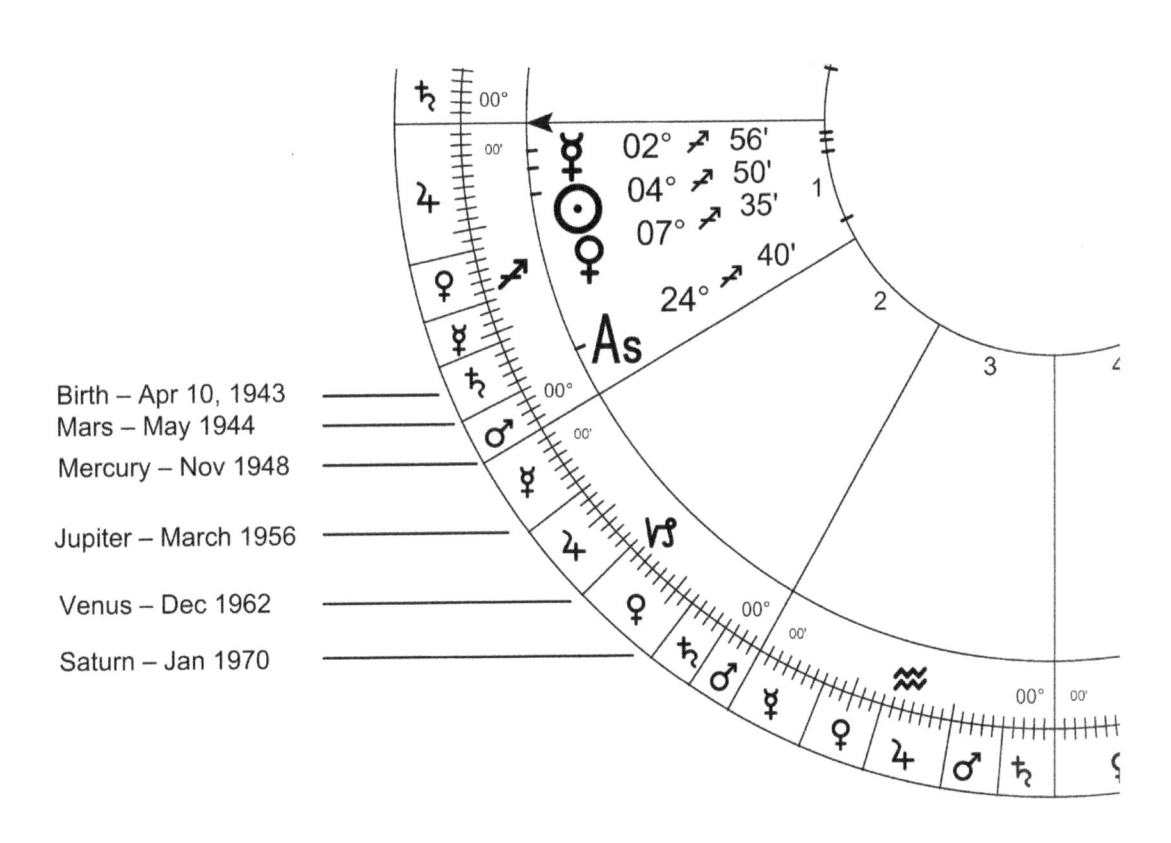

This is the lower left quadrant of the Jimi Hendrix chart. I have the dates marked on which the directed Ascendant moves into a different bound. At birth, the Ascendant in Sagittarius is in the bounds of Saturn. About a year later, May 1944, the Ascendant directs into the bounds of Mars. Mars continues as the bound lord until November of 1948, when the Ascendant moves into the bounds of Mercury at the beginning of Capricorn. The direction continues through to the entry into the Saturn bounds in Capricorn in January 1970, and Hendrix died later that year. **Remember, the Ascendant is standing still while the zodiac rotates clockwise past it. We view that as the Ascendant directing through the bounds, as in the above diagram.**

The Participator or Partner

Working with the bound lord is the participator or partner, which is the last planet in the natal chart to make a whole sign Ptolemaic aspect with the point being directed - conjunction, opposition, trine, square or sextile.

While the bound lord is the dominant influence to consider, the participator represents other people who have an influence on the person in this area. The participator thus colors or flavors the work of the bound lord, and can be either positive or negative, depending on its condition and its relation to the bound lord in the natal chart.

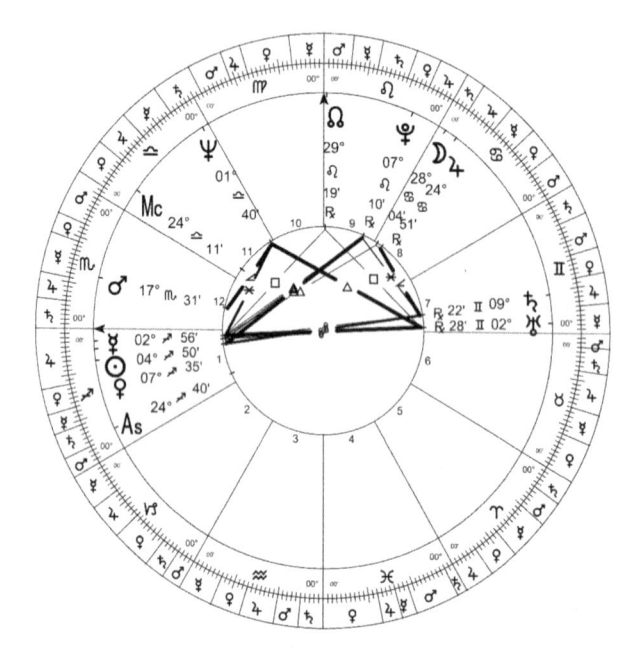

Again this is the natal chart of Jimi Hendrix.

The Ascendant is at 24 Sagittarius, and the last aspect it made was an opposition to Saturn at 9 Gemini in the 7th house. This means that Saturn is the participator planet when Hendrix was born.

Saturn stays the participator until the Ascendant directs to 17 Capricorn, in the bounds of Venus, when it makes a sextile aspect to Mars at 17 Scorpio. At that point Mars becomes the participator while Venus is the bound lord.

We will examine how these directions played out in the life of Hendrix later in this chapter.

The bound lord is primary, the participator is supporting or secondary. The bound lord is in charge of implementing this point, the participator represents supporting people or outside influences. I find from my own work with the bounds that the participator also has a strong internal and psychological component.

In referring to bound lord and participator I use a shorthand notation, with the two planets separated by a slash, bound/participator. For example, Asc in Venus/Saturn refers to the bounds of Venus with Saturn as participator.

William Lilly and Directing through the Terms

Book three of Lilly's *Christian Astrology* is devoted to natal interpretation. Here are some examples from Lilly describing how the planet ruling the terms of the Ascendant sets the tone for activities in that period.

On the Ascendant moving into the terms of Saturn.

> *The Native is then usually slow and dull in his actions, little mind to speak, dogged and reserved, full of Envy and Malice, hard to please, waspish, it represents the Native not caring which end goes forward...(p. 657)*

By contrast, this is the Ascendant in the terms of Venus.

> *The Native's Complexion and Disposition inclines to cheerfulnesse, he is active, and much delighted in Womens companies, prone to Musick, Dancing, to all honest and pleasant Sports and Pastimes, happy in the affaires he undertakes, and in his Trade. (p. 662).*

Later in the book Lilly analyzes the natal chart of a merchant with directions year by year. Here is his description of a direction of the Sun.

> *Sun to the Terms of Mercury induces the Native to be studious, and to pursue his Books of Accounts, and to call in some Moneys owing, which may happily be returned, because Mercury immediately comes to a semisextile of Jupiter in Scorpio, and in the tenth house; the aspect may produce some preferment to the Native, or acquaintance with some Jovial person, or Merchant of quality, from whom afterwards much good may be expected. (p. 785)*

Note that Lilly is influenced by Kepler here, and uses a semisextile or 30 degree aspect. The semisextile is not one of the traditional Ptolemaic aspects, so in this particular instance Lilly is departing from tradition. Given that, the description is a good example of how the aspected planet affects the Sun's expression.

Significant Points to Direct

Different points in the chart can be directed for different subject areas.

The Ascendant is first and primary to consider, and I find it the most consistently useful when I use it with readings and can interact with the subject. In looking at celebrity charts for this study I did not find it as consistently useful, and I suspect that is because we often do not get a good sense of what is going on with celebrities as whole people with multiple aspects to their lives. We see only the thin and distorted picture that is displayed through the warped filter of the media limelight.

In the traditional usage of directions there are other main points that are consistently used along with the Ascendant.

The Midheaven concerns career, reputation and work in the public eye. I find the Midheaven is often the most useful point to consider when working with the directions of politicians and military leaders.

These two points, Ascendant and Midheaven, are the most consistently important and useful to direct. This makes sense, since primary direction is a system that looks at movement of the angles through the zodiac, and symbolically treats all of the planets as if they were angles in order to calculate their directions.

Traditionally there are two other main points to look at in directions.

The Sun is worth considering for reputation and for general health and vitality.

The Moon is often useful for matters concerning physical health, and also for emotional state.

Traditional writers often refer to directing the Lot of Fortune also. I have not researched that enough to speak on the topic.

Along with those four key points, the planet to direct may also depend on which planets are particularly strong in the natal chart, and on which are activated in the solar return and profection for the year.

It is often worth looking at the two malefics, Saturn and Mars, when there is a particularly negative, violent or stressful event like a death. We will note that in in some of the examples.

Like pretty much any other technique in astrology, general rules and guidelines will take you only so far. You really need to look carefully at each chart individually and determine its particular strengths and weaknesses before you can determine which directions are important. To use traditional predictive techniques you need to master the use of dignity and debility in chart evaluation.

How to Read the Directions Listings

Throughout the examples in the book I will be using directions as they are printed out by the software program *Morinus*. For instructions on using Morinus please see he section at the end of the book. Here are two lines from the directions for Jimi Hendrix, and how to read them.

Z Sextile Mars D --> Asc 23.275900 1966.03.08

The Z stands for zodiacal directions, which is the kind we are using.

The point we are directing is after the arrow - in this case, the Ascendant. The planet Mars is making an exact sextile aspect to the Ascendant here. At the point the Ascendant was directed to 17 Capricorn, in the bounds of Venus. The number, 23.275900, is the number of degrees of arc that the Ascendant has been directed from its natal position to meet the exact sextile to his natal Mars position. March 8, 1966 is the day in Hendrix's life that this exact aspect happened. Always keep in mind that even though we have an exact date here, directions have to do with blocks of time rather than exact dates. Approximately March 1966 would be when Mars became the participator or partner planet at the Ascendant. Venus was the bound lord at that time.

Any lines in the listing with just a planet name and no aspect indicate that the directed point has moved to a conjunction with that planet.

Z (Capricornus)Saturn D --> Asc 27.129650 1970.01.13

When you see a zodiac sign in parentheses listed to the left of the arrow, it means that the directed point is moving into a different set of bounds. In this case the Ascendant has directed to the bounds of Saturn in the sign Capricorn beginning January 13, 1970. Saturn being the bound lord, you would look at the location and condition of Saturn in the natal chart to see how that might play out.

Put these two lines together, and we see that in January 1970 the Ascendant directed to the bounds of Saturn, with Mars continuing as participator since it is still the last aspected planet. Saturn is the primary influence, and Mars is secondary.

Start with the Ascendant

If you are new to working with directing through the bounds, a good place to start is with the directions of the Ascendant for your own chart.

Run a listing of the Ascendant directions and partners for your entire life. Notice what blocks of years correspond to what bound rulers. I find it helpful to write in what age the bound lord changes took place. Next, jot down major life events within the periods. Notice in which bounds those events happen to fall. If you have a specific planetary bound lord that has repeated in your life, think about whether there are parallels or similar themes between those periods.

Always remember that how a bound lord plays out depends on the location and condition of that planet in your natal chart. Your Jupiter is not the same as my Jupiter, and your Saturn is not the same as my Saturn, because the planets differ in their natal starting conditions.

I found it very useful to draw up the list of directions for my life, and then keep coming back and looking at it over time. I find that I keep seeing new patterns emerge.

I'll give you an example of what I mean, by talking about the kinds of things I noticed looking at bound lord periods in my own life.

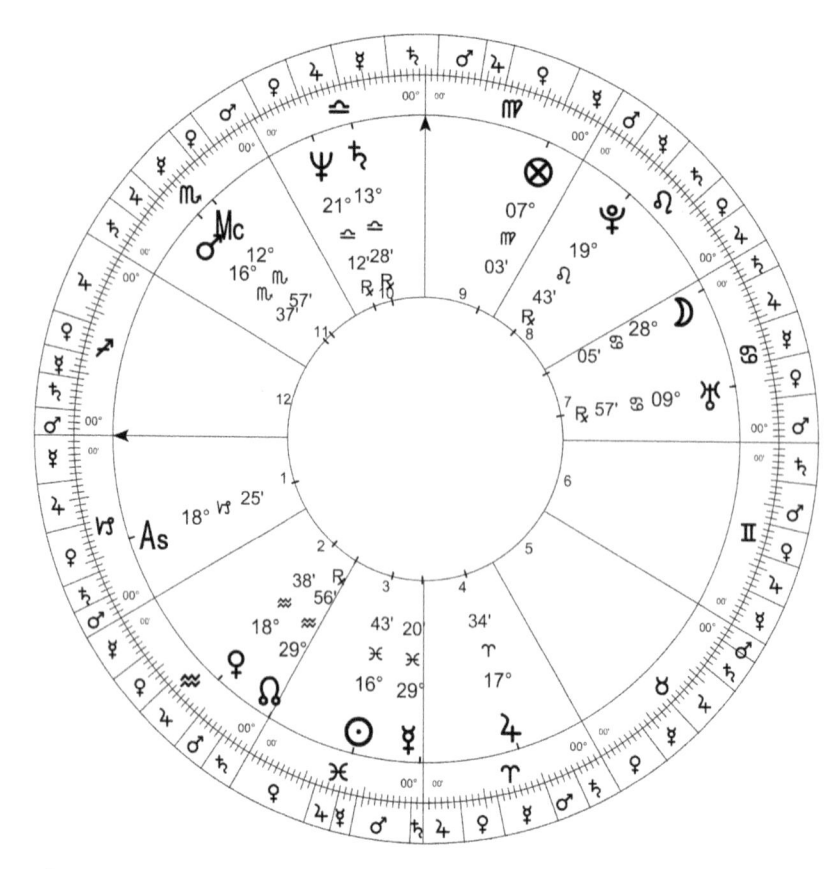

Charles Obert, March 7, 1952, 3:38 AM, Queens, New York. Rodden Rating A,

Saturn is exalted in Libra in my chart, but retrograde, and in mutual reception with Venus, tenth house to second house. Saturn bound periods are definitely not fun - Saturn is always Saturn, in good shape or bad - and Saturn periods are often a lot of work and involve delays, but they often involve my doing okay financially and earning money, always by my own effort - tenth house to second house connections. Saturn bounds sometimes involve interactions with work superiors who discipline me, but in ways where they are trying to be fair, that work out as growing experiences for me - Saturn exalted in the tenth house of work and bosses.

Interestingly, Mars periods are often times when I take some kind of initiative involving a sense of spiritual purpose or calling - I have Mars in Scorpio conjunct my Midheaven so it is very strong and prominent, and related to my sense of vocation. These are periods when want to I go my own way, make my own decisions, and work on the things that are the most important to me spiritually.

Not surprisingly, Mercury periods often involve a lot of focus on reading, thinking, writing, often involving philosophical speculation, and sometimes going off in many directions at once - I have Mercury in Pisces, in detriment and fall, in the third house. Mercury periods are fun, but they can get very scattered.

Again I want to emphasize that you need to get to know how the planets act as bound lords in the context of your own life as they emerge from the potential of your particular natal chart.

If you are using directions with another person, and you have a particular planet coming up as bound lord, if that planet was bound lord in a previous period, it is worth giving the person those dates and asking what that period was like. It will likely give you some clues as to how the recurrence of that bound lord will work out. That is a good example of predicting backwards to predict forwards - if we know how a planet acted in the past, we have a guideline as to how it will likely act in the future.

You cannot determine everything about a period or event just from the bound lord of the Ascendant, but a bit of intelligent questioning and thinking should help you perceive the patterns and similarities between recurring bound periods with the same planetary lord.

Jimi Hendrix

To illustrate how directing through the bounds is used with traditional methods of evaluating condition, we will take a closer look at the Ascendant directions for the brief career of the wildly creative and pioneering guitarist, Jimi Hendrix.

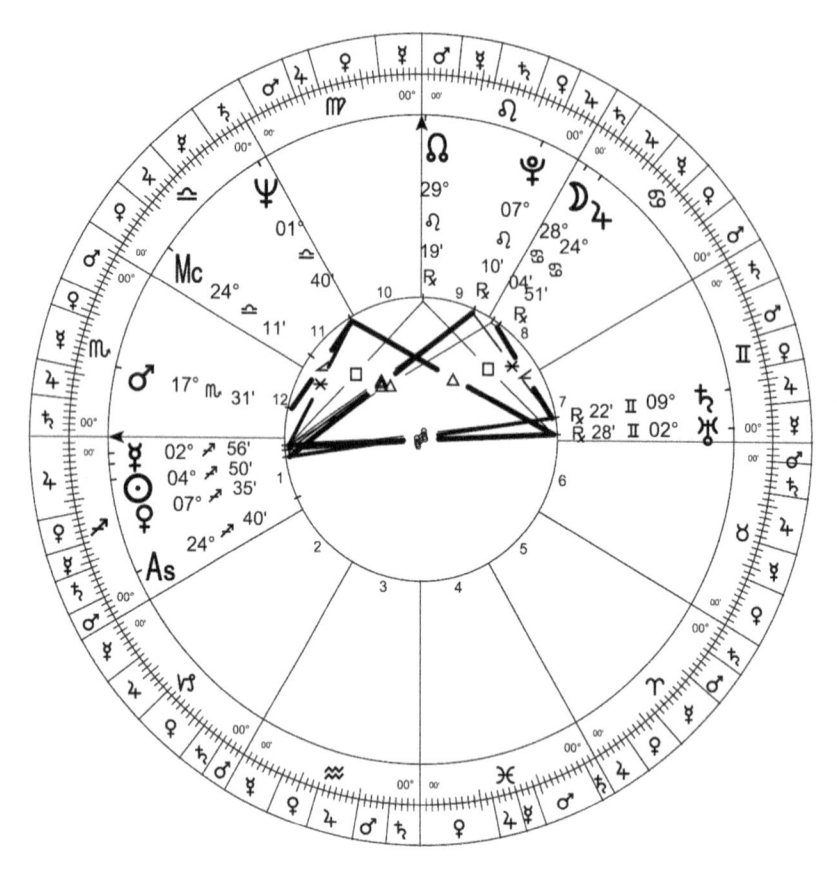

Johnny Allen Hendrix, November 27, 1942, 10:15 AM Seattle, WA. Rodden Rating AA.

I will be looking at the period of Hendrix's primary musical creativity and fame, through to his untimely death.

Z (Capricornus)Venus D --> Asc 20.080430 1962.12.26

In late 1962 the Ascendant directed into the bounds of Venus in mid Capricorn, so we start by looking at the location and condition of Venus in the natal chart.

Venus in Sagittarius in the first house is the ruler of his Midheaven. Venus is ruled by Jupiter which is in its exaltation in Cancer, conjunct the Moon in rulership in Cancer. Venus is part of a three planet conjunction of Mercury, Sun and Venus, and all three are in the rulership, triplicity and bounds of Jupiter. Jupiter controls three of the five dignities for those planets, so the influence of Jupiter is overwhelming here.

It is that strong Jupiter/Moon combination in the water sign Cancer, influencing the three planet cluster in the first house, which accounts for the wild, strongly emotional nature of Hendrix's work. The ruling Jupiter is averse the Ascendant, meaning it does not make any whole sign aspect, so there is an out of control quality to his music.

This period, beginning in 1962 after his honorable discharge from the US Army, is the beginning of his musical career.

During this period the partner planet is Saturn, since the last major aspect that the Ascendant made is an opposition to Saturn in Gemini in the seventh house. Ascendant in opposition to Saturn suggests Hendrix's opposition to any kind of restriction or restraint, and his emphasis on a wild and unrestrained freedom. That theme runs through all of his musical creations.

Z Sextile Mars D --> Asc 23.275900 1966.03.08

Things really took off for Hendrix in the Venus bound period beginning in 1966, when the participating planet switched from Saturn to Mars. In shorthand notation, the Ascendant moved from Venus/Saturn to Venus/Mars.

Mars is quite strong in his rulership in Scorpio, but is in the twelfth house of self-undoing, and is also averse the Ascendant. Mix Venus (ruled by Jupiter) and Mars (who rules himself and tolerates no restraint, thank you very much) and you get the wild, crazy, borderline out of control intensity of his best music.

The trio that was the Jimi Hendrix Experience is the most successful band he ever had, with Mitch Mitchell his best drummer. Mars as partner planet represents supporting or contributing people, and in this case it could represent his band, especially the drummer. Since Mars is in the 12th house it could point to a self-destructive streak, and it could also speak to enemies out of his awareness who were working against him. That last point is just conjecture on my part.

This period represents the peak of his musical career, his climb to worldwide fame with the Jimi Hendrix Experience, and his best recorded musical work.

All of the albums released in his lifetime except one were recorded during this period.

Z (Capricornus)Saturn D --> Asc 27.129650 1970.01.13

In 1970 the Ascendant moved into the bounds of Saturn. Saturn is problematic in this chart, being retrograde in the seventh house and in a mutually applying opposition to the three planet cluster in the first house. With mutual application you have three planets here moving forward to meet Saturn who is moving backward to meet them. Traditionally mutual application is bad news with any two planets, and more so with a malefic. In this period we have Saturn as bound lord with Mars as the partner, the two malefics in control.

Hendrix's best work was behind him at this point, and he had only a short time left to live.

The final album released by Hendrix (Band of Gypsies, 1970) was recorded in January 1970, right around the time of change of bound lord. This album was marked by a complete change of band, and the album is generally not rated as being at the same level as his previous recordings. For me it does not have the same fire and craziness of his peak work - Hendrix is nearly always good, but it is not his best work.

It is during the first year after the Ascendant entered the Saturn bound period that Hendrix died, September 18, 1970.

Anita Bryant

Anita Bryant was famous as a singer and Miss Oklahoma beauty pageant winner, and for many years she was brand ambassador for the Florida Citrus Commission and orange juice. She scored four Top 40 hits in the United States in the late 1950s and early 1960s, including "Paper Roses", which reached #5 on the charts.

Today Bryant is most remembered as an outspoken opponent of gay rights, and for her 1977 "Save Our Children" campaign to repeal a local ordinance in Dade County, Florida, that prohibited discrimination on the basis of sexual orientation. This involvement significantly damaged her popularity and career in show business.

This is an example where just looking at the directing of the Ascendant through the bounds correlates with the main ups and downs of her life.

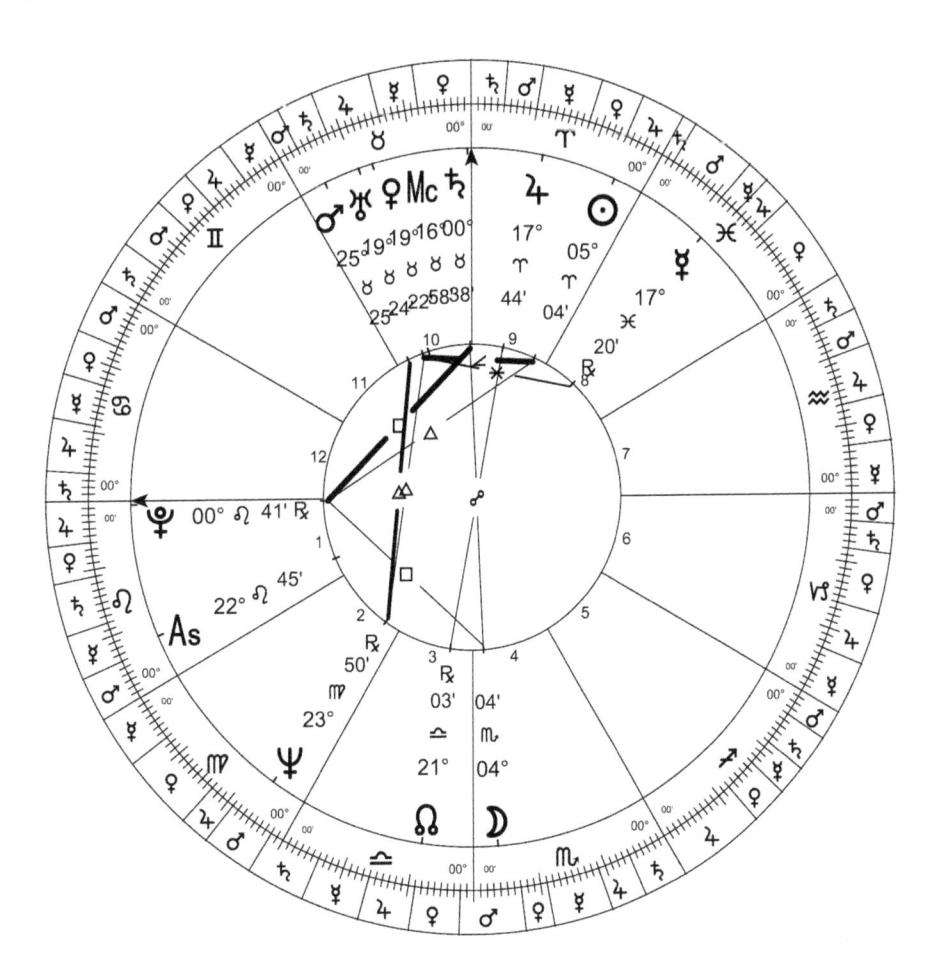

The Ascendant in this chart is Leo, ruled by the Sun, and the Sun is exalted in Aries in the 9th house, near the top of the chart. The Sun is in the same sign as Jupiter, and is in the Jupiter bounds, and Jupiter has dignity by triplicity in Aries. Even with Jupiter being very near the Sun, with their shared dignity the two planets do work well together, and Jupiter likely adds an expansive quality to the Sun's expression. (I suspect maybe just a teeny tiny bit of inflated sense of self-wonderfulness.) Since the Ascendant is ruled by the Sun, one of the most positive and visible planets in her chart, it makes sense that the directions of the Ascendant should correlate with her public life and general fortune.

Z Sextile Moon D --> Asc 13.926553 1954.02.27
Z (Virgo)Venus D --> Asc 17.514411 1957.09.29

Starting in 1957 the Ascendant is directed to the bounds of Venus, in the middle of Virgo, with Moon as participator. Venus is very strong in this chart in her ruling sign Taurus, in the terms of Jupiter, and angular in the tenth house very near the Midheaven, so we should expect this Venus period to be very positive. Sure enough, this is the period when she first became famous as a beauty queen - Venus in Rulership right on the Midheaven + Sun ruler of Ascendant exalted = shining beauty.

In 1958 at age 18 Bryant became Miss Oklahoma, and in 1959 she took second place in the Miss America pageant. She also had a moderately successful singing career, and all of her most popular singles and albums were released during this period. Venus bounds were very positive for her.

Bryant also married in 1960 during this period, and had 4 children. There could be a connection between the marriage and her children, and the Moon being the participating planet. (Note that the Moon is opposite Saturn - we will comment on that again later.)

Z (Virgo)Jupiter D --> Asc 29.714593 1969.12.11

In 1969 the Ascendant moved into the bounds of Jupiter. Also in 1969 Bryant became a spokeswoman for the Florida Citrus Commission, and nationally televised commercials featured her singing "Come to the Florida Sunshine Tree" with the tag line "Breakfast without orange juice is like a day without Sunshine." Sunshine - think Sun exalted in Aries, and the relationship between Sun and Jupiter in the same sign.

Z Opposition Mercury D --> Asc 30.135445 1970.05.14
Z Trine Venus D --> Asc 32.602552 1972.10.31
Z (Virgo)Mars D --> Asc 34.576507 1974.10.22

In 1974 the Ascendant went into the terms of Mars, with Venus now the participating planet. Mars is poorly placed in his detriment in Taurus, still in the tenth house, so it highly visible, and note that Mars rules her ninth house of religion. This is a day chart, and Mars is often problematic in day charts, and being in its detriment we can expect it to be argumentative and contentious. It was during this period that she became involved in anti-gay activism starting in 1977, driven by her conservative religions convictions. This cost her much of her public reputation, and that eventually led to her losing her position as spokesperson for the Florida Citrus Commission in 1979.

Z Trine Mars D --> Asc 39.940388 1980.03.03

It was when the Ascendant was in the bounds of Mars with Mars also as partner, that she went through her divorce - and a contentious divorce fits a Mars partner. It also fits that she says the divorce was for reasons of abuse - think ill-tempered and ill-controlled Mars, and recall that her Moon in the fourth house (participating planet when she married) is opposite Saturn, lord of the seventh house.

This divorce alienated a lot of the Christian fundamentalist support base that had stayed with her during the anti-gay incidents, so her career and popularity went downhill from here.

Z (Virgo)Saturn D --> Asc 43.070300 1983.04.20
Z (Libra)Saturn D --> Asc 45.495497 1985.09.22

Her second marriage took place in 1990 under Saturn bounds for Ascendant, with Mars still the participator. Saturn rules her natal seventh house, Aquarius. I suspect that the second marriage was at least partly for convention and to honor tradition since she was a very conservative Christian, and it is just more proper for a woman to be married.

Z Opposition Sun D --> Asc 51.644306 1991.11.16
Z (Libra)Mercury D --> Asc 52.772650 1993.01.01

Her bankruptcy took place in 1997 during Mercury bounds. Mercury is the weakest planet in her chart, in Detriment and Fall in Pisces in the weak and ineffective eighth house, and retrograde. Mercury also rules her second house of finances.

(Note that eighth house is specifically linked with bankruptcy in vedic astrology, and it fits the general traditional Western sense as also being related to lawsuits concerning money.)

Herman Melville

Today Herman Melville is considered to be one of the greatest writers in America's history, and his landmark (or, perhaps, sea-mark) book, *Moby Dick*, is considered one of the great novels of all time. During his lifetime he had only a brief period of popularity. Much of his writing career was accompanied with increasing popular and critical disfavor, fostering disillusion and depression on Melville's part. The directions of the Ascendant for Melville follow the ups and downs of the central part of his career.

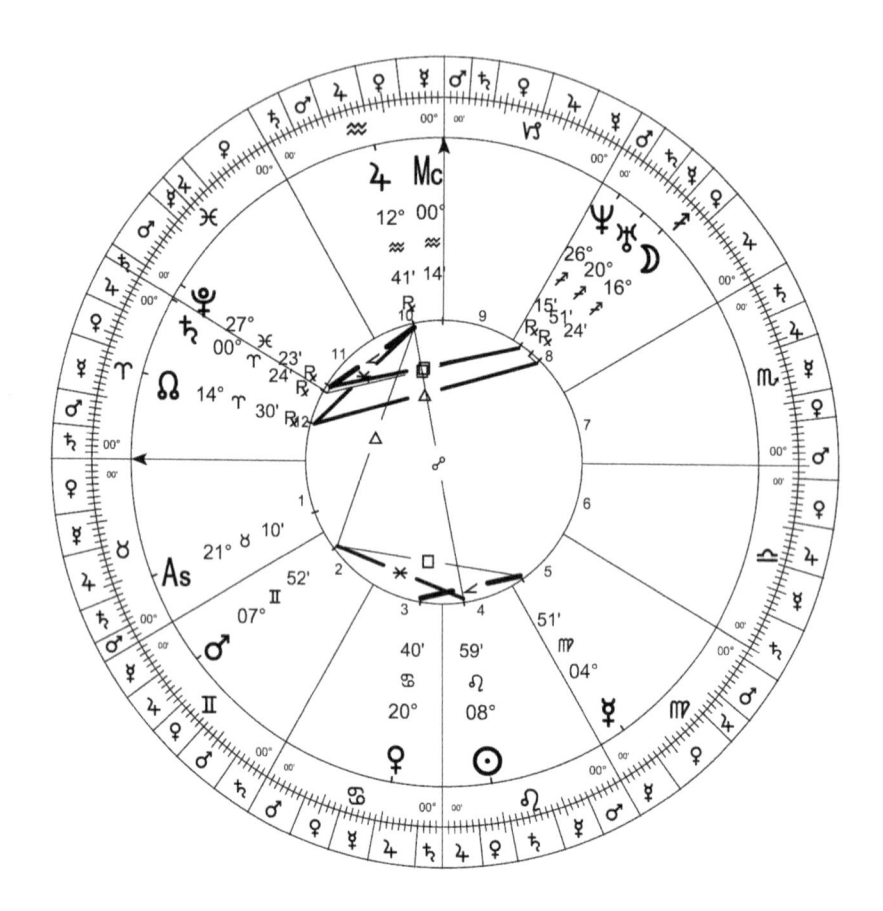

Mercury in this chart is very strong in terms of essential dignity in Virgo, in rulership and exaltation and in Mercury bounds. It is in the positive fifth house, which is linked in modern astrology to creativity like writing. However, note that Mercury has no influence or dignity on either of the angles.

Mercury rules the peregrine Mars in the second house, and we will see the Mercury/Mars connection show up in some of the directions. The second house is Gemini, ruled by Mercury, and for most of his life Melville made his living in Mercury professions - most notably, as a writer. When his writing career fell apart he became a lecturer, and then spent most of the rest of his life as a government clerk, which is also a Mercurial profession.

Saturn is by far most difficult planet in the chart. This is a night chart, where Saturn is especially malefic. Saturn is also in his fall in Aries in the twelfth house. We have themes here of being ignored or miSunderstood, of hidden enemies out to get him, and also of self-undoing, where it is his own actions that alienate people. Saturn rules his ninth house of publishing, travel, religion and religious or spiritual quests, and also his tenth house of career and reputation.

The combination of rulers of the sign Capricorn in the ninth house is very interesting. We have the main sign ruler Saturn (his very Saturnine mature writings and philosophy) with Mars exalted there (the wanderlust, the quest, also the compulsive urge to be writing about the quest).

Z (Gemini)Venus D --> Asc 17.444397 1837.01.10
Z Trine Jupiter D --> Asc 18.089303 1837.09.03

It is during this Venus/Jupiter period that Melville first goes to sea, in 1839.

Z Opposition Moon D --> Asc 21.618956 1841.03.15
Z (Gemini)Mars D --> Asc 22.200195 1841.10.13

We will see a recurring connection with Mars and travel in later Mars periods. It was in this period during his second sea voyage in this period that he was captured by cannibals in Polynesia and spent four months with them before escaping. This experience became the basis for his first two novels, which began his popular fame as a writer. He first made his name in stories (Mercury) of his wanderings and adventures (Mars) around the world.

Melville wrote the two novels that were the most popular during his lifetime, *Typee* in 1846 and *Omoo* in 1847, in a Mars period. Mars is in his second house in Gemini which is ruled by Mercury. The partner planet here is the Moon, in the eighth house in Sagittarius, applying to conjunction with Uranus and Neptune, and completely dominated by Jupiter as far as dignity. I wonder whether that Mars opposition to Moon/Uranus/Neptune is part of what contributed to the flavor of the wild and exotic sea adventures in his popular fiction.

Also, Melville's sea stories are very Mars ruled by Mercury in flavor - the wayfaring male wanderer having his adventures - and almost all the characters are men.

Z (Gemini)Saturn D --> Asc 29.244384 1848.10.29

Melville's later books, from *Mardi* through *Pierre* in this period, became increasingly serious and philosophical - and increasingly less popular. This is also the period where his work took on a much more saturnine tone, and where he became increasingly convinced he had enemies in the publishing industry that were working against him.

We have some complex and interesting symbolism of a malefic Saturn in the twelfth house at work here - the hidden enemies in publishing he was convinced were out to destroy him - his own self-destructive tendencies in how he dealt with some of his writing - and the deep metaphysical and philosophical themes with an increasingly dark, disillusioned and even nihilistic tone in the later works, that alienated his earlier audience. I also think that this twelfth house Saturn in fall was evident in his increasingly bleak mature spiritual quest and philosophy. My own sense is that this Saturn in fall is embodied in the character Captain Ahab in *Moby Dick*.

And it was, indeed, during this period, in 1851, that Melville published this masterpiece, *Moby Dick*, which was a complete critical and popular failure at the time.

This whole period, in which Melville's writing career declined and fell apart, was in the bounds of Saturn, 1848 through 1855. In 1855 the Ascendant moved into Mars bounds with Saturn the participator.

Z (Cancer)Mars D --> Asc 35.630887 1855.03.20
Z Square Saturn D --> Asc 36.079988 1855.08.31

It was in 1857, after his novel *The Confidence Man* was published and was another critical and popular failure that Melville quit writing and went on a 3 year lecture tour. Again we see Mars bounds connected to traveling. In addition, Melville's 9th house of travel is Capricorn, with Saturn ruler and Mars exalted, and this lecture tour took place when the pair was the bound lord and partner.

Saturn may have added a depth and profundity to Melville's thought and writing, but it had a very harsh negative affect on his career during his lifetime.

Harry Belafonte

In this example I want to look at the chart of Harry Belafonte, singer, actor and civil rights activist. This particular example will include directing the Midheaven, and how it interacts with the profection for a particularly critical and beneficial year in Belafonte's life.

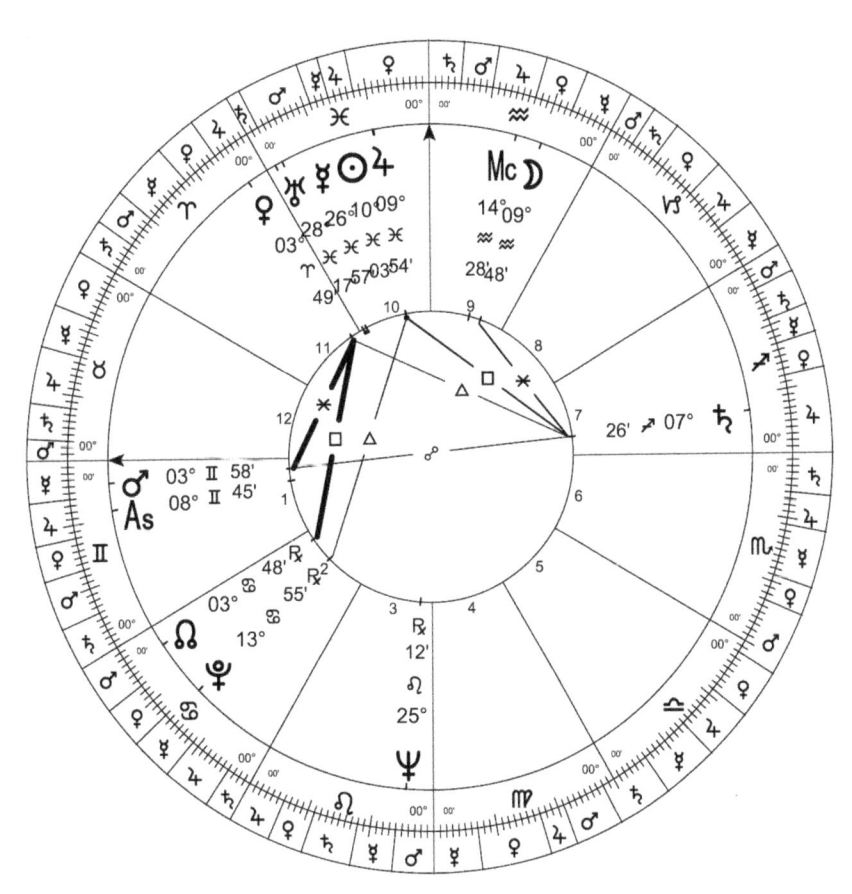

The outstanding feature of this chart is the very tight conjunction of the Sun and Jupiter in Pisces, in the 10th house. The conjunction is exact to within 9 minutes of orb, and this is called cazimi, or at the heart of the Sun, and it is considered about the most propitious place that a planet could be. Add the fact that the conjunction takes place in Pisces, where Jupiter is in rulership, and you have a very powerful, rare and positive configuration, right in the 10th house of career and reputation. At his peak Belafonte had an amazing charisma and magnetism, and was also very handsome.

Note also the angular Mars in the first house, just above the Ascendant is in an applying opposition with Saturn in Sagittarius in the 7th house. I associate this Mars/Saturn opposition with Belafonte's very outspoken speaking and action on civil rights, and I associate the extremely dignified Jupiter with what he would call his 'moral compass' - he had very strong beliefs concerning civil rights, and he was completely consistent in his words and actions, including putting his life and reputation on the line for his civil rights work. Note also that both Saturn and Mars are in a pretty tight square to that Sun/Jupiter conjunction - Belafonte primarily used his fame as a way to further his civil rights work.

59

Looking at the Midheaven, note that it is in the 9th house in Aquarius, a sign ruled by Saturn. The Midheaven is also in the triplicity and bounds of Jupiter. Since the Midheaven will be directed counter clockwise, it makes sense to pay attention to when it reaches the Sun/Jupiter conjunction. And finally, note that the Jupiter bounds in Pisces are just slightly after the Venus bounds where Jupiter and the Sun are, so that the Midheaven will be in these Jupiter bounds shortly after its conjunction with Sun and Jupiter.

Here are the directions for the Midheaven for the period we are looking at.

Z (Pisces)Venus D --> MC 15.153138 1942.04.26
Z Square Mars D --> MC 18.933662 1946.02.05
Z Square Saturn D --> MC 22.199317 1949.05.12
Z Jupiter D --> MC 24.512766 1951.09.04
Z Sun D --> MC 24.649753 1951.10.24

That Midheaven directed to conjunct Sun and Jupiter in 1951, and stayed the participating planets all the way through 1967. (Strictly speaking the Sun is the participator, but since the two planets are so tightly conjunct we can effectively view the pair as being participators.) In 1951 the Midheaven is still in the bounds of Venus.

Z (Pisces)Jupiter D --> MC 26.463376 1953.08.17
Z (Pisces)Mercury D --> MC 30.177944 1957.05.04
Z (Pisces)Mars D --> MC 32.950857 1960.02.11

The Midheaven entered the bounds of Jupiter, with Sun/Jupiter participating, in 1953, and stayed there until mid 1957 when it entered the bounds of Mercury. (Note that the Midheaven went into the bounds of Mars in 1960, which is the beginning of his most serious civil rights activism.)

The peak period, where his career took off and he ascended to worldwide fame, coincides exactly with the Jupiter bound period for the directed Midheaven, with Sun and Jupiter together the participators, from 1953 through mid 1957. Here is some biographical information for this period.

Debuting on Broadway in 1953, Belafonte won a Tony Award for his performance in John Murray Anderson's Almanac, in which he performed several of his own songs. He also appeared in another well-received musical revue, 3 for Tonight, in 1955.

Around this time, Belafonte launched his film career. He played a school principal opposite Dorothy Dandridge in his first movie, Bright Road (1953). The pair reunited the following year for Otto Preminger's Carmen Jones, a film adaptation of the Broadway musical. Oscar Hammerstein II had written the musical as a contemporary, African-American version of the opera Carmen, by Georges Bizet. Belafonte received an Academy Award nomination for his portrayal of Joe, a soldier who falls for the title character, played by Dandridge.

The success of Carmen Jones made Belafonte a star, and soon he became a music sensation. After signing with RCA Victor Records, he released Calypso (1956), an album featuring his take on traditional Caribbean folk music. "The Banana Boat Song (Day-O)" proved to be a huge hit.

This was the first vinyl album in recording history to sell more than one million copies.

Here I want to look at the solar return and profected chart for the year 1956, which is the year that the album *Calypso!* was released and Belafonte rose to worldwide fame. 1956 was the peak of the peak.

For this example I am primarily interested in the condition of the two planets, the Sun and Jupiter, since those are the planets that are active in the directions.

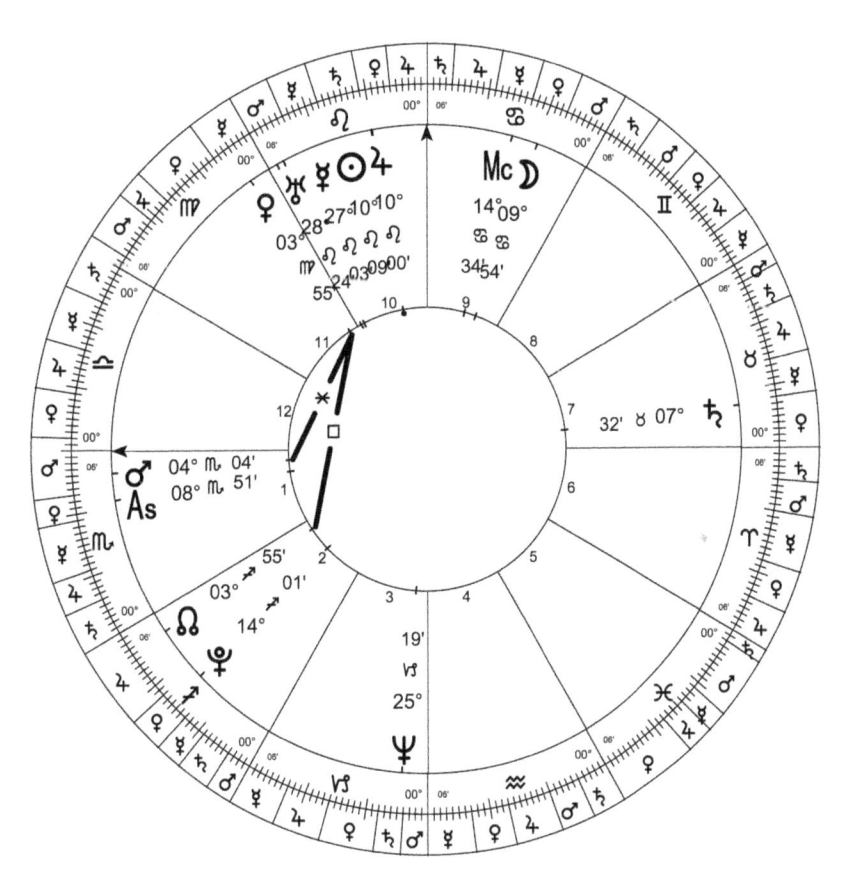

Here is the profected chart for 1956. Note that the Sun/Jupiter conjunction is in Leo, the sign of the Sun's rulership, so it is especially strong in this year's profected chart. This coincides with its special strength in the Midheaven directions. Also note that Mars on the Ascendant has profected to Scorpio, and Moon on the Midheaven has profected to Cancer, both being the signs of their rulership, so those two planets will likely be particularly helpful and effective during this period.

In this case the directions are extremely positive, and the profections very strongly supported and fulfilled that positive character. The very strong directions of a very strong point in the chart, supported by the very strong profections, was enough to make this the year that Belafonte's worldwide musical career went nova.

Transits

Not all transits are equal in impact. The system that we have been examining here provides a context to help decide which transits are likely to be the most important. The same general principle applies that we have used throughout.

Transits which align with the general directions of the predictive systems will likely have the biggest effect.

Any planet, point or house that is particularly emphasized in the directions and other charts should be watched in transits. Transits of that point, and transits to that point, are both important.

These are points that should be watched.

1) Transits of the LOY in the natal chart and in the solar return.

2) Transits to the LOY in the natal chart and in the solar return.

3) Transits through the profected sign of the year, especially by planets which are otherwise emphasized. Transits through the stakes, the signs in square and opposition to the profected sign of the year, can also be significant. All four of those signs are activated by the profection.

4) Transits to the solar return Ascendant of the year, and transits through the SR first house.

5) Eclipses on any of the above points also take on extra significance. Planets stationing and changing direction on any of those points, especially by the slower moving planets, are especially strong.

Along with these points, which are specific for a given time period, there are other transits I always watch. I pay attention to the transits of the slow moving planets, from Saturn on out, whenever they make hard aspects to the personal planets (Sun, Moon, Mercury, Venus) or to the angles. I find that Saturn transits in particular are always important, and I mark what house Saturn is moving through, and whenever Saturn changes signs.

LOY and Transits - Charles Obert

In this example I want to use the solar return and profections for myself for the most recent year, 2017, and show how the two together related to what was the most significant transit of the year. This shows my natal chart in the center surrounded by the profections for 2017 in the outside wheel.

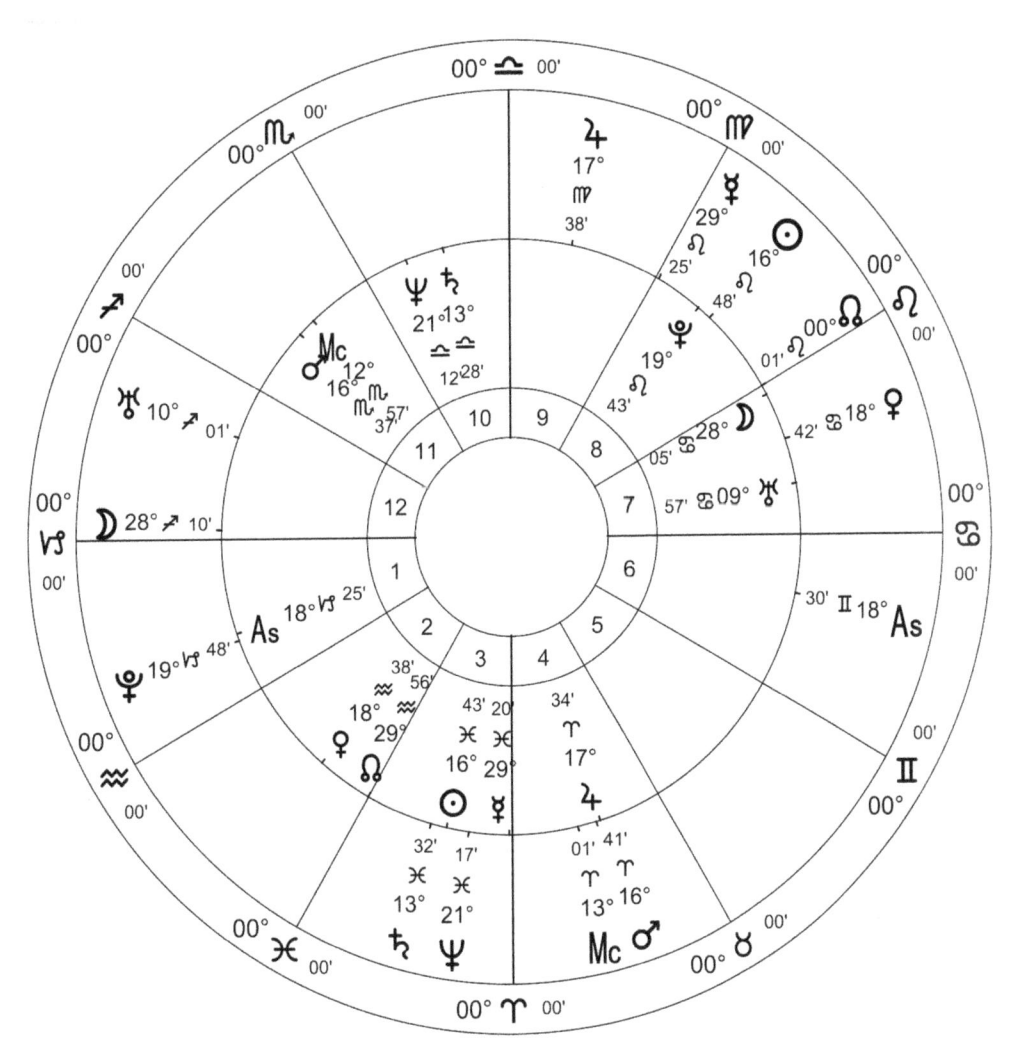

The profected sign of year is Gemini, and the profected house is the sixth, which is a house of illness. The profected LOY is Mercury, the ruler of Gemini.

Looking at the profected chart as a whole against my natal, there are a couple of close conjunctions that gave me pause. Profected Pluto is sitting right on my natal Ascendant, the profected Sun is sitting right on natal Pluto, and Profected Saturn is very close to my natal Sun. That shows two stressful hits involving my Sun, and two stressful hits involving Pluto. I pay attention to redundant aspects. When aspects like that show up only in the profected chart I question how important they are, but I note them when they correlate to qualities in the solar return chart and in other directions.

As it turns out, there is a significant correlation involving Pluto, which we will see later on.

This chart shows the solar return for the year 2017.

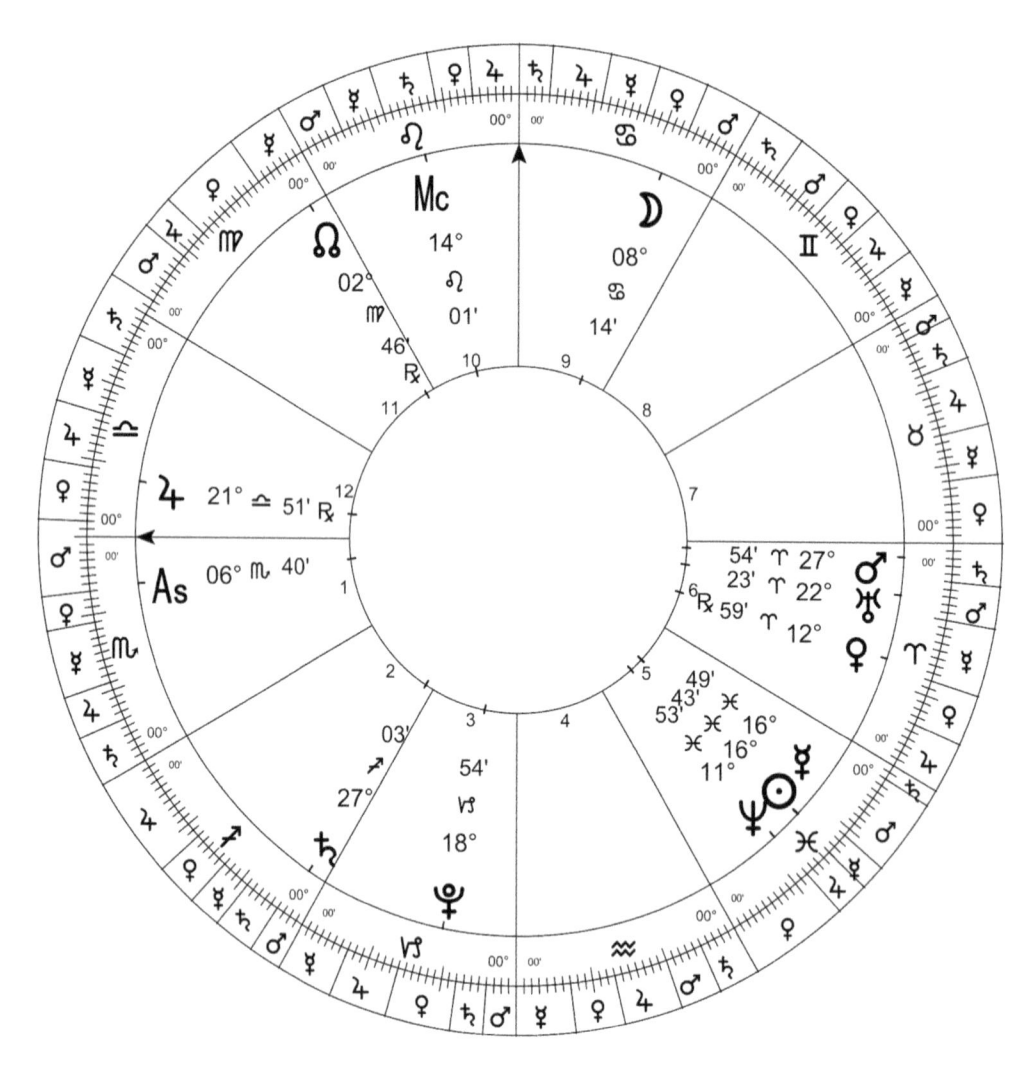

First note the rising sign is Scorpio ruled by Mars, and the SR Mars is in the sixth house - so again we see a sixth house connection. There is also a first and sixth house connection by rulership in two ways - the ruler of the sixth house, Mars, is in the first house, and also rules the first. First plus sixth house could equate to me getting sick. Fortunately, Mars in the sixth is in Aries in his rulership where he is strong, so that is good. Mars is in a cardinal fire sign which could correlate to some sort of acute or sharp illness, probably painful but not of long duration, and one that would likely turn out okay given Mars being in good condition in both my solar return and in my natal chart. The sharpness of it might be accentuated by Mars being loosely conjunct Uranus, but that is a five degree separating orb so I don't weigh it very highly.

LOY Mercury is in the fifth house in Pisces, in detriment and fall, but Mercury is also cazimi, just six minutes from exact conjunction from the Sun. Being cazimi greatly strengthens and greatly emphasizes Mercury, so I expect Mercurial activities to be important this year, possibly involving fifth house matters like creativity. (In my case I was 65 this year and not in a relationship, so it would be unreasonable to expect me to have a child.)

This next chart shows the solar return in a bi-wheel around my natal chart.

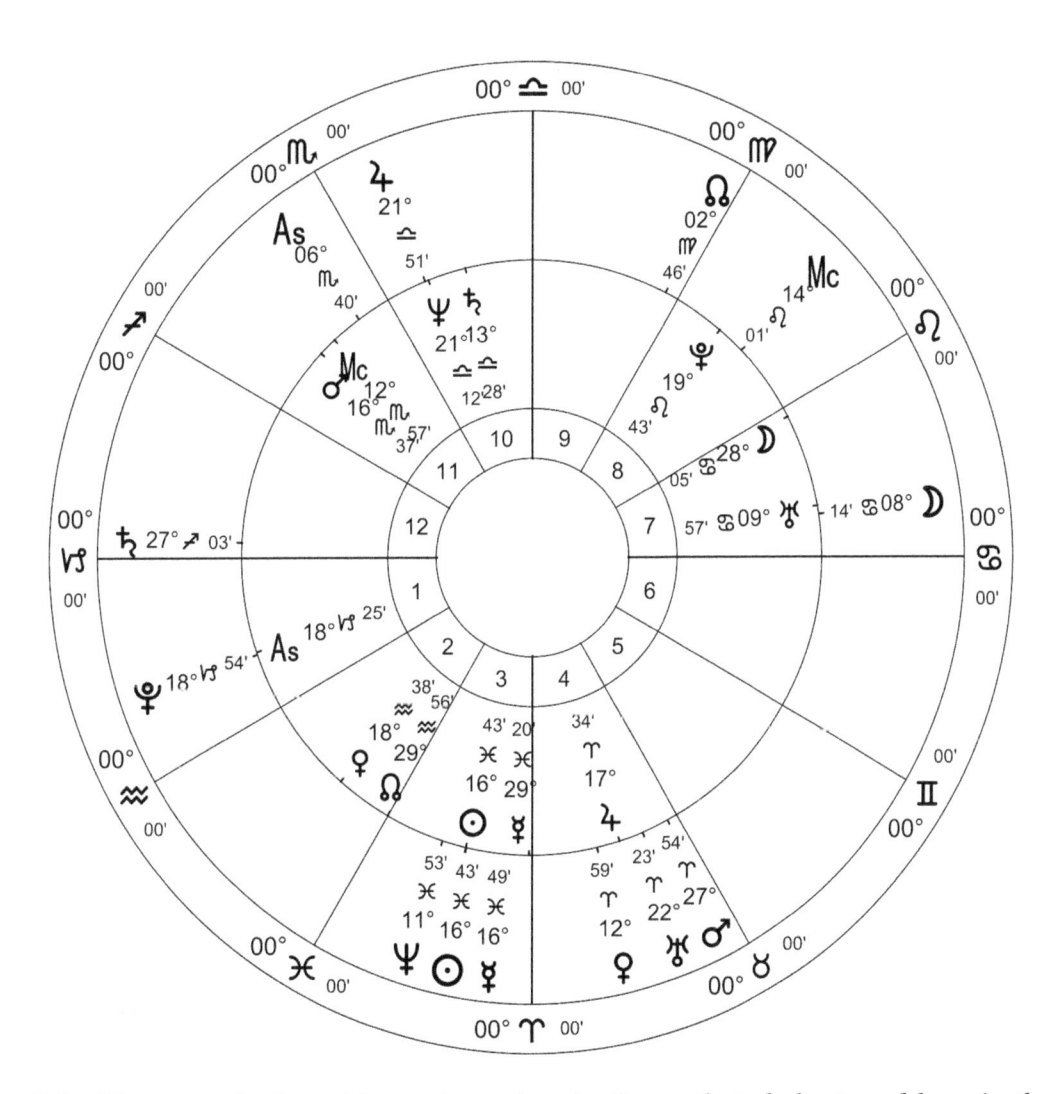

I mentioned the Pluto correlation with my Ascendant in the profected chart, and here in the SR chart Pluto is sitting right on my Ascendant, tightly conjunct. Time to sit up and take notice. I've worked enough with the outer planets to have a healthy respect for them, so in this case I expect a year of some far reaching changes, possibly involving health challenges.

Also note that solar return Moon is sitting tightly conjunct natal Uranus in the seventh house. The Moon often correlates to health issues, and in my case Moon in Cancer often means digestive issues. The seventh house location could also indicate relationship issues, but that is not emphasized anywhere else.

The next chart flips the two wheels, and puts the solar return in the middle with the natal chart around it. The house structure and angles of the solar return are emphasized in that view.

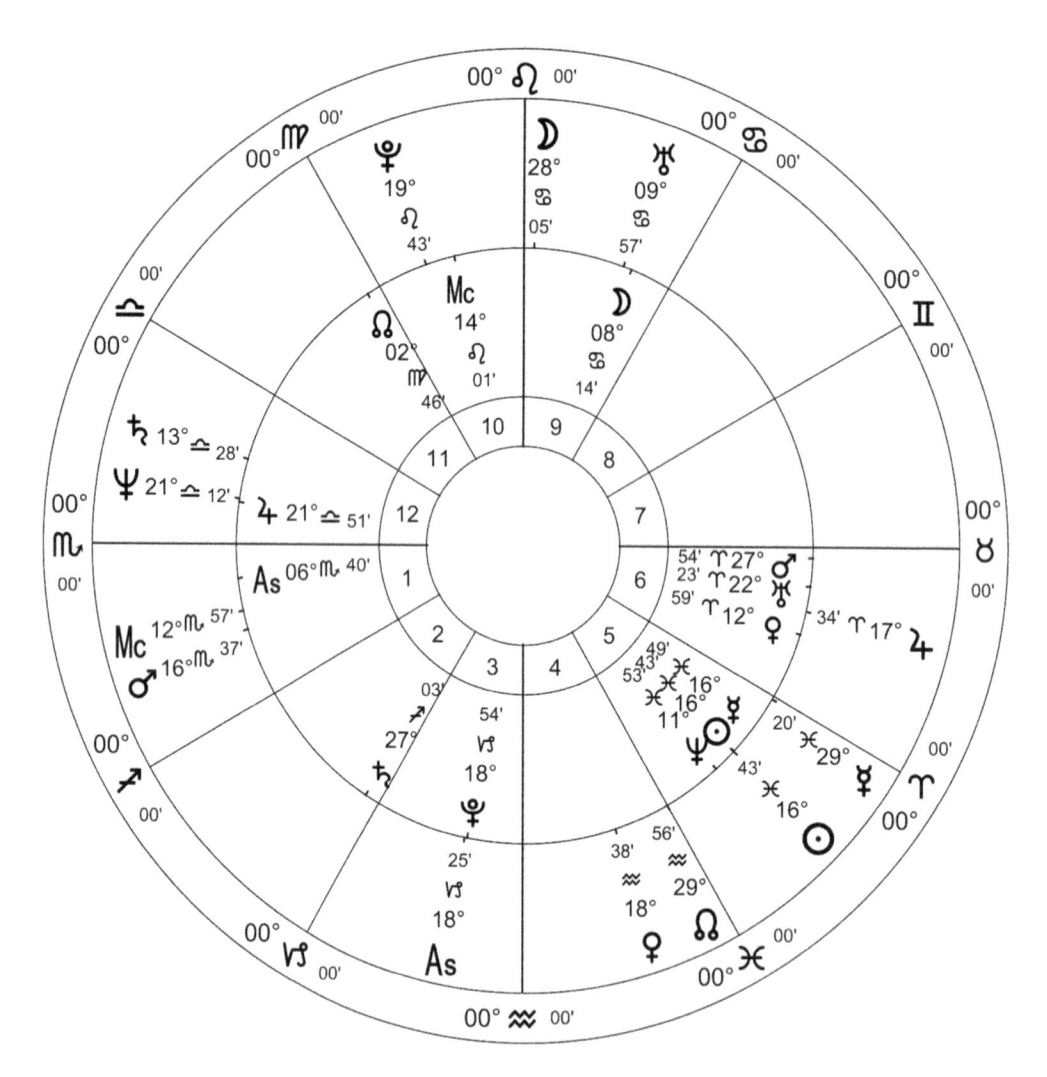

In this chart LOY Mercury in the outer ring is at very late Pisces, just about to enter the sixth house when it moves to zero degree Aries. My natal Mars is rising in the SR chart, so again we have the first and sixth house connection. A significant transit to that Mercury triggered a major health event that ended up setting a big part of my agenda for the first part of the year.

The Sun entered Aries, moving into the SR sixth house and transiting my natal Mercury who is LOY, at the beginning of Spring in late March. That coincided with the peak of a series of gall bladder attacks over a three day period that was the first major illness I have had in many years. It also marked the beginning of a several month period in which I severely controlled my diet, cleared up the gall bladder problems, and lost a great deal of weight. That sort of strict self-discipline fits with SR ruler Mars being in the SR sixth house, and with that same Mars in my natal chart rising in the SR chart since it affected my physical self.

Regarding LOY Mercury being cazimi, the entire year was very important and active in terms of reading new material and doing a great deal of writing. Philosophically I was drawn to Mars kinds of individualistic and libertarian of writers, so Mars set much of the tone for my reading.

66

Yearly Solar Return Directions

For the solar return, directions are done for the Ascendant, moving it all the way around the wheel of the signs for the year. Within the space of that year the directed Ascendant moves through all the signs and makes all possible aspects to the planets in the chart.

The free program Morinus can create the listing of annual solar return directions, and I think you will find that running a listing for a solar return of your own will help clarify how they work.

The following example listing illustrates how the annual directions work.

Z (Scorpio)Venus D --> Asc 2017.03.07
Z (Scorpio)Mercury D --> Asc 2017.03.12
Z Trigon Mercury D --> Asc 2017.03.20
Z (Scorpio)Jupiter D --> Asc 2017.03.22
Z (Scorpio)Saturn D --> Asc 2017.03.29

Z (Sagittarius)Jupiter D --> Asc 2017.04.06
Z (Sagittarius)Venus D --> Asc 2017.04.21
Z Quadrat Mercury D --> Asc 2017.04.27
Z (Sagittarius)Mercury D --> Asc 2017.04.27
Z (Sagittarius)Saturn D --> Asc 2017.05.02
Z (Sagittarius)Mars D --> Asc 2017.05.07
Z Trigon Mars D --> Asc 2017.05.09

Z (Capricornus)Mercury D --> Asc 2017.05.12
Z (Capricornus)Jupiter D --> Asc 2017.05.19
Z (Capricornus)Venus D --> Asc 2017.05.26
Z Sextil Mercury D --> Asc 2017.05.29
Z (Capricornus)Saturn D --> Asc 2017.06.03
Z (Capricornus)Mars D --> Asc 2017.06.06
Z Quadrat Mars D --> Asc 2017.06.08

Z (Aquarius)Mercury D --> Asc 2017.06.10
Z (Aquarius)Venus D --> Asc 2017.06.16
Z (Aquarius)Jupiter D --> Asc 2017.06.20
Z (Aquarius)Mars D --> Asc 2017.06.25
Z (Aquarius)Saturn D --> Asc 2017.06.28
Z Sextil Mars D --> Asc 2017.06.30

This is a portion of the annual directions listing from my own solar return chart for the year 2017.

My birthday is March 7 and the solar return Ascendant is in Scorpio, so the annual directions start in the bounds of Venus in Scorpio on that date, and move to Mercury bounds on March 12. On March 20 the Ascendant made a trine aspect to Mercury.

The direction changed signs on April 6, when it moved into the bounds of Jupiter in Sagittarius. The Ascendant moved through Sagittarius in April and early May, also making a square aspect to Mercury around April 27 and a trine to Mars on May 9.

On May 12 the directed Ascendant changed signs again, moving into the Mercury bounds in Capricorn. It moved through the various bounds in Capricorn through May and into early June, changing signs again on June 10 when it moved into the Mercury bounds of Aquarius.

The directions continue in this way, going all the way around the chart in the space of the year, returning back to Venus bounds in Scorpio on March 7 of the next year.

Important Points in Yearly Directions

As with transits, the important directions to look for are those involving the profected sign and planets activated for the year.

Note the direction of the Ascendant to the LOY by aspect. This includes the LOY in both the natal and the SR. The major aspects are used - conjunction, opposition, square, trine - and traditionally sextile is not included. I am finding that the hard aspects are more likely to be significant than are trines.

Note the direction of the Ascendant through the profected sign of the year, and to the signs in square or opposition. This includes the signs of the same mode - so for example, if the profected sign is cardinal then directions through any of the cardinal signs are important.

Those are the general rules featured in the traditional literature. I am finding that, like everything else, the important directions depend on which planets and houses are standing out that year, including any significant aspect patterns in the solar return. For instance, if the most important configuration in the SR chart is a strong square or opposition, direction to the points in that pattern by conjunction can mark critical events.

The traditional points listed above are most likely to be significant when those points are also involved in major aspect configurations or are angular in the SR chart.

For really significant events you are likely to see significant transits and significant directions coinciding in time, sometimes to the same point.

On the following page is an illustration of how the yearly directions work, using my solar return chart for the year 2017. This shows how I work with charts in my practice - I print out the solar return wheel of the year, by itself with the bounds, and in a bi-wheel with the natal chart, and mark the dates the directed Ascendant changes signs around the rim. This makes it easier for me to graphically time the directions.

In this example Gemini is the profected sign of the year, so Mercury is Lord of the Year. This means that exact aspects by the directed Ascendant to either natal or SR Mercury mark significant times. It also means that periods when the Ascendant directs through Gemini and the other mutable signs mark times of increased significant activity relative to the theme of the year.

This is a bi-wheel, with my 2017 solar return chart on the inside, and the natal on the outside. I have put the dates in the year that the SR Ascendant changes signs outside the rim.

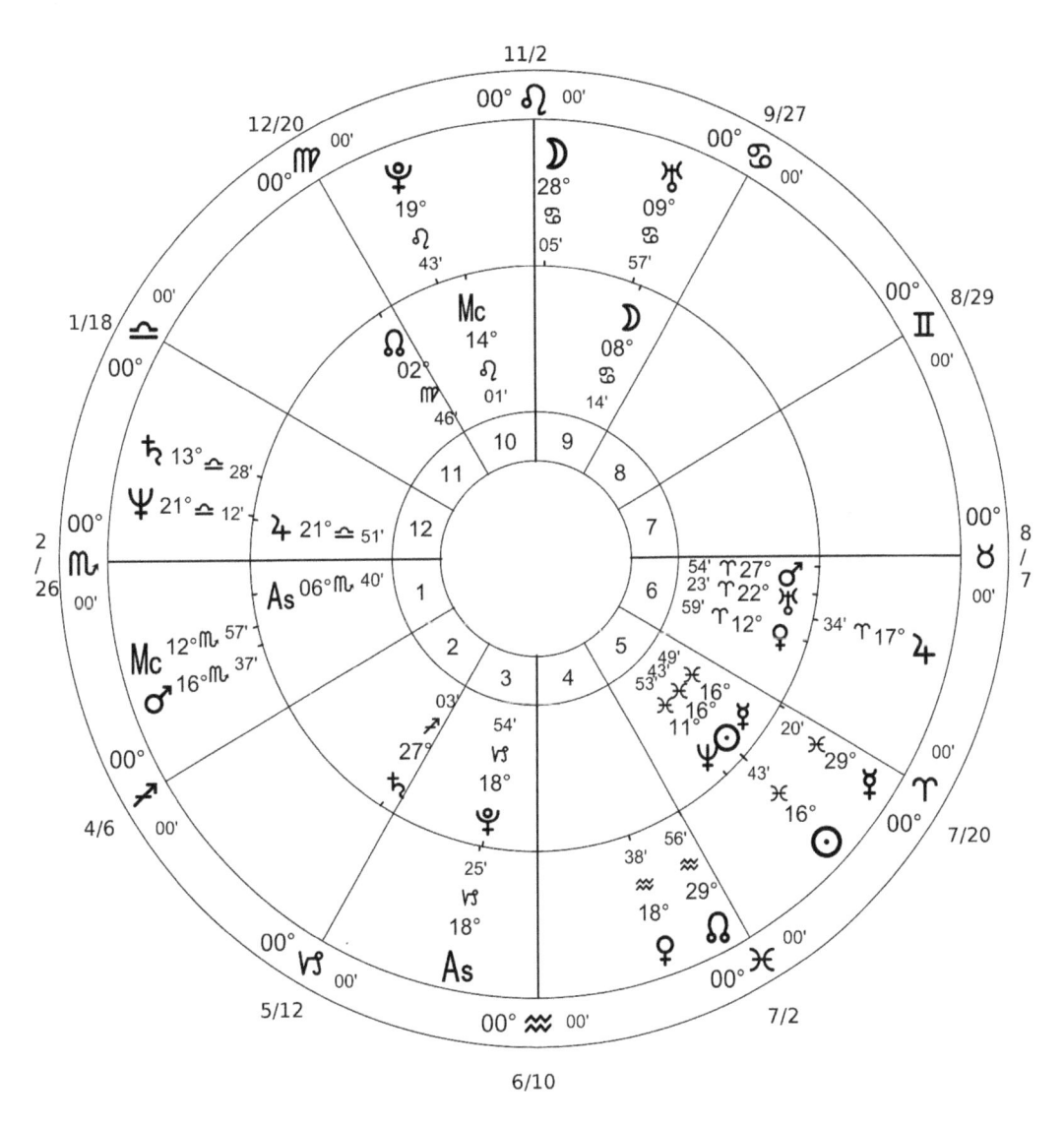

The listing below shows excerpts from the annual directions for two periods during the year. The Ascendant starts at its SR location at 6 degrees Scorpio and moves around the wheel from there. I marked the lines of a change of signs, and of an exact aspect to Mercury, in bold. The directed Ascendant entered Sagittarius around April 6, and entered Pisces around July 2. It made an exact square aspect to SR Mercury on April 27, and an exact conjunction on July 12.

(Sagittarius)Jupiter D --> Asc 2017.04.06   ...
(Sagittarius)Venus D --> Asc 2017.04.21   **(Pisces)Venus D --> Asc 2017.07.02**
Quadrat Mercury D --> Asc 2017.04.27   (Pisces)Jupiter D --> Asc 2017.07.09
(Sagittarius)Mercury D --> Asc 2017.04.27   (Pisces)Mercury D --> Asc 2017.07.12
(Sagittarius)Saturn D --> Asc 2017.05.02   **Mercury D --> Asc 2017.07.12**

This next diagram has the solar return chart by itself, in a wheel that also shows the bounds around the outside edge, so it is easier to graphically watch the bound rulers change. Again I have marked the dates the directed Ascendant changes signs around the edge. I have also marked the natal position of the LOY Mercury, at 29 Pisces, in the outer rim of the chart with the letters ME.

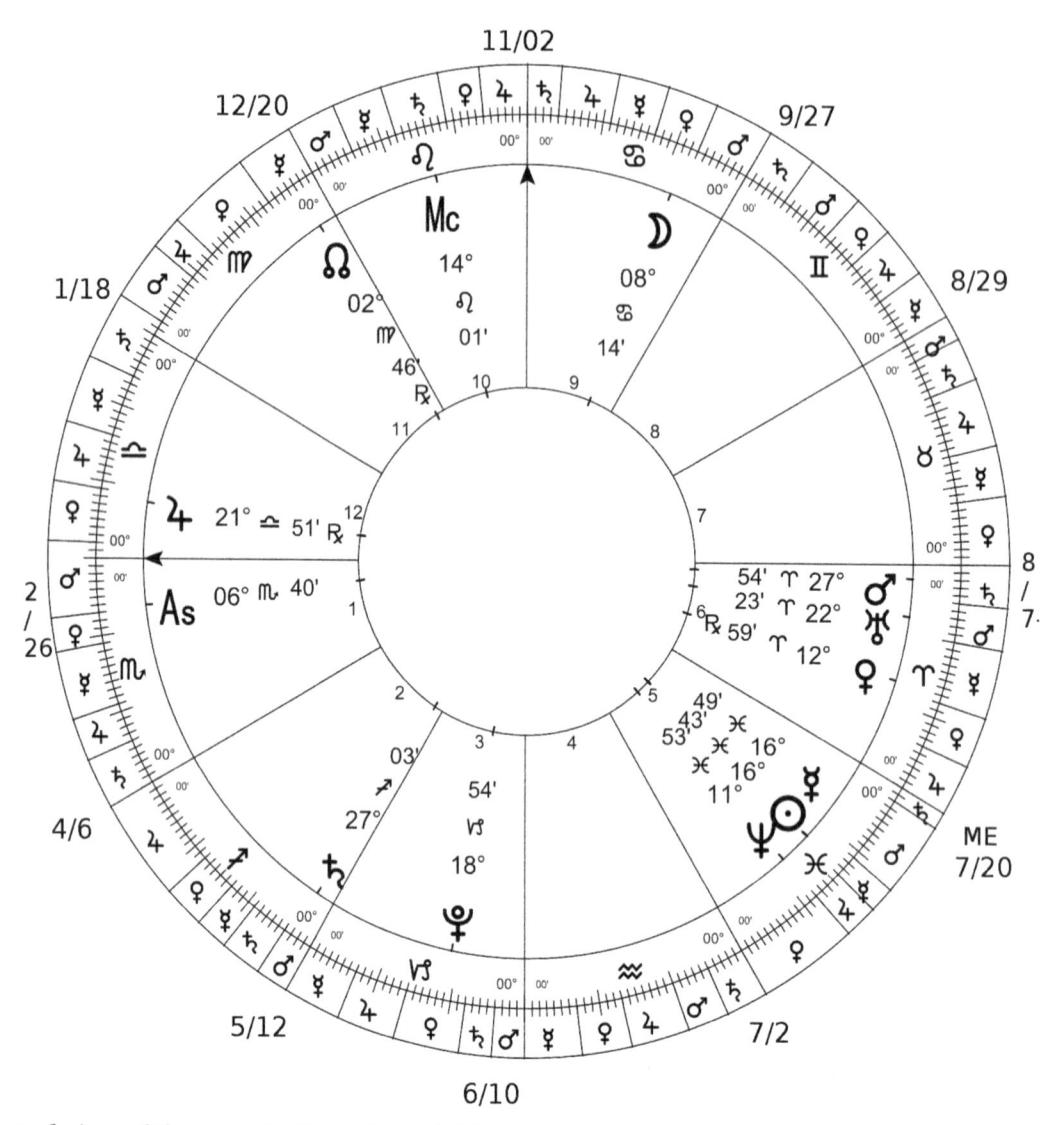

The profected sign of the year is Gemini, and LOY is Mercury, so directions to the mutable signs and to Mercury are especially important.

The period during April, when the Ascendant directed through the mutable sign, Sagittarius, I was very busy reworking my diet and recovering from a serious illness.

The period in July, when the Ascendant directed through the mutable sign Pisces, I started a major new teaching, writing and reading project that set the theme for the rest of my year's work. Both of those periods also included major aspects to the SR Mercury location (by square from Sagittarius, by conjunction in Pisces), so they were significant by both sign and by aspect to the Lord of the Year.

Franklin D Roosevelt

In this section we are going to look at a significant year in the life of Franklin D Roosevelt, who was elected President of the United States in 1932 and guided the country through the years of the Great Depression and into World War II, dying in 1945, the year the war ended.

The year we will look at is 1921, the year he contracted the disease that left him paralyzed from the waist down for the rest of his life.

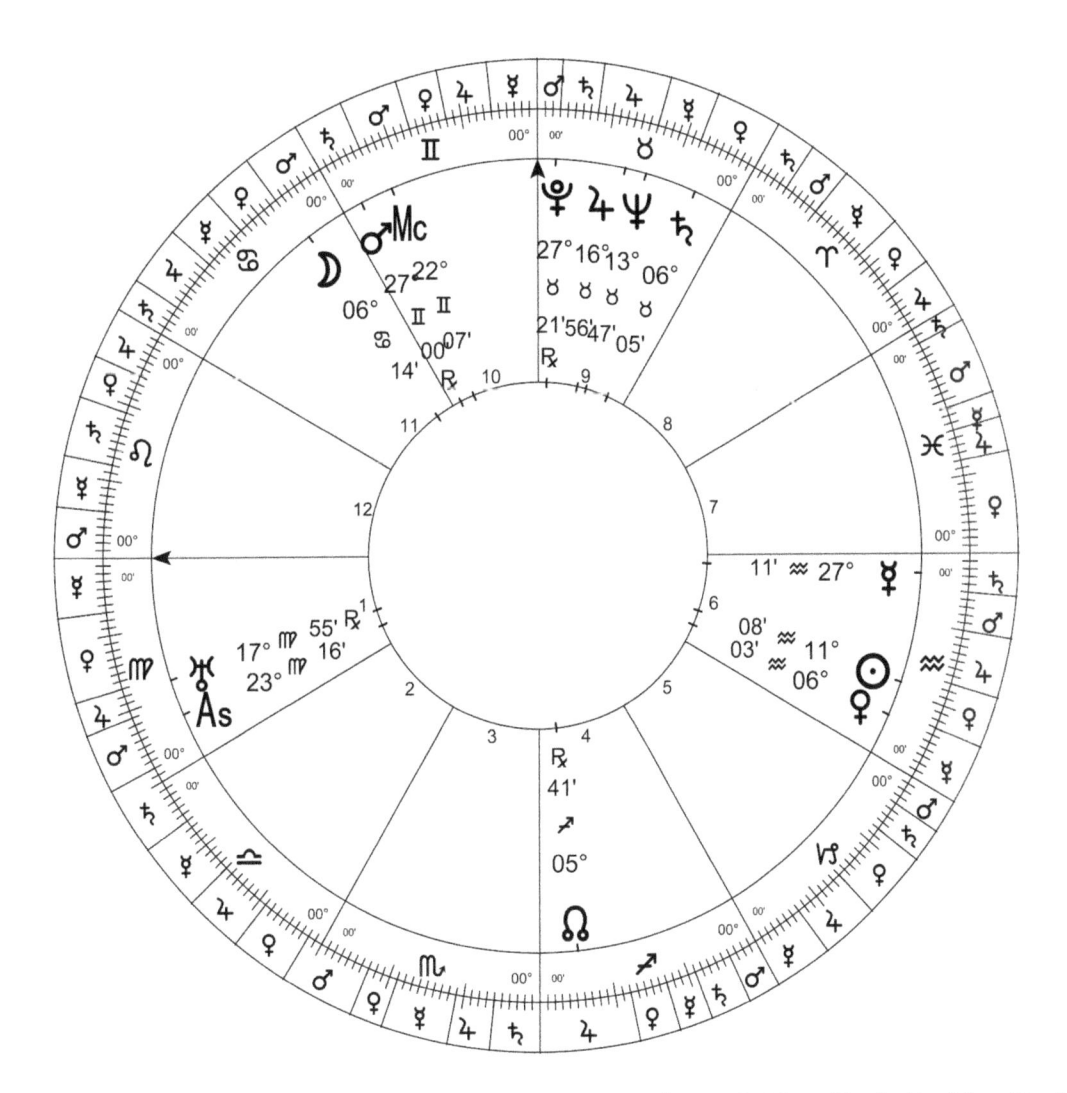

Franklin Delano Roosevelt, January 30, 1882, 8:45 PM, Hyde Park, New York. Rodden Rating AA.

We are going to look at the chart to find evidence of the potential for the paralytic disease. (Note that in a later chapter I talk about the usefulness of approaching a chart or a reading with a defined theme or question, to draw out useful data relevant to that theme.) That evidence shows the seeds of potential, and we should see those seeds sprouting by being prominent in the predictive data for 1921, the year he fell ill.

The logical place to start for questions of illness is the sixth house, and Roosevelt has three of the inner planets there, the Sun, Venus and Mercury. None of the three is strong - the Sun is peregrine and in detriment, Venus has dignity by face only and is greatly weakened by being combust, approaching the Sun, with no reception to soften the condition. Mercury has dignity by triplicity in air signs.

And - the sixth house is ruled by the peregrine malefic Saturn in Taurus, part of the four planet stellium in the ninth house with Pluto, Jupiter and Neptune.

All three of those sixth house planets are stressed by hard aspects to difficult planets, squares from the stellium in Taurus in the ninth house. Venus is in a very tight applying square, within two minutes of exact, with Saturn. Fortunately Saturn and Venus have a very strong mutual reception by both rulership and triplicity, and that takes a lot of the hard edge off of that aspect.

The Sun is less fortunate, being in a hard applying square with Neptune in Taurus. Hard aspects to Neptune can manifest as health issues that are weakening and debilitating, and Neptune health problems are often mysterious and hard to diagnose - note that there is disagreement to this day as to exactly what disease Roosevelt contracted. Since Roosevelt's illness has the marks of a Neptune disease, we should expect a badly stressed Sun in the predictive material, and it would be confirming to find that as a stressed aspect from Neptune as in the natal.

Mercury also has a very stressed aspect, a tight mutually applying square to Pluto retrograde in Taurus. Mercury is associated with diseases of the nervous system, and that fits Roosevelt's ailment also. We can expect stressed Mercury in the predictive data.

It is worth noting that Mercury also has a tight trine with Mars, who is retrograde and strong on the Midheaven. Since this is a trine and Mercury rules Mars, this is not as negative an aspect.

Whenever there are questions of health it is always worth keeping the Moon in mind. The Moon in this chart is pretty strong, being in her rulership in Cancer and near enough to the Midheaven to be angular - think of Roosevelt's homey, personable fireside chats on the radio while he was president. The Moon is in a tight sextile with Saturn in Taurus, and there is one-way reception there - Saturn is in the exaltation and triplicity of Taurus, but the Moon is in Saturn's detriment. Note that Venus, Saturn and the Moon are all at six degrees - that can be significant when the chart is rotated in profections, because those planets will repeatedly end up right on top of each other by the profected movement.

We can expect that the stressful planets in the Taurus stellium will show up in the data for the illness.

We will start our examination of the 1921 data by looking at the profected chart for the year, seeing where the profected sign of the year is, and how the profected chart in general lines up with the natal chart.

This wheel shows his natal chart in the center, with the profected chart for that year around the outside edge.

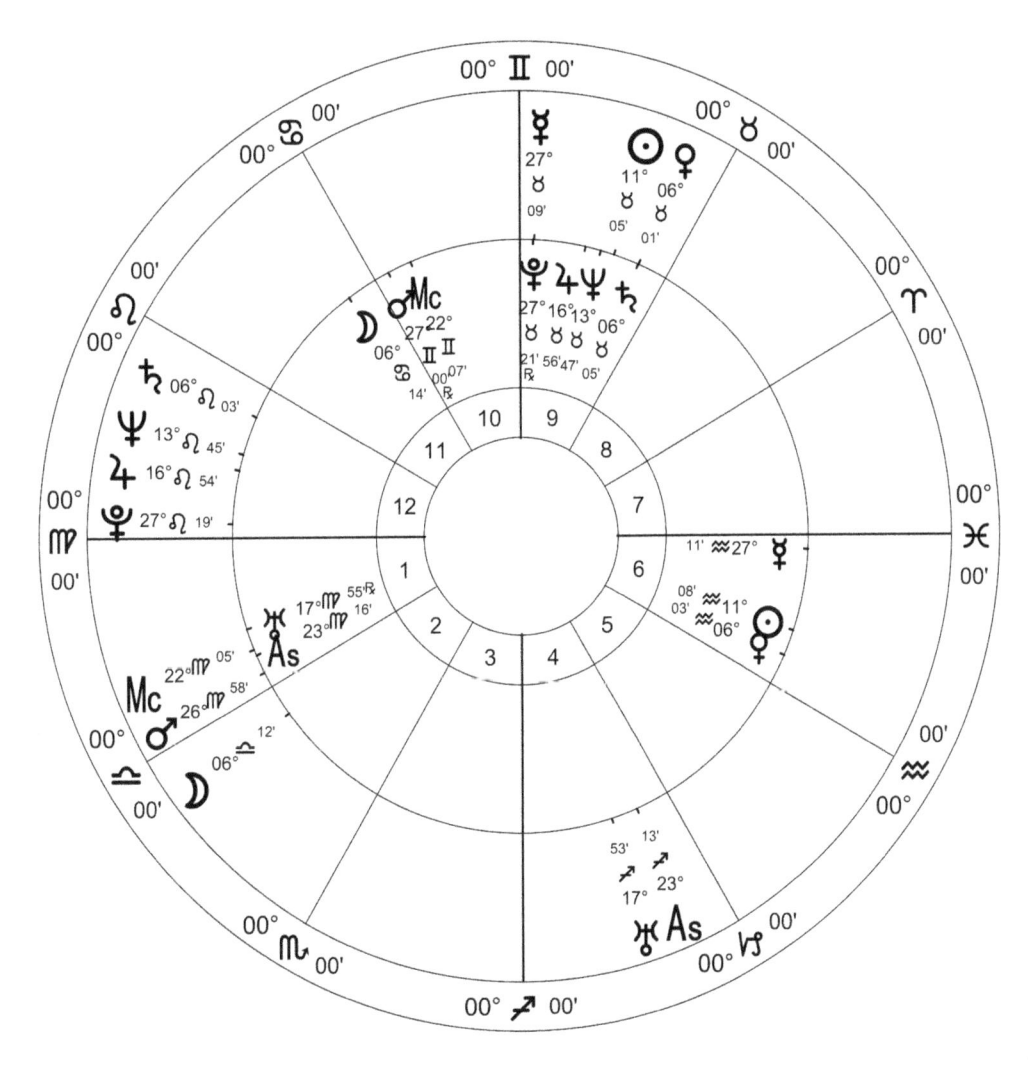

Franklin Delano Roosevelt, January 30, 1882, 8:45 pm, Hyde Park, NY. Rodden Rating AA.

The profected sign of the year is Sagittarius, ruled by Jupiter, and profected Jupiter is in the 12th house which is also associated with illness. **The entire Taurus stellium has rotated around to the twelfth house, and is sitting opposite the three planets in the natal sixth**.

Natal Mercury is exactly opposite profected Pluto, and profected Mercury is conjunct natal Pluto. Redundant markers like this are important, especially since this reflects the tight square between Mercury and Pluto in the natal chart.

Profected Mars is rising conjunct the Ascendant in Virgo, a sign ruled by Mercury in the sixth house. Recall that Mars and Mercury are in a tight trine in the natal. Mars being on the Midheaven in the natal, this could be a marker for political prominence or activity, or for the stress of illness.

Most ominously, *natal Sun is opposite profected Neptune 6th to 12th house, and natal Neptune is conjunct profected Sun in the 9th* - two stressed Sun/Neptune aspects between the charts, reflecting the stressed Sun/Neptune square in the natal chart.

Also note that *natal Venus is exactly opposite profected Saturn, and natal Saturn is conjunct profected Venus*.

There are three planets in Roosevelt's natal sixth house - Sun, Venus and Mercury - and all three of them are stressed in multiple ways in this profected chart.

Just in general, every time this profected chart came around in Roosevelt's life there would be potential for illness. Roosevelt died in 1945, 24 years later, when this same profected chart was active.

This next chart is the solar return for the year 1921.

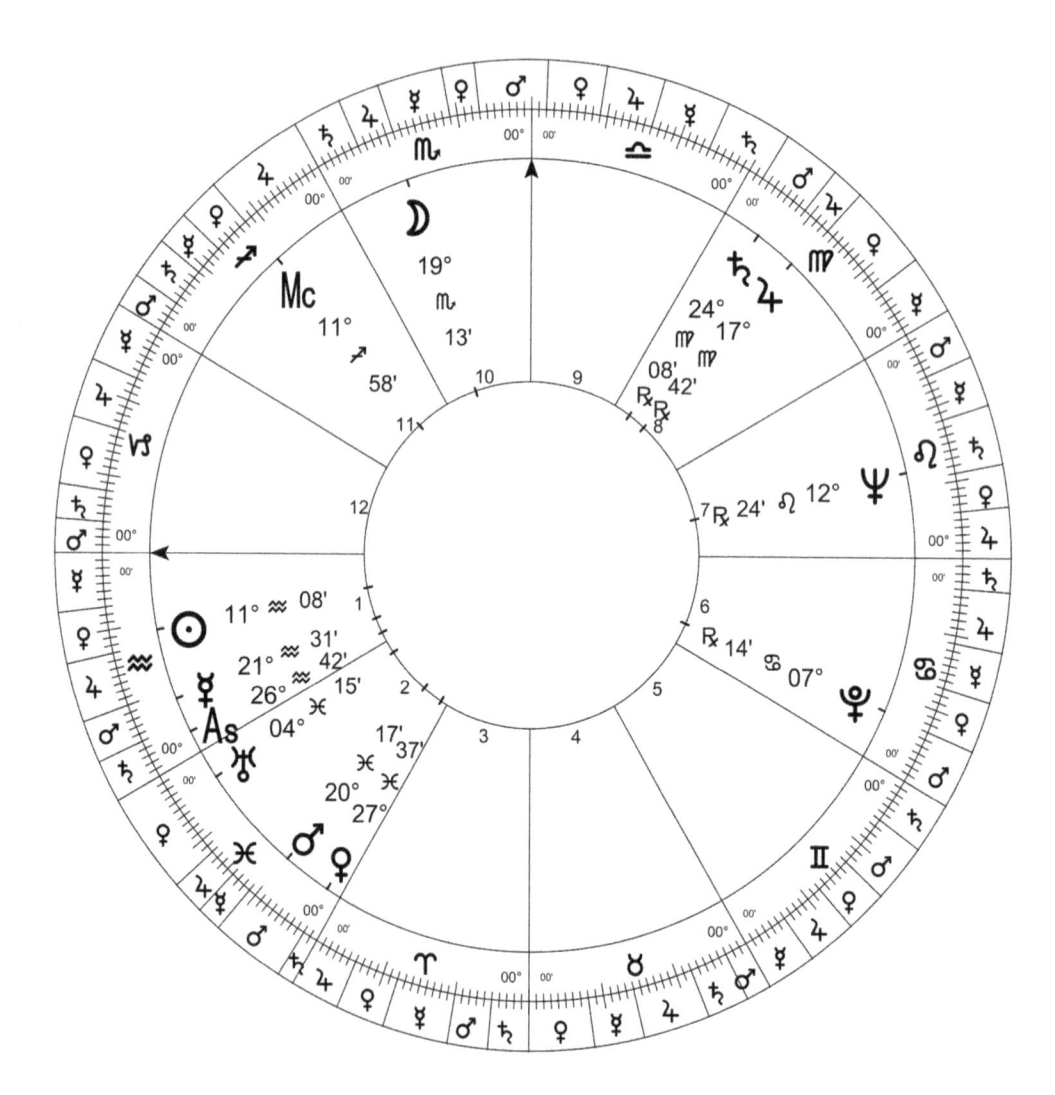

Aquarius is rising, ruled by Saturn - *Aquarius is Roosevelt's natal sixth house*. LOY Jupiter is in detriment in the 8th house which can relate to illness, conjunct the SR Ascendant ruler Saturn. Mars is in Pisces, separating from opposition to Jupiter and applying to opposition to Saturn - so both malefics are involved in hard aspects to each other and to the LOY.

The Sun is opposite Neptune, which echoes the Sun/Neptune configurations in the profected chart. There are two very difficult oppositions in the solar return chart, and they involve two of the three stressed sixth house planets in Roosevelt's natal.

Also note that the solar return sixth house is Cancer, ruled by the Moon - and the Moon is in bad shape, in fall in Scorpio.

This next chart is a bi-wheel with the natal chart in the center and SR in the second ring.

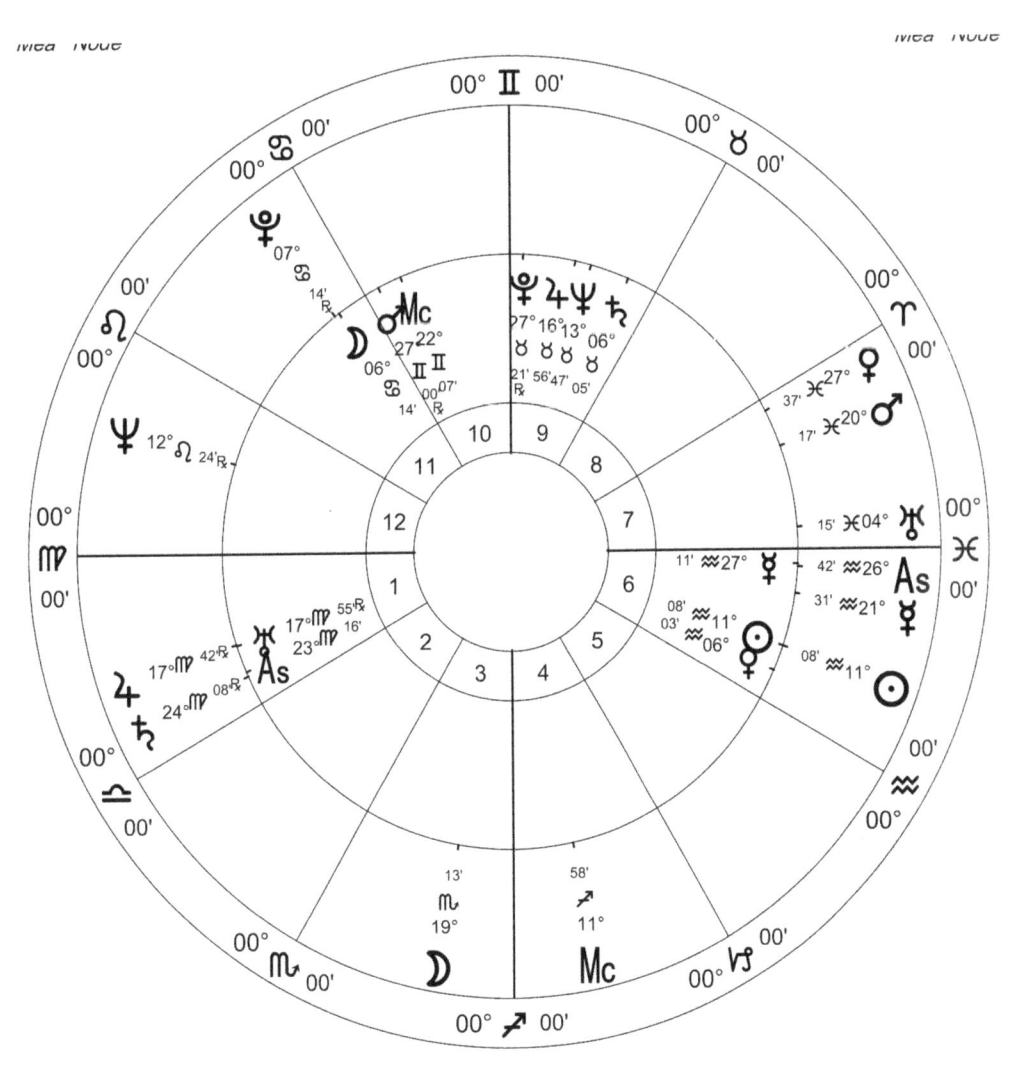

The SR Ascendant falls in the natal 6th house of illness, conjunct natal Mercury. **SR Saturn is retrograde sitting conjunct the natal Ascendant** in the first house and ruling natal the natal sixth - Saturn transits to the Ascendant often mark health issues, and this is a three pass transit. The ruler of the sixth house in the first is another marker for illness. Saturn is also conjunct LOY Jupiter on the Ascendant, and Jupiter is further weakened by being retrograde and in detriment.

SR Pluto is retrograde in mutually applying conjunction with natal Moon in the 11th, and we noted that the Moon is often associated with health issues. We also noted two significant aspects with Pluto involving the profected chart.

This next wheel flips the two charts and puts the natal around the solar return.

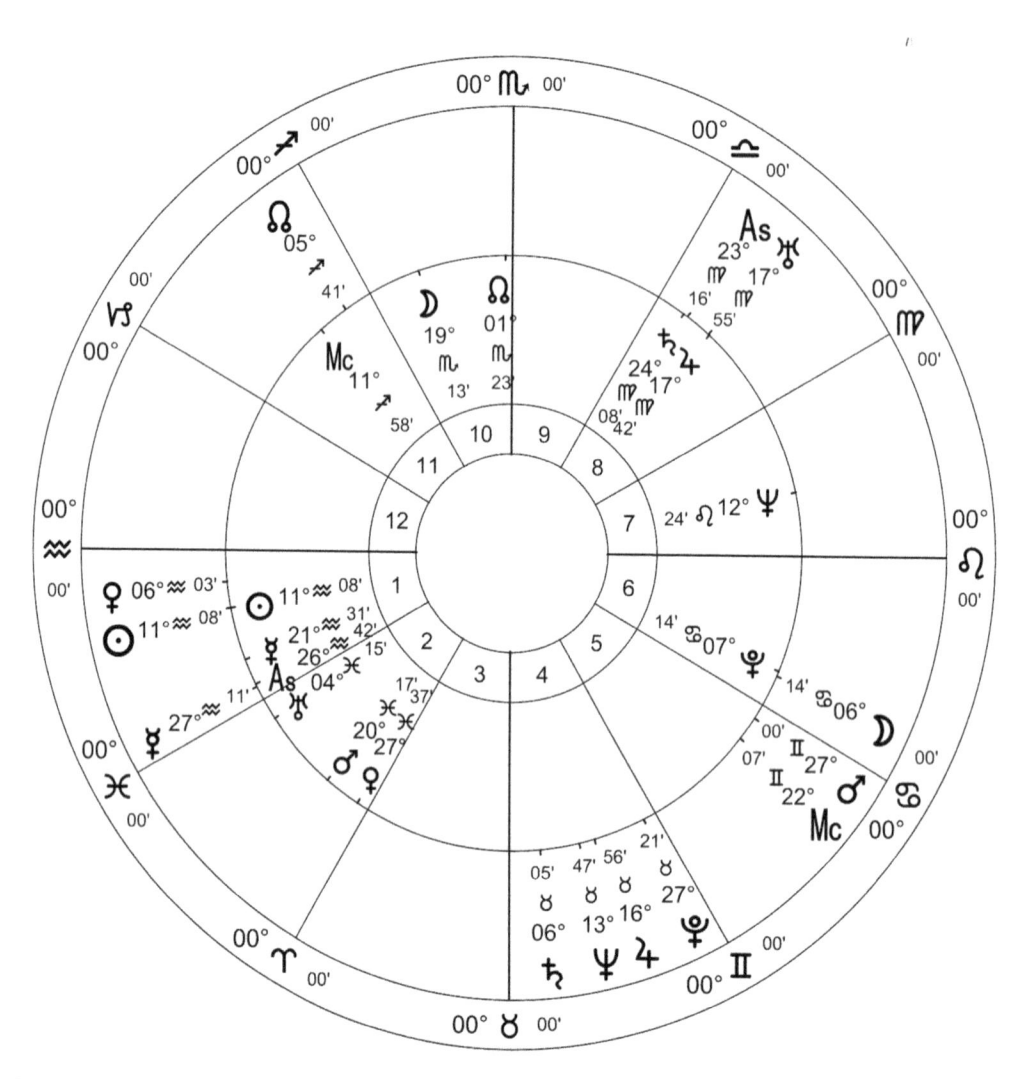

Note that **the SR Pluto to natal Moon conjunction falls in the SR sixth house**. Natal Uranus is conjunct SR LOY Jupiter in the eighth house, and the natal Ascendant is conjunct SR Saturn right next to it. Natal Jupiter, LOY, is opposite SR Moon which is in fall in Scorpio. By sign, the SR Moon is opposite the stressing Taurus stellium in the natal. The SR opposition of Mars to Jupiter and Saturn falls right on the natal Ascendant/Descendant axis, and the natal Ascendant falls in the eighth house.

LOY Jupiter is stressed in the SR chart and is angular relative to the natal chart.

The next chart is a bi-wheel of the natal with chart with the transits for August 10, which is day he became seriously ill and consulted a doctor. I drew the chart for noon, so I do not consider the transiting angles to be important, but the planetary positions are valid.

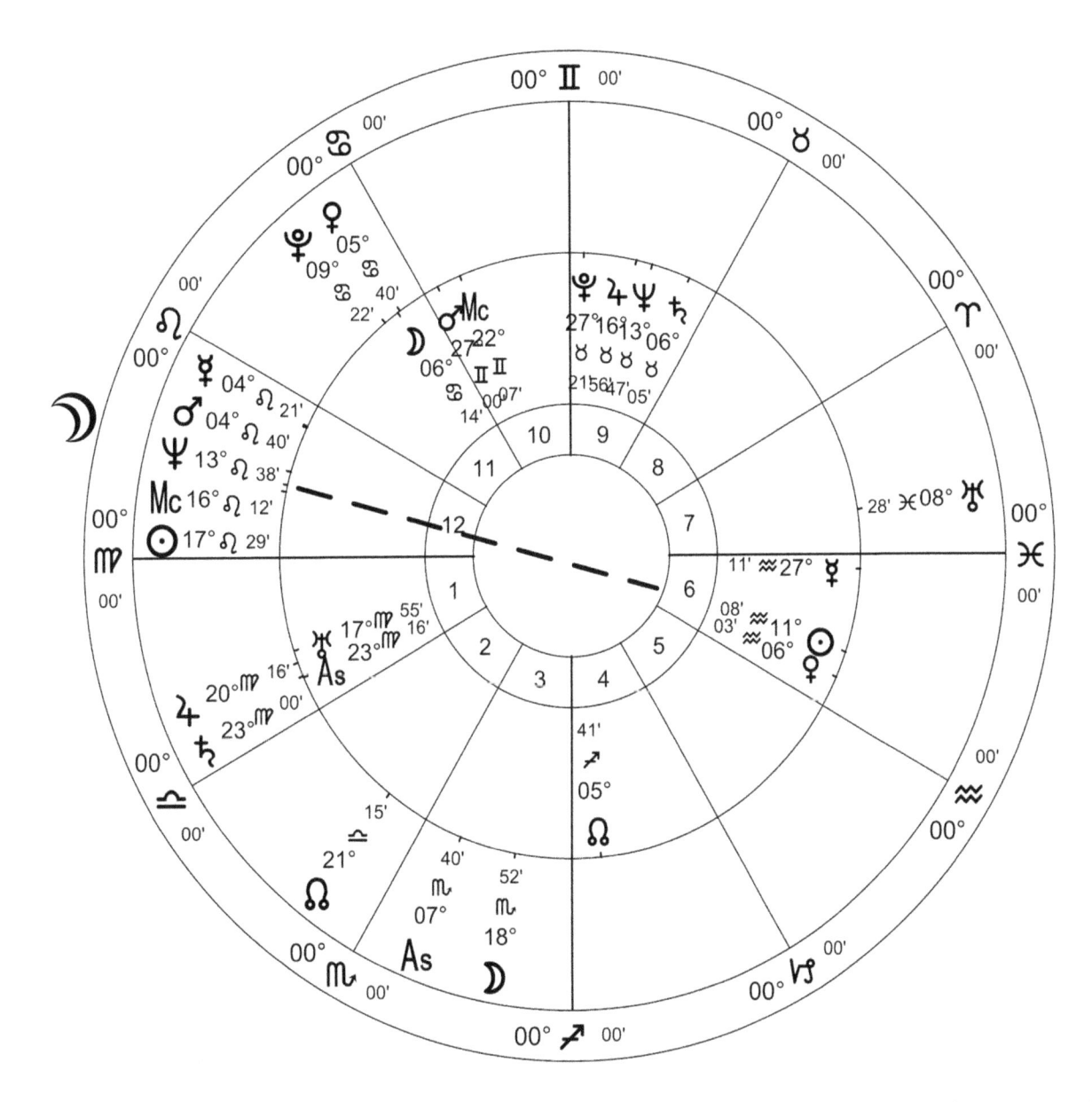

Note especially the stellium of transiting planets in Leo in the natal 12th house - the same sign and house as the stellium in the profected chart. Transiting Mercury in the twelfth is applying to a very tight conjunction to Mars, and the Sun is 4 degrees (4 days by transit) past conjunction with Neptune in the 12th - so again we have a Sun/Neptune connection, with the Sun transit being one of the likely triggers for the onset of the disease. Transiting Saturn is now moving direct approaching tight conjunction with the Ascendant - since Saturn was retrograde in the SR it made a triple pass over FDR's Ascendant that year. We already noted that Saturn rules FDR's natal sixth house.

The primary directions active at this time are: Asc -Venus(Libra)/Sun, MC -Saturn(Cancer)/Jupiter, Sun - Mercury(Pisces)/Mercury, **and Moon - Saturn(Leo)/Sun**. These involve the same planets we are seeing stressed in this group of charts.

The Moon being in bounds of Saturn is especially significant. Note that the directed Moon is opposite the natal Sun from 12th to 6th house, very near the position of solar return and transiting Neptune. This ties in with the transits in August when he became ill - *the directed Moon is being transited by the stellium in Leo opposite his natal sixth house the month he fell ill*.

Finally, we look at the annual directions of the SR Ascendant for the year. I am repeating the image of the SR here, and then the list of directions. Around the chart is the position of the directed Sun, and of the directed solar return Ascendant

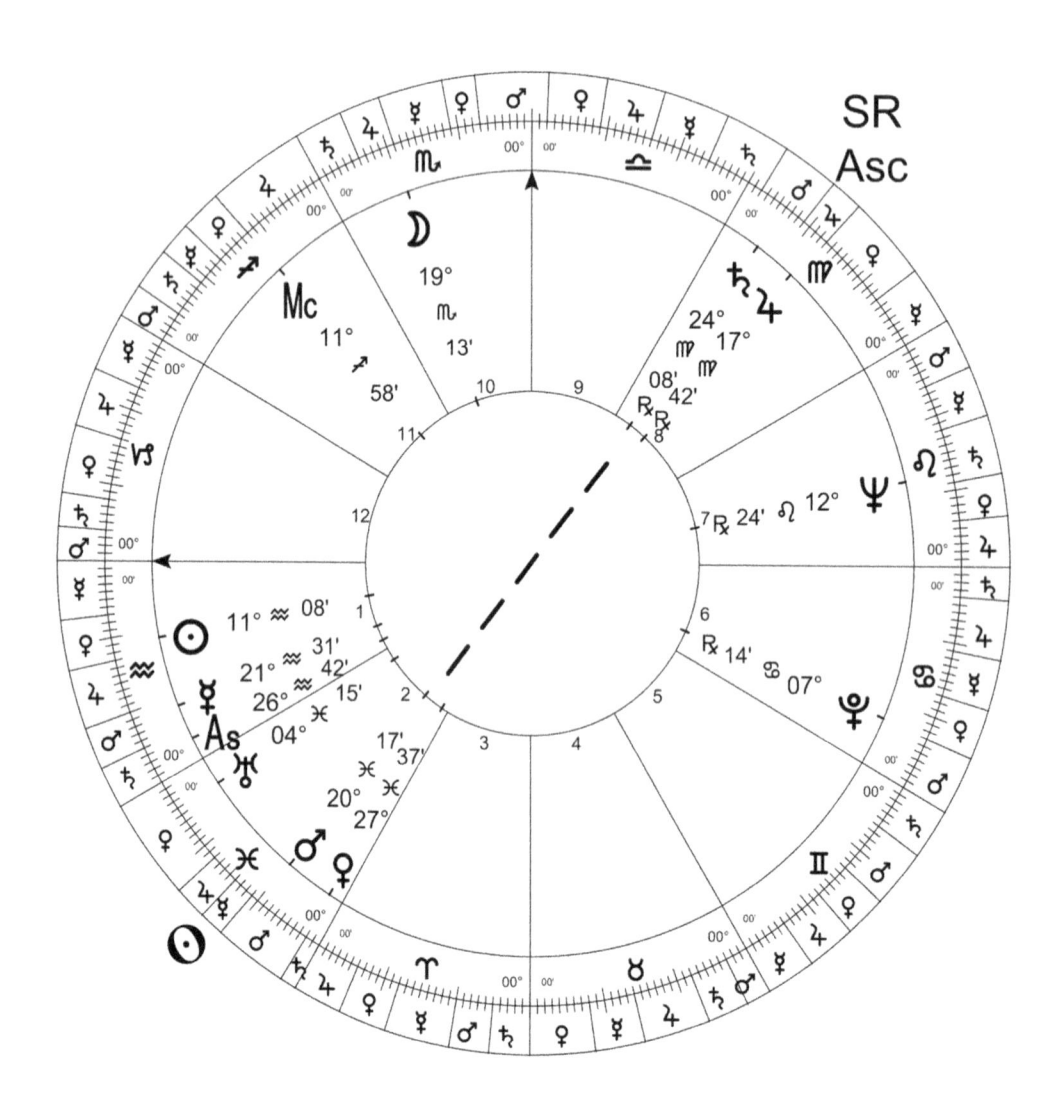

Recall that the profected sign of the year is Sagittarius, LOY Jupiter. This means that Jupiter and the mutable signs are activated for the year and are sensitive points for the annual directions. Jupiter in detriment is conjunct Saturn in the SR 8th opposite SR Mars. Both Saturn and Jupiter are in the mutable sign Virgo, and Mars is in mutable Pisces.

Z (Virgo)Jupiter D --> Asc 182.907136 1921.08.05
Z Jupiter D --> Asc 183.814268 1921.08.06
Z Sextile Moon D --> Asc 185.740094 1921.08.07
Z Opposition Mars D --> Asc 187.097085 1921.08.09
Z (Virgo)Mars D --> Asc 188.009754 1921.08.10
Z Saturn D --> Asc 192.022628 1921.08.14

In early August the yearly directions reached Virgo and the SR eighth house, making aspects to Jupiter, to Saturn and to the axis of the Saturn/Mars opposition in the SR, and directly opposite the directed Sun.

Margaret Thatcher

Margaret Thatcher, the "Iron Lady", was the first woman Prime Minister of England and the longest serving PM in the 20th century, from 1975 to 1990. She was politically conservative, and her leadership style was strong, severe and uncompromising.

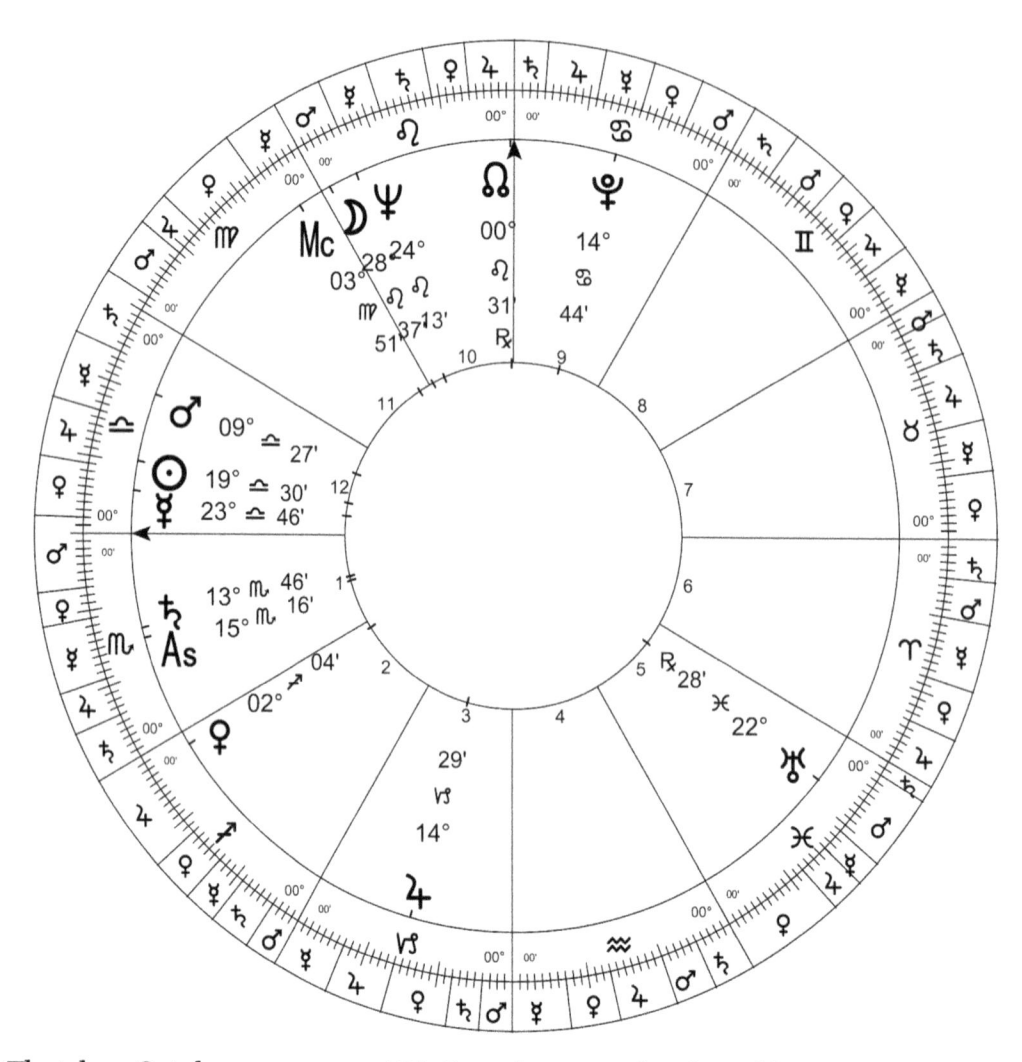

Margaret Thatcher, October 13, 1925, 9 AM, Grantham, England. Rodden Rating A.

The obvious dominant planet in this chart is Saturn, sitting right on the Ascendant in Scorpio. Mars, the Ascendant ruler, is a lot stronger and more important than it looks in first glance . Even in detriment in Libra and in the 12th house, Mars has a strong mixed mutual reception with Saturn (Saturn in Mars' rulership, Mars in Saturn's exaltation). With the two planets averse (making no aspect to each other), and three planets hidden away in the 12th house, I wonder how much of her political work involved private back-room maneuvering out of the public eye.

There is another interesting configuration worth noting. The Moon is angular and strong in Leo about 5 degrees from the Midheaven, loosely conjunct Neptune. The Moon is ruled by the Sun, which is in

Libra in its fall in the twelfth house, conjunct Mercury, and sextile the Moon/Neptune pair. Planets in fall are not heard, not respected, and the Sun being in the twelfth house emphasizes not being seen. It is noteworthy that the Sun is sextile that very visible Leo Moon, pushing to get the recognition that its ruler the Sun wants.

With the two planets Saturn and Mars being so important, we should expect to see them be strong and emphasized during significantly positive years for Thatcher. That is exactly what we find.

Thatcher was elected Prime Minister in 1979. I want to start our study by looking at the primary directions for that period. I added in the directions for Mars and Saturn to the usual four points. I also show a chart wheel with the directed positions around the outside edge.

Asc - Saturn(Sag)/Mercury
MC - Mars(Scorpio)/Moon
Sun - Jupiter(Sag)/Venus

Moon - Mars(Libra)/Mercury
Mars - Saturn(Scorpio)/Jupiter
Saturn - Saturn(Sag)/Mercury

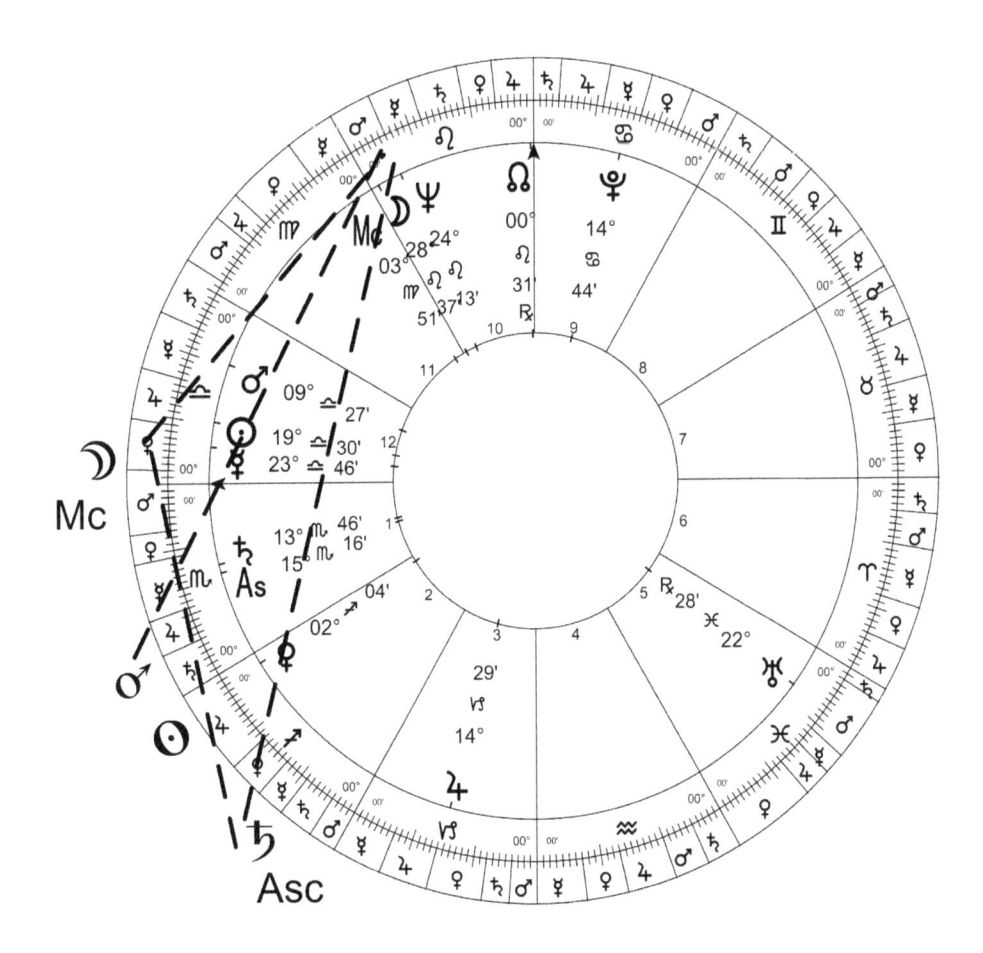

The dominance of Saturn and Mars is striking. The directed Ascendant, Mars and Saturn are all in Saturn Bounds, and the MC is in Mars bounds.

Directed Mars is in the first house along with Saturn, and I surmise that may increase the communication and coordination between the two. Directions can mark periods where planets that are averse in the natal chart are working together better. I also surmise that we could trace her rise to power previous to the election as Mars was directing through the first house, hitting Saturn and then the Ascendant.

It is also very striking that **Thatcher was elected shortly after the Midheaven directed into her first house.** The Midheaven directing into the house representing herself is an obvious marker for rising to prominence and power.

Notice the interesting and suggestive aspect configuration shown between the directed planets and the Leo Moon up at the top of the chart conjunct the Midheaven and Neptune. These are marked outside the wheel in the preceding chart.

1) The directed Moon is now sitting on the Sun Mercury conjunction and is sextile natal Moon.

2) The directed Ascendant and Saturn are both now trine that natal Moon and sextile directed Moon and natal Sun/Mercury.

3) Directed Mars is now square that same natal Moon/Neptune.

That strikes me as forming a powerful aspect pattern, all the directed planets working together to highlight that elevated Moon so that it gets the attention it is craving.

This is her profected chart for 1979, the year she was elected - I ran the profection for 1978 since she was born late in the year, and the election was in May.

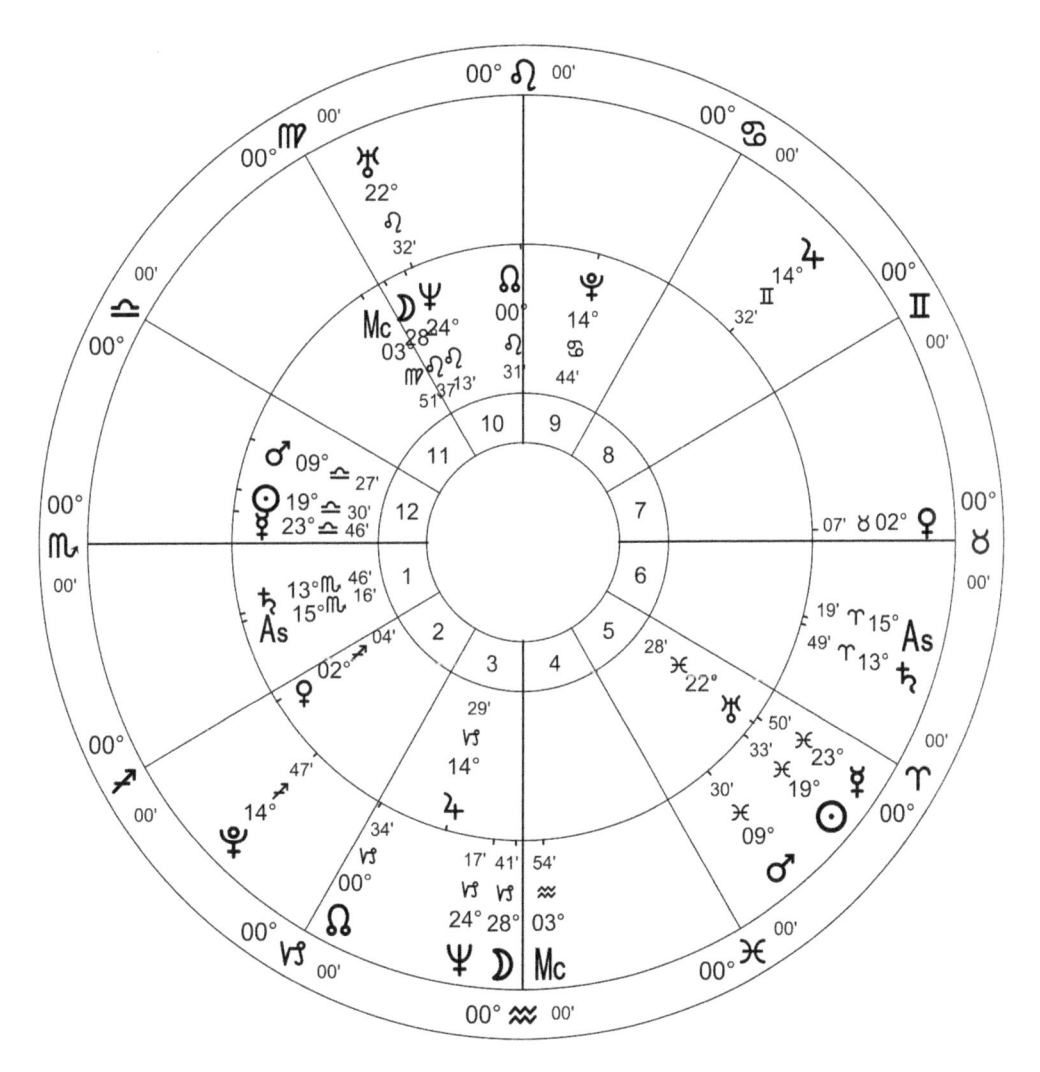

The profected sign of the year is Aries, so the LOY is Mars. Aries is a cardinal sign, and all of the other cardinal signs are also activated because of their hard aspect to Aries. These are called the signs in the stakes to Aries, those signs that are square or opposite.

Aries is opposite Libra, the sign where natal Mars resides, so Mars is additionally activated by being in the stakes with the profected sign.

Also note that profected Mars is angular, near the natal Midheaven/IC axis.

This is the Solar Return for 1978.

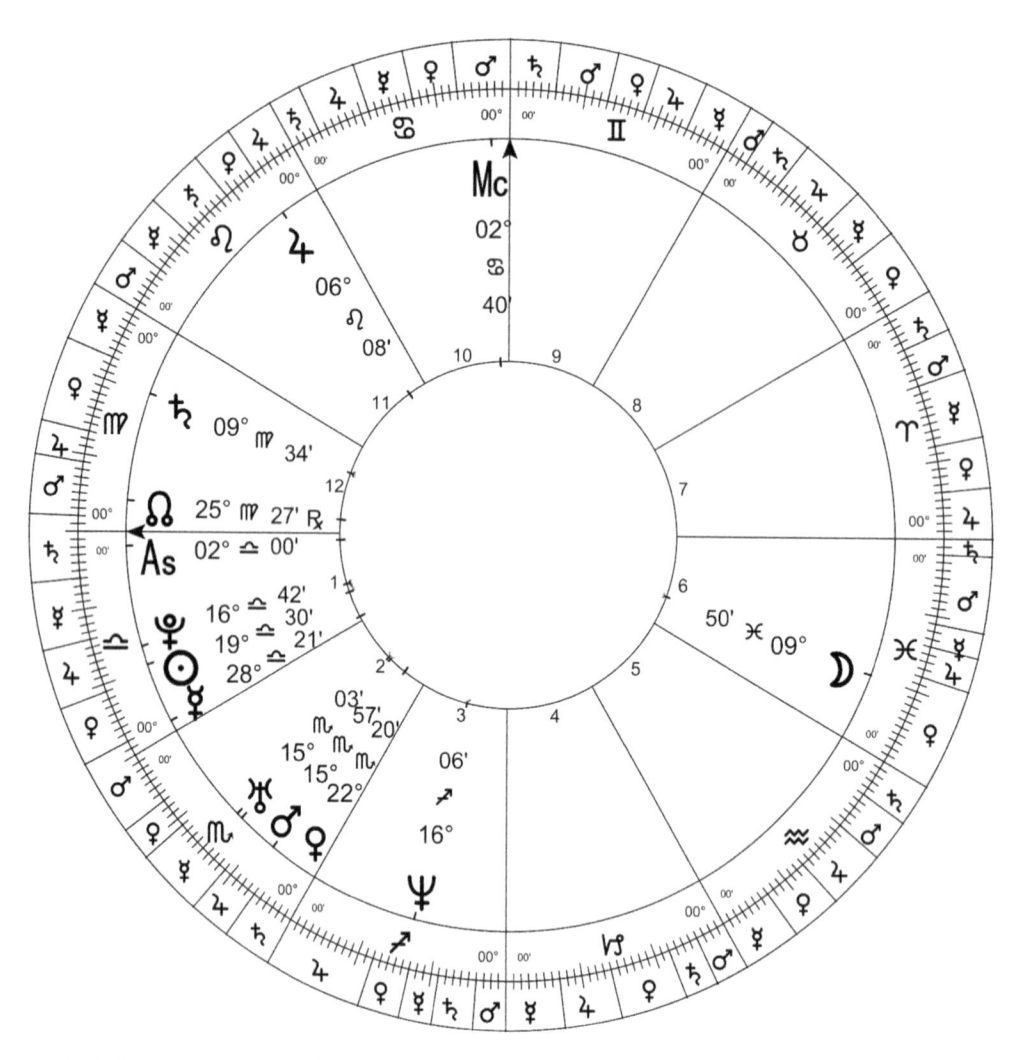

The rising sign is Libra, where natal Mars resides, and Libra is also activated by the profection. LOY Mars is strong in his rulership in Scorpio. Note the tight opposition Moon to Saturn, sixth to twelfth house.

There is a major mixed mutual reception between Saturn and Mercury, but averse, out of contact. I keep thinking that there likely was a good amount of behind the scenes political scheming that went on to help get Thatcher elected.

LOY Mars, in Scorpio, is also conjunct Uranus, and is in a wide separating conjunction with the SR Ascendant ruler Venus. The rising planet in the chart is Pluto, which is conjunct her Sun.

Thatcher's Sun is in its fall in Libra, and planets in fall often feel like they are not given the attention, credit and respect they deserve, so they can overcompensate by demanding attention and respect.

This solar return chart will look a lot more significant when we view it combined with her natal chart.

This wheel has the natal in the inner ring and the 1978 SR in the outer.

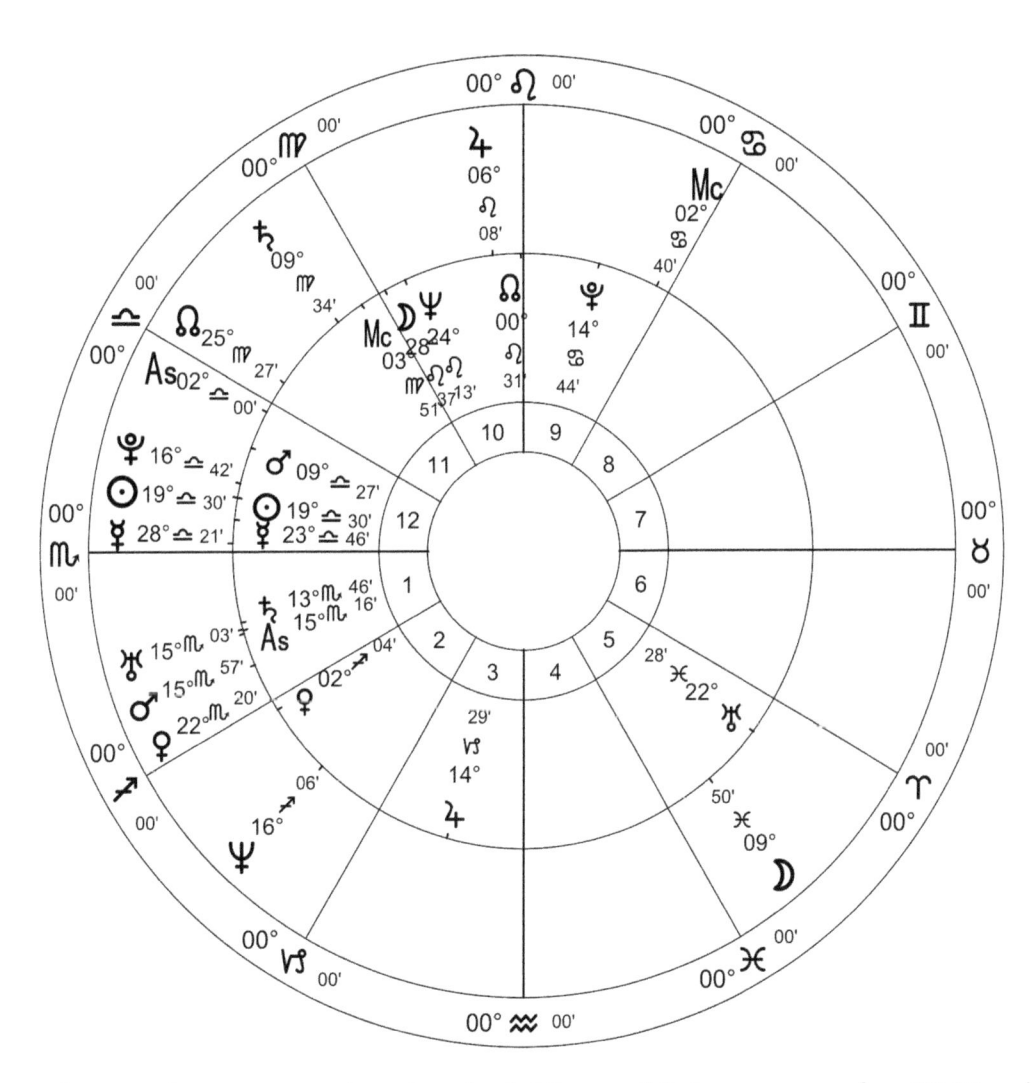

When we put the two charts one on the other, both Mars and Saturn are angular. SR Mars is conjunct her natal Ascendant as is SR Uranus, and SR Saturn is 6 degrees from the Midheaven. The mutual reception between Mercury and Saturn takes on more importance with Saturn's prominence.

Natal Jupiter is also strong in the SR chart, being in the tenth house conjunct the SR North Node which amplifies its effect.

The strong Moon Saturn opposition is now tightly angular along her natal Midheaven axis, and the Moon is making a strong applying trine to SR Mars and her natal Ascendant.

This next wheel shows the Election Day chart in a bi-wheel with the natal. The election was May 3, 1979. I ran the chart for noon, so I don't place heavy emphasis on the angles in the outer wheel.

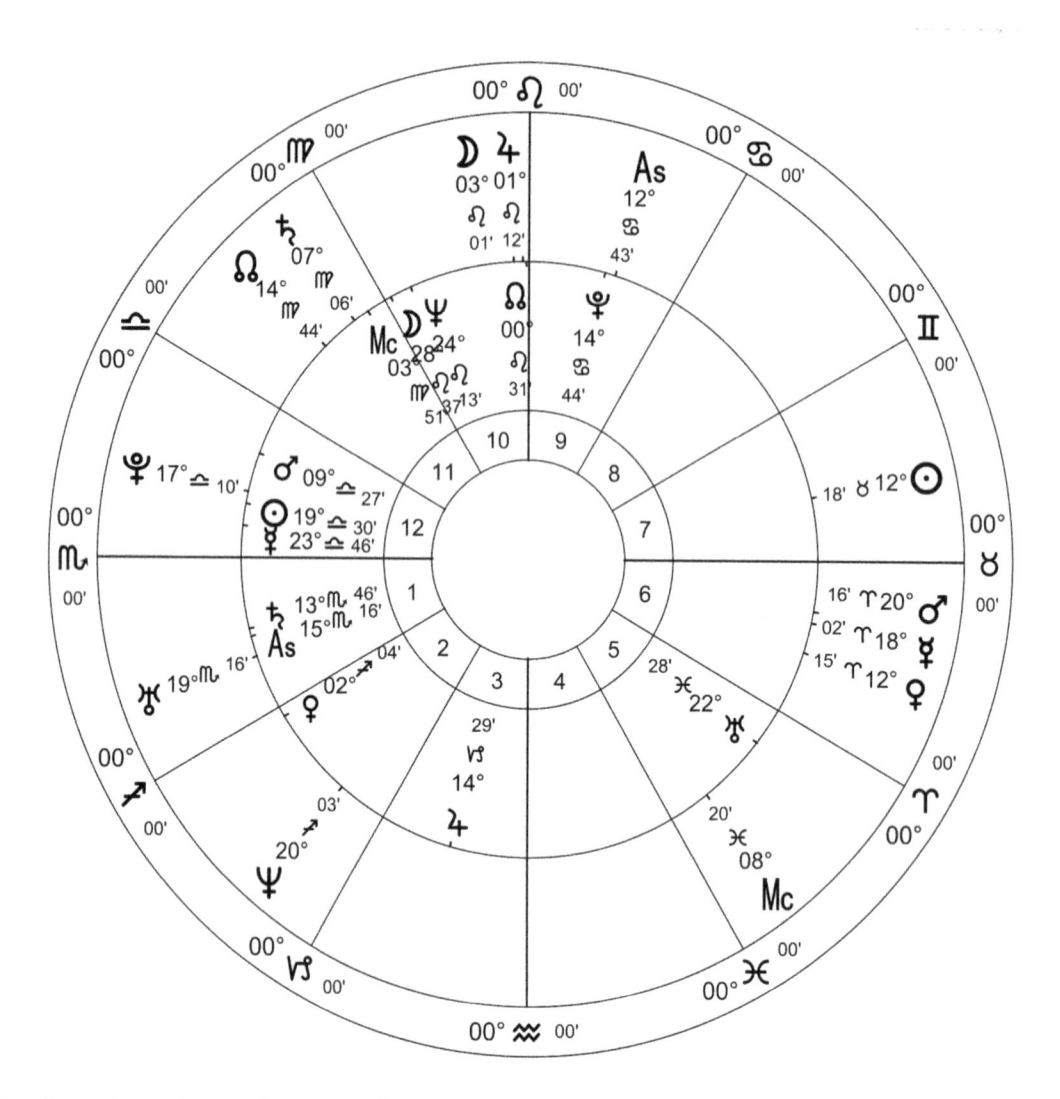

Note LOY Mars is again in his rulership, having moved to his other sign Aries, and Aries is the profected sign of the year. Transits by the LOY through the profected sign mark key periods and events. At election time Mercury and Mars are conjunct and are making an opposition to natal Sun and Mercury. Transiting Pluto lines up conjunct the Sun.

Transiting Uranus is still sitting on the Ascendant, and now transiting Sun in Taurus is in opposition to natal Saturn and Ascendant. Her natal Ascendant is strongly and repeated activated in this series of charts.

This last bi-wheel has the SR in the inner ring and the election in the outer.

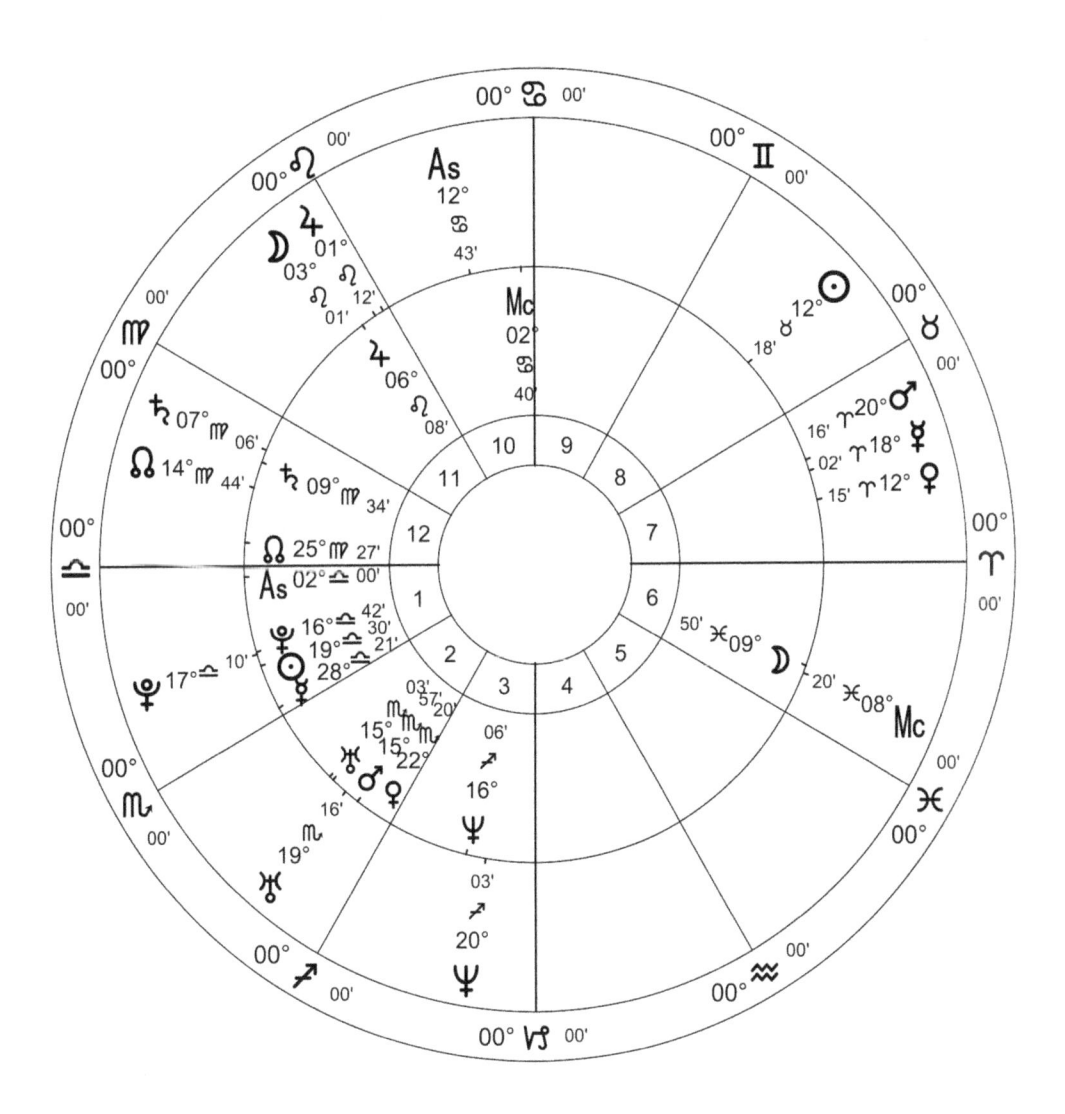

Here it is worth noting that transiting Mars on Election Day is angular and strong in his rulership in Aries, tightly conjunct transiting Mercury, opposite the Sun. The repeated strength of both Mars and Saturn in this entire series of charts is very striking.

Putting the icing on the cake, these are the yearly directions of the SR Ascendant around the wheel for around May 3, the day of the election.

Z (Taurus)Jupiter D --> Asc 196.289199 1979.04.30
Z Opposition Mars D --> Asc 197.345289 1979.05.01
Z (Taurus)Saturn D --> Asc 200.795126 1979.05.04

The election was May 3. 1979. *The directed Ascendant is making an opposition to LOY SR Mars in Scorpio, shortly after opposition to her natal Saturn and Ascendant.* The directed Ascendant is marked in italics in the seventh house in the diagram below. Both her natal Ascendant and SR Mars are activated by the yearly direction.

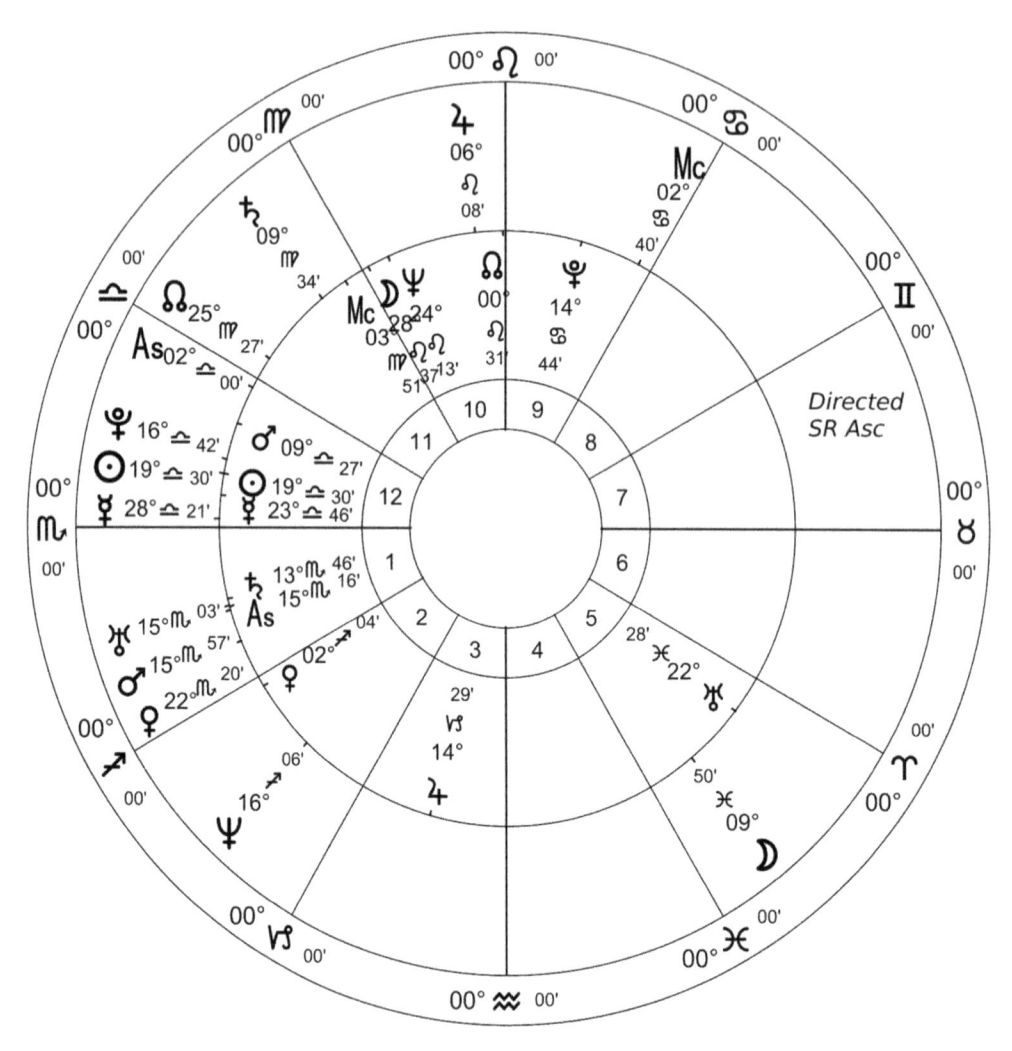

It follows the rule that hard aspects to the LOY in the yearly directions mark significant events. *This coincides in time with the significant transit of Mars through Aries, the profected sign of the year.* Mars is doubly emphasized by both direction and transit at election time.

Preparing for a Client Reading

In this chapter I want to discuss how I use these predictive techniques to prepare for a client session, and during the course of the reading itself.

I do not think astrology is primarily about prediction or fortune-telling. I also do not think that astrology is something that the astrologer does as a solo act, putting on a kind of miracle show while the client just sits back and watches.

I am convinced that astrology is not well suited for vague "tell me what's going to happen to me" readings. Astrology is a sacred art, a consultation with the Gods, and we can use this predictive tool because the ordered and symbolic movement of the heavens mirrors the divine order. When we study astrology we are contemplating divine order. We are peering into the mind of the Holy.

Astrology works best in response to a heartfelt need for guidance from the Gods. The medieval astrologer Guido Bonatti lays this out very clearly in the first sections of his *146 Considerations* chapter from his landmark compilation, *The Book of Astronomy,* and William Lilly echoes that setting in his *Christian Astrology*.

Here is what Bonatti has to say. This quote is from the Ben Dykes translation of Bonatti's *146 Considerations.*

"...he must observe this manner of asking, plainly that he ought to pray to the Lord God, from Whom every good beginning leads, and to entreat Him (with all devotion and with a contrite spirit) that it should fall to him to reach an understanding of the truth of those things about which he intends to ask. Then with this truth he ought to go to the astrologer with intention concerning that about which he is going to ask, ...and the intention for which he retains in his heart for a day and a night (or more), not touched by just any motion of the mind.

...the beginning statement of which, however, is always the name of the Highest; for certain people sometimes do otherwise, and for that reason they come to be deceived in themselves, and they sometimes pressure the astrologer - or rather, they often lie; for a stupid querent makes the responding wise man deviate sometimes; and men, not knowing the folly of him who asks poorly, sometimes defame and revile the astrologer when the astrologer is not guilty..."(p 265)

Consider the implications of this lovely statement of Bonatti's.

An astrology reading is ultimately seeking guidance from God, the Gods, the Holy, the Order of the Universe - I don't care what you call it, the Principle and the Reality is the same. As such, it is a sacred endeavor, and not to be taken lightly.

The quality of the reading depends as much on the client as it does on the astrologer.

Focused intent produces a focused, quality reading. Fuzzy intent produces a fuzzy reading. A hostile client who walks in with a chip on their shoulder, looking to pick holes in what the astrologer does, is likely to have their expectations confirmed, and end up with a garbage reading. This is important enough that both Bonatti and Lilly have a series of *Considerations Before Judgment* that are designed to help weed out hostile clients.

The astrology reading is a sacred transaction, and both astrologer and client must prepare themselves and step into the sacred space together.

Given a good intent on the part of the client, I have developed my own procedure to maximize the potential for a quality reading.

This first step is the most important part of the process.

Step One: Get the Agenda from the Client. This is prior to the reading. For me it happens before I put a date and time for a reading on my calendar. I ask for feedback on what is on their mind for the reading, what are their main concerns, their questions - what is the purpose of the reading. The more focused this is, and the more detailed, the better I can prepare, and the more useful they likely will find the reading.

The question from the client provides the focus of the reading. That provides the frame within which the symbols of astrology make the most sense. A good question acts like a lens that helps the astrologer know where to look, what factors to weigh up.

Given that agenda from the client, this is what I draw up, usually in this order.

1) **The natal chart** - and I include a detailed study of the dignity and debility of the chart. Everything else grows out of that.

2) **The primary directions** of the Big Four, Ascendant, Midheaven, Sun, and Moon. If there is any clear preponderance of a single planet across those, I will be on the alert for that planet being prominent in the other systems. Remember the general principle of converging systems. Depending on what I find in the following steps, I may come back and run directions for any other planets that seem to be particularly important for the period.

The next two steps I do together for a sequence of two or sometimes three years - previous, current, and next. I want to get a feel for the year leading up to the reading, and the year following.

3) **Profections** - I draw up a profected chart in the outer rim of a bi-wheel around the natal chart. I first note the profected sign and house, and planets activated there. I also look for how the profections line up with the natal chart, and I am especially looking for planetary overlays, where a profected planet has moved to sit on a natal planet. This is used in combination with the next chart, which is -

4) **Solar returns** - This is where I spend the most time with analysis for predictive purposes. I treat each solar return as a stand-alone chart, and I read it keeping in mind the profected sign and LOY, and planets activated in that sign. I check to see if any of the returns has the markings of a Big Year. In this analysis, I am comparing the dignity and condition of the planets in the SR with their condition in the natal chart.

For each solar return I draw up
    A) a stand-alone return chart.
    B) a bi-wheel with natal in center and SR around.
    C) a bi-wheel with SR in center and natal around.
I am looking for how planets in the two charts line up, and the relative house positions.

5) I run the **yearly direction of the Ascendant** through the current solar return chart, and mark the periods when it moves through the signs of the same mode as the profection, and direct major aspects to the profected LOY. Depending on the timing of their birthday relative to the reading, I sometimes run the yearly directions for more than one year.

6) I always run a 2 year listing of **transit to natal aspects** for the planets from Jupiter on out. With the planets I use only conjunctions, oppositions, squares and trines, and I usually don't place a lot of weight on trines to trigger action. I give most weight to hard transits to the personal planets, Sun, Moon, Mercury, Venus and Mars, and to the angles.

I use the directions plus the transits for a given year to help pinpoint the most important periods, marked by the yearly direction of the SR Ascendant to signs in hard aspect to the sign of the year. I am particularly scanning for a coincidence of directions and transits. If a period of the year looks particularly significant, it is worth checking an ephemeris for transits of all of the planets for that period. The directions help narrow down which parts of the year need that detailed focus.

7) It is worth checking **solar and lunar eclipses** for the year, to see how they intersect with the sensitive points in the natal and solar return charts.

(Note that, in addition to these, I add a listing of lifetime secondary progressions, looking just at progressed lunar phases, and planets changing signs or stationing. I usually look at that list early in the process, to get a feel for the overall sweep of the person's life, especially where they are in the lunar phase cycle. Secondary progressions are not usually used with the Cycle of the Year techniques in the traditional literature, so I have not covered them in this book.)

At this point, after printing out all of these charts and listings, I pause, take a deep breath, say a prayer asking forgiveness from the gods of trees, and write a check to the Canadian Forestry Preservation Foundation.

If this sounds like a lot of material, you're right, it is. I maneuver through this mass of material by focusing only on the big standouts in the process, and I am looking for the places that the various systems converge. Almost without fail I can see major configurations and themes emerge.

The more important the question is to the client, the more likely I am to see those concerns clearly mirrored in the prominent configurations for the period.

This is where having a topic of focus for the reading is so very valuable. It helps to figure out what to look at.

Note the following point, which is key to using this material with clients.

After I have gone through this material, I come out of it basically with a list of questions that I am ready to ask the client during the first part of the reading.

Underline that - I come out of the preliminary analysis with more questions than answers. The analysis gives me a preliminary orientation and a list of dates and issues. The purpose of the questions is to map the significant points from my analysis to their concrete life situation. I include questions concerning past periods, which lets me get data about what actually happened.

How I phrase the questions will depend on how well-versed the client is with the language of astrology. The questions are generally something along this line:

I see that, two years ago, there was an important point where Mercury stationed and turned retrograde. This was likely a time when you had a major change in how you use your mind, and may have become more withdrawn or introspective, or more drawn to your inner life. Can you tell me how your life changed around that time?

or

Last year at your birthday the area of home and family was coming up, and this was likely a major focus in the year. Is that correct? How did that play out?

I start with a series of leading questions like this, focused on a previous period. I try to phrase the questions in a way that is inviting rather than demanding. I am trying to give them a safe space within which they can share at the level they feel comfortable.

My purpose of doing these questions for past periods is to get a feel for how the planets act in their particular life, and to get a feel for where things are headed. This process also typically builds a great deal of credibility - if a person can say, "Why Yes, here's what happened then and it was like this", then you have shown that these predictive techniques do work.

For the great majority of clients, I find that they are more than eager to talk about what is happening to them since I have provided an understanding framework within which they are welcome to talk about what is most important to them. There are precious few areas in most people's lives where we get permission to talk about what really matters to us, so this is welcomed by most people.

The more information the person is willing to share, the better the reading goes, and the more useful feedback I can offer. Given their sharing I can then take the language of the astrology symbolism and show how it plays out in the details of their life.

The astrology and my questions provide a shape, a framework, a way of making sense of what they are going through. The actual reading of the details is done by the client, and as astrologer I am just helping to tie it together. That framework also helps to determine which upcoming directions or transits are likely to be important. Within that, I find that it is much more reliable to look at general periods than at specific dates.

Also, if the client has a question about a specific time frame or event they have planned, that framework gives me a way of determining how it will turn out.

Another very important point - clients often come for help in making a decision. My job is not to make the decision for them, but to provide them the data and framework they can use to make the decision for themselves.

That gets tricky, because sometimes clients come in wanting me to tell them what to do. That way, if things don't turn out the way they want, they have someone to blame. I gently try to turn the question back on them, present the data, and help them realize they must choose for themselves. Blame is a useless game to play - ultimately we are each responsible for how we deal with our own life situation.

I have to present the data as I see it mirrored in their chart, rather than give them my own opinion. I have figured out from experience that astrology knows more than I do. More than once I have seen the client's question and thought, wow, that won't work - and then looked at the data to see the charts pointing in a very different direction from what I would have said on my own. That is an ongoing challenge and art for me, separating out what the chart is saying from my own opinion about what should be happening.

Very often it feels that the answers to the client's questions emerge from the astrological data. The work of the reading happens in the interchange between my knowledge of astrological symbolism, and the client's knowledge of their life situations and their desires. That is where the magic happens.

There is one last thing I need to add - I always try to start the actual sessions with a brief period of quiet and inner alignment, and a prayer for guidance, and then end with another centering and a prayer of thanksgiving. (The prayers are private and internal, before and after the client meeting.) I am very serious when I say that astrology is an art involving consulting with the gods, and the more I practice this art, the more aware I am that there is no way that I could do this without divine guidance. It really does help to consciously place myself in the divine presence.

When the session works well I sometimes have the feeling that I am allowing the gods to speak to the client through the reading, and my job is to provide a sacred space, a kind of magic circle, within which that can happen. I have done my homework by studying the details of the symbols of astrology in general and of this particular group of charts, and I offer that language to be used by the gods.

When you approach astrology, remove your shoes and take a moment to compose your heart; you are walking on sacred ground.

Introibo ad altare Dei...

Tying it All Together - Examples

The purpose of this part of the book is to give some examples worked out in more detail, to show how the system as a whole can work. All of these examples are of significant years, which means you will see strong correlations between the different predictive techniques. For less eventful years you will often find that the correlations are less frequent and exact, or that you have contradictory indications.

For all of these examples I include all the necessary charts and listings to be able to follow the analysis. The descriptions are designed for you to pick out the aspects and correlations in the charts as you read, to understand how the analysis is done.

The first example takes Marilyn Monroe and looks at the year of her death. There are some striking points regarding primary directions of planets that are involved in the natal chart configuration that was likely the weak point where her death played out.

The next long example is that of the mass shooting in Las Vegas, Nevada in October 2017. We have a tightly timed chart for the shooter, and a time for the event accurate to within a few minutes. The number of correlations across all of the predictive systems is mind-boggling.

The next section takes two significant years from the life of Napoleon Bonaparte, when reflecting his rise, and the other reflecting his fall. It shows how different parts of his natal chart are activated on the way up as opposed to the planets active on the way down.

The next example is from a peak year in my own life, showing an unusually strong emphasis on a single planet in directions, that is then echoed in the other charts.

The final example looks at a very interesting and multi-dimensional solar return from a pivotal year in the life of the writer Maya Angelou.

Marilyn Monroe

The life of the famed, legendary, very nearly deified film star and media goddess, Marilyn Monroe, is a messy and disturbing story of professional fame and personal tragedy. In this example I want to focus on a particular group of planets that were likely involved in her early death in 1962, and how her death is reflected in the directions of those planets at the time of her death.

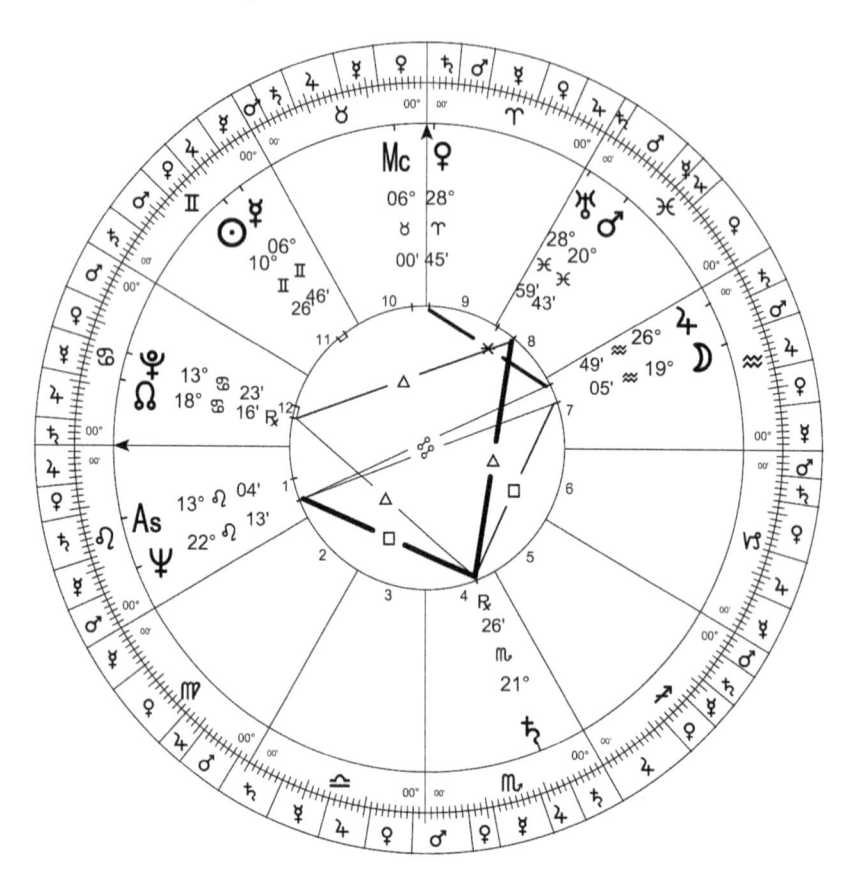

The tightest aspect configuration in this chart is the nasty applying t-square between Neptune at 22 Leo in the first house, opposite the Moon at 19 Aquarius in the 7th house of marriage, both planets tightly square to a retrograde Saturn in Scorpio in the 4th house. Since this is a day chart, the most dangerous planet is Mars, in the 8th house of death in Pisces, having dignity by triplicity and by bound. Mars in turn is in a tight applying trine to Saturn in the 4th house, and Mars rules that Saturn. Mars controls Saturn and the two work together with that trine, to the detriment of the Moon - think abusive relationships here.

The likely cause of death was suicide from drug overdose (Neptune) from serious depression (Saturn square Moon).

It occurred to me that, at the time of her death, it would be logical to look at the directions for the Moon (which represents the physical body and her emotional state) and the two malefics, Saturn and Mars. This is what I found.

Z Sextile Moon D --> Saturn 28.549927 1954.12.19
Z Sextile Moon D --> Mars 29.792243 1956.03.17
Z Square Mars D --> Saturn 30.304514 1956.09.20
Z (Sagittarius)Saturn D --> Saturn 30.593424 1957.01.03
Z (Aries)Mars D --> Mars 30.747974 1957.03.01
Z (Pisces)Mercury D --> Moon 31.728474 1958.02.22
Z (Pisces)Mars D --> Moon 35.225602 1961.08.22
Z (Sagittarius)Mars D --> Saturn 35.999166 1962.06.01
Z (Aries)Saturn D --> Mars 36.068099 1962.06.26

The Moon - her body, her health, and her emotions - is in the bounds of Mars - and in this case the exact location of the direction is significant - *it is directed to the bounds of Mars in Pisces, which is in the 8th house of death and is almost exactly conjunct with natal Mars itself* - and remember, natal Mars rules natal Saturn, which is in square to both the Moon and Neptune. The participating planet is Mercury, but it is within a degree or two of natal Mars in his own bounds, so we can justifiably take Mars to effectively be participator here also. If you consider the symbolism of bound as meaning a delimited or confined space, then the Moon is directed right into the room that Mars rules and is currently occupying.

Saturn is in the bounds of Mars with Mars as most recently active participator - and Saturn is already ruled by Mars in the natal - so this is an example of fulfilling the promise of the natal chart.

In addition, Mars is in the bounds of Saturn, with Saturn as participator. Directed Mars is in Aries, so it is practically conjunct her natal Venus.

Saturn is in Mars/Mars, and Mars is in Saturn/Saturn. Each of the two malefics is in the bounds and partner of the other malefic.

Since Neptune is involved with the tight aspect to Saturn and the Moon, I tried running the directions for Neptune - and this is what I found.

Z (Virgo)Mars D --> Neptune 33.490009 1959.11.27
Z Sextil Saturn D --> Neptune 33.998436 1960.05.31

Neptune is in the Bounds of Mars with Saturn participator. Again, the two malefics are involved. The cause of death was drug overdose.

Monroe's death was very early morning August 5, 1962 - she was found to be unresponsive at 3 am that day.

Here is the solar return for the year of her death.

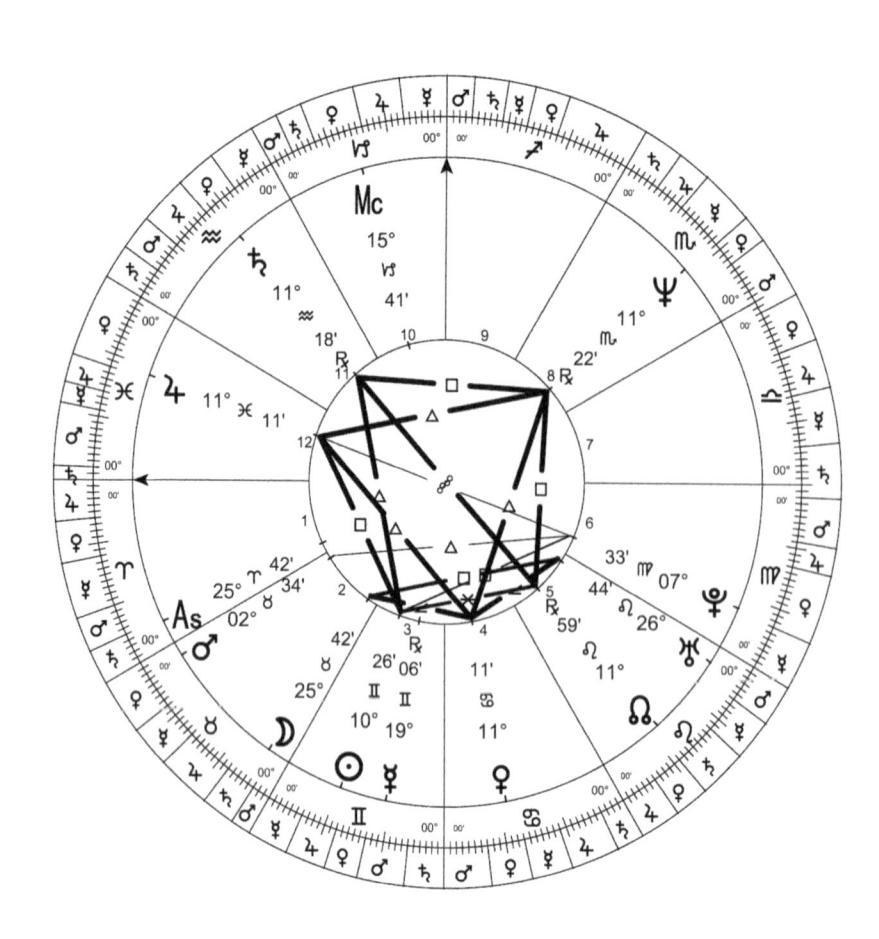

The solar return has Aries rising. The solar return Ascendant at 25 Aries is pretty closely conjunct her natal Venus at 28 Aries. **This is practically conjunct directed Mars, and is in the bounds of Saturn.**

The ruler of the solar return Ascendant is Mars, who is the rising planet, but from early Taurus - so in his detriment. Note that **Saturn and Neptune are in a very tight applying square**, which duplicates the tight square between those planets in the natal chart, and the square is in fixed signs both here and in the natal - Saturn in the same sign as natal Moon, Neptune in the same sign as natal Saturn. Mars in this chart, in the fixed sign Taurus, is applying to opposition to Neptune and square to Saturn. So, we have Mars, Saturn and Neptune featured in the solar return as they are in the natal - fulfilling the natal promise.

The solar return Moon is exalted in late Taurus, the same sign as Mars here, and is in very late balsamic phase, approaching New Moon, the end of a cycle. **Solar return Moon is in the bounds of Saturn.**

As a curious side note concerning this chart, it struck me that there are a very large number of planets that are at eleven degrees of a sign - Jupiter in the 12th, Saturn in the 11th, Neptune in the 8th, the nodal axis in Leo/Aquarius, and Venus in Cancer in the 4th - and the Sun is very close, at 10 degrees Gemini, here and in the natal. That is five planets plus the nodal axis.

98

This is a chart for the approximate time of death - we don't know the exact time, but it was likely between late evening August 4, and 3 am. I ran this chart for 1 am, a couple of hours before she was found unresponsive.

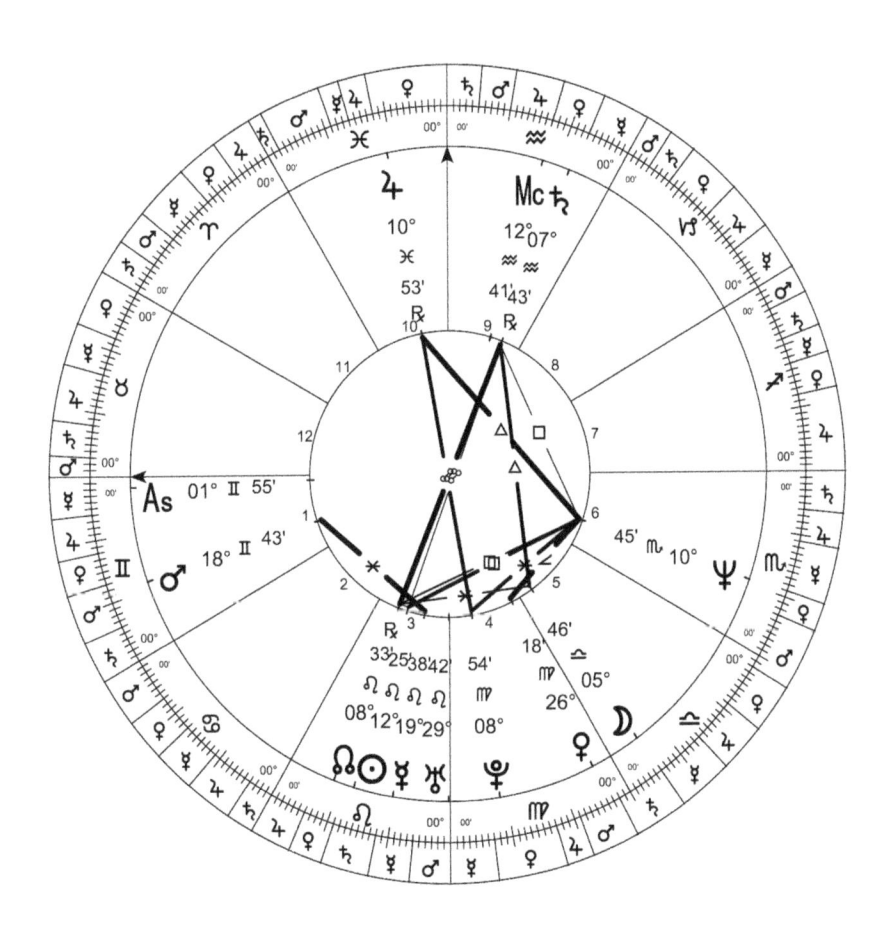

This next is only conjecture, but if I had to guess a time of death I would put it at around 2 am, since that was very close to the time when the Ascendant would have been conjunct Mars at 18 Gemini. The Ascendant would have been in Gemini from roughly 1 am to 3 am, so there is at least a reasonable chance that Mars was the rising planet at the time of her death.

Transiting Mars at time of death is 18 Gemini, square natal Mars at 20 Pisces. Transiting Sun at 12 Leo is very near her natal Ascendant at 13 Leo, and transiting Mercury at 19 Leo is quite near her natal Neptune at 22 Leo - recall that, at the time of death, the Moon was in the bounds of Mars with Mercury as the partner, and here we have Mercury near her natal Neptune in her first house.

The Las Vegas Shooting, October 1, 2017

One of the main rules of astrological timing is that any major event should show multiple significant correlations pointing at the event. The more major the event, the more correlations there should be.

Another main rule is that the angles - the Ascendant and Descendant, Midheaven and IC - are the places of action, so that event timing should show significant planetary triggers at angles.

These correlations should not be subtle. They should be significant, redundant, and tight. In your face.

Accurately timed charts are helpful to have since the angles shift quickly as time passes.

With the mass shooting that took place in Las Vegas on October 1, 2017 we have a very exact time for the event. News sources say that the call to the police dispatcher was at 10:08 pm, so the shooting must have started a few minutes before that. I am using 10:05 pm.

We also have a reliable timed birth chart for the shooter, Stephen Paddock. The astro.com site gives his birth time as April 9, 1953, at 11:05 am in Clinton, Iowa, and cites reference to a birth certificate, which is considered the highest level of reliability.

We have an accurate time for the event, and an accurate birth time for the shooter. When I started researching this event I expected to see some significant hits, but I was not prepared for the flood of correlations at all levels that I kept finding. The sheer number and tightness of them made the hair of my neck stand up.

I want to use this example to show how the predictive techniques -direction through the bounds, profections, solar return and transit - all fit together in with the sort of eerie, everything converging at once kind of synchronicity that shows up only very, very rarely, in freaky major events like the shooting.

This is the natal chart of the shooter, Stephen Paddock.

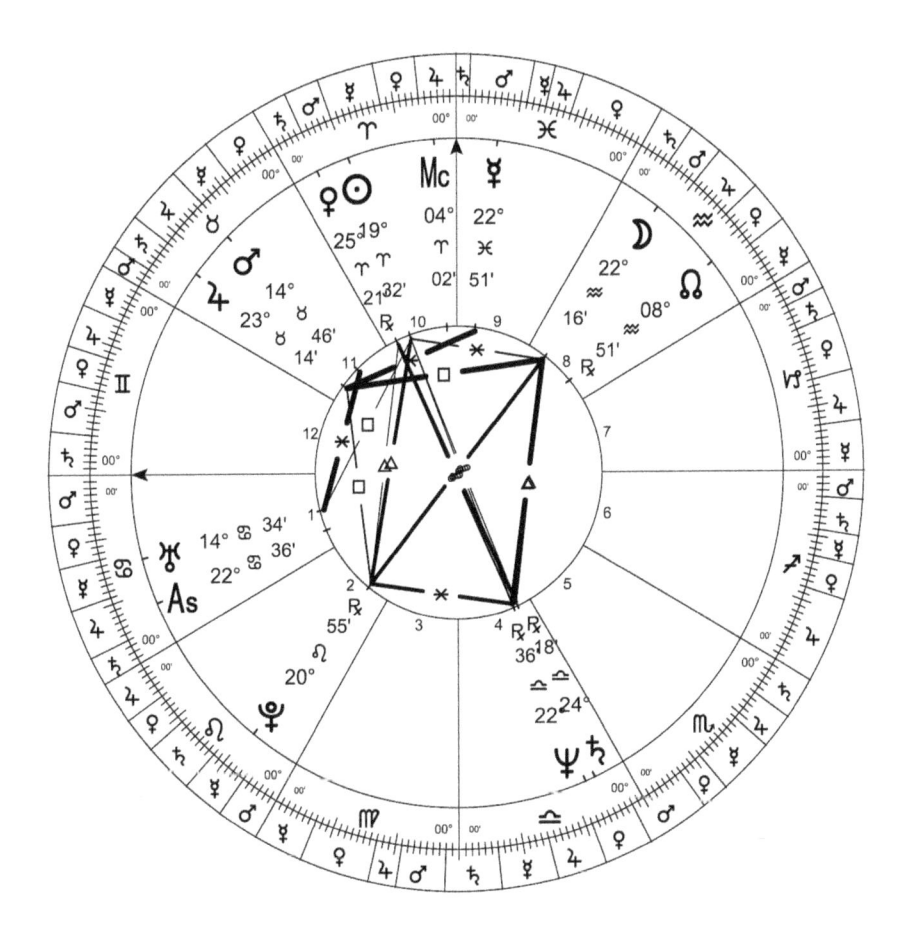

I will focus on the parts of the chart that relate to the timing of the shooting.

There are two very nasty oppositions in this chart, and oppositions are aspects that are tense and potentially explosive.

The natal Sun is in Aries, loosely conjunct Venus, and those two planets are in opposition to Saturn and Neptune in Libra. These planets are in the strong and angular tenth and fourth houses, so they are prominent, visible and active. The Sun to Saturn opposition is particularly nasty since the reception between them is very bad, with the Sun is in the sign of Saturn's fall, and Saturn is in the sign of the Sun's fall. You could describe this as saying the two planets despise each other. Oppositions are difficult, and the bad reception makes it a lot worse. This opposition is in a tight square to the Ascendant, which makes it stronger yet.

The other opposition is between the natal Moon, which is Aquarius in the eighth house, and Pluto in Leo in the second house. Eighth house planets typically are difficult to express or control. The Moon is particularly important since it rules Cancer, which is the Ascendant in this chart. Also, the Moon in Aquarius is ruled by Saturn, and Pluto in Leo is ruled by the Sun, which are the two planets in the other opposition.

Jupiter is in tight square to the Moon/Pluto opposition, and Mars is in an applying square. Mars here is in his detriment in Taurus, so he is off balance, edgy, irritable.

Keep those two oppositions and the squares in mind.

Before we start looking at the charts specific to the year of the shooting, I want to list the most important directions for the planets we are watching that were in affect at the time of the shooting.

Z (Gemini)Saturn D --> Sun 63.092568 2016.05.12
Z Trine Saturn D --> Sun 63.433971 2016.09.14

The Sun is in the Bounds of Saturn with Saturn participator - reportedly Paddock had been despondent and depressed for a period prior to the shooting. Recall that Saturn and Sun are in opposition in the natal, in each other's fall, so they basically detest each other.

Z Sun D --> Moon 63.490470 2016.10.05
Z (Aries)Mars D --> Moon 63.999264 2017.04.08

The Moon is in the bounds of Mars starting mid 2017, with the Sun as participator. The Moon is in bad shape square to Mars in bad shape in the natal, and this direction activates that. Moon plus Mars is an unpleasant combination at best, and here they are in a tough aspect in bad shape.

Z Trine Venus D --> Saturn 59.720472 2012.12.28
Z (Sagittarius)Mars D --> Saturn 60.409081 2013.09.05/

Saturn is in the bounds of Mars, with Saturn participator. One malefic being in the bounds of the other malefic is bad news.

Z (Cancer)Mercury D --> Mars 59.260622 2012.07.13
Z Sextile Mars D --> Mars 61.245482 2014.07.08

Mars is in the bounds of Mercury, with Mars participator.

Z Jupiter D --> Mercury 59.762729 2013.01.12
Z (Taurus)Mars D --> Mercury 63.741503 2017.01.04

Mercury is in the bounds of Mars, with Jupiter participator. I find it worth noting that Mars and Mercury are in each other's bounds.

Z (Cancer)Jupiter D --> Jupiter 58.067500 2011.05.04
Z Square Saturn D --> Jupiter 64.125315 2017.05.24

Jupiter is in his own bounds, square Saturn participator.

We will return again to these directions, and note their exact locations, at the end of this study.

This is the chart of Paddock's solar return for this year, 2017.

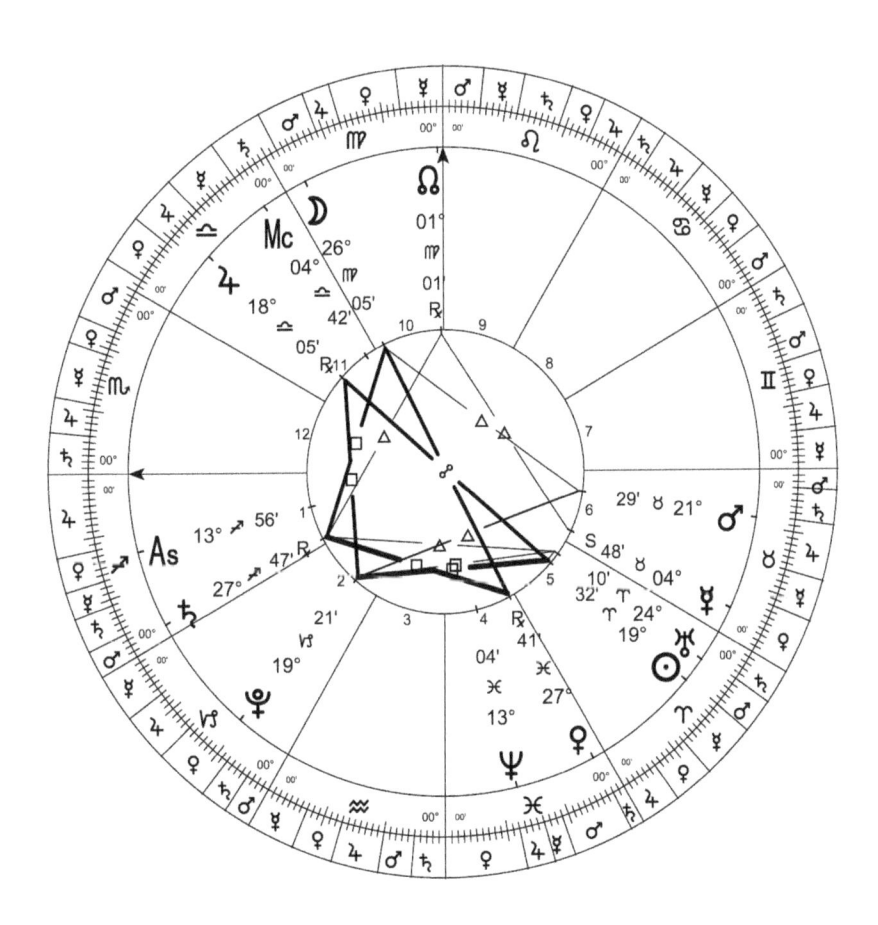

First, note that the Ascendant axis of the chart is Sagittarius and Gemini - this means that those two signs are particularly activated this year. That will end up being very important later.

Saturn is rising in this chart, which activates the potential of the natal Saturn, including the opposition.

The ruler of the solar return Ascendant is Jupiter - and **Jupiter in the solar return is in tight opposition to the Sun in Aries, which activates the Sun/ Saturn opposition in the natal**. Jupiter, ruler of the Ascendant in the solar return, is sitting right on top of Saturn and Neptune in the natal chart. Saturn is doubly activated now.

In this solar return Uranus is in Aries conjunct the Sun, sitting right on top of the Saturn - Neptune conjunction in the natal. That is strong, and explosive. Recall that Uranus is conjunct the Ascendant in the natal chart. Saturn is now triply activated.

Finally, Mars is now at 21 Taurus - **so Mars, by degree, has perfected the applying square aspect to Pluto and the Moon in the natal chart.** The Moon to Mars connection is also activated by Moon being in the bounds of Mars, which we noted earlier. This is a very good example of fulfilling the promise of the natal chart.

Next I want to look at the profected chart for Paddock for this year.

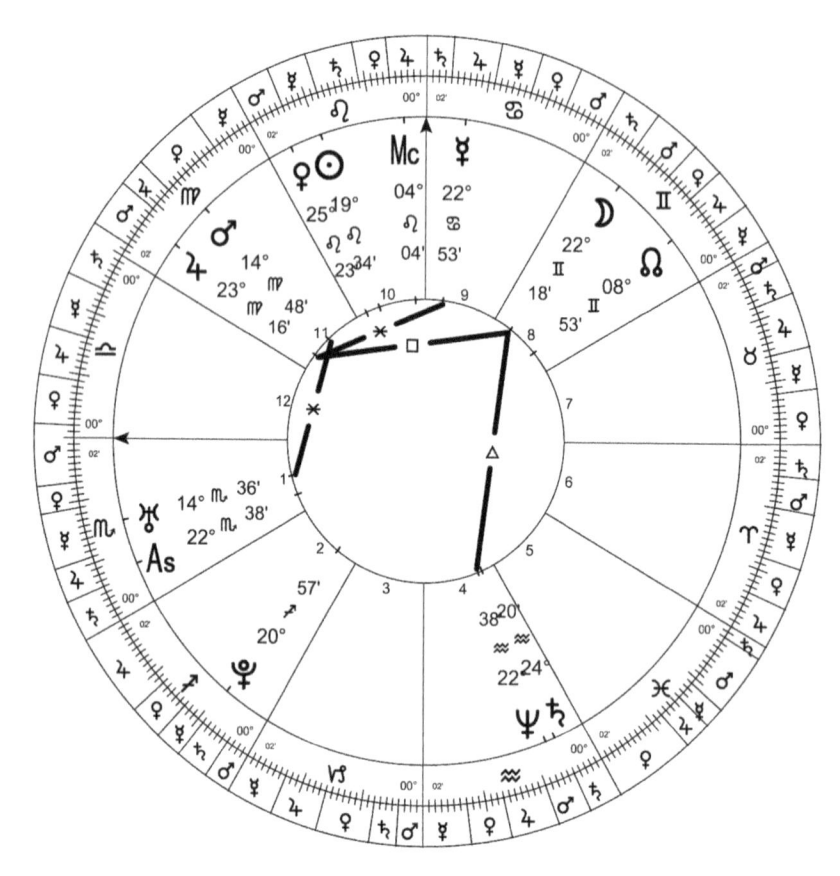

First, note that **the Sun/Saturn opposition has moved to Aquarius/Leo - so it is sitting right on top of the Moon/Pluto opposition in the natal chart. The two oppositions are coinciding here.**

Also note that **the profected Moon/Pluto opposition has moved to Gemini/Sagittarius - which are the signs along the Ascendant/Descendant axis in the solar return chart.** The Moon in Gemini is considered to be debilitated since it is in the 12th sign from its home sign of Cancer, and it falls in the twelfth house in Paddock's natal chart, and the twelfth house is related to self-undoing. Again we see the two oppositions in the natal chart coinciding.

Note that the profected Moon is at 22 Gemini. We will see that degree again in a moment.

This next chart is of the time of the shooting, October 1 at 10:05 pm.

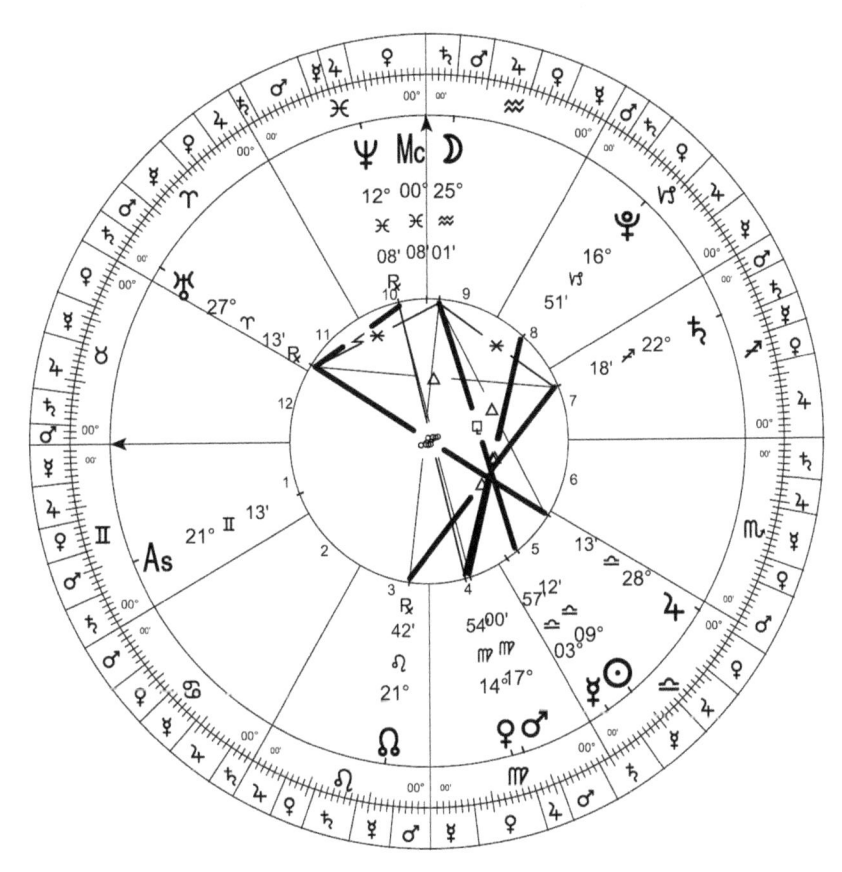

Note that **the Ascendant of the chart is 21 Gemini - again the Gemini/Sagittarius axis which we saw in the solar return chart.**

Most ominously, note the position of **Saturn - at 22 Sagittarius, it is sitting right on the Ascendant/Descendant axis** at the moment of the shooting. Again Saturn is activated.

Note that **Mars is at 17 Virgo, in applying square to that Ascendant/Saturn axis**. Mars activates Saturn.

Jupiter at 28 Libra is in tight opposition to Uranus in Aries, and the two planets sit on the axis of the Venus/Saturn opposition in the natal. Saturn is activated yet again.

This next chart is a bi-wheel, which has the chart of the shooting in the center, and the profected chart of the year in the outer ring.

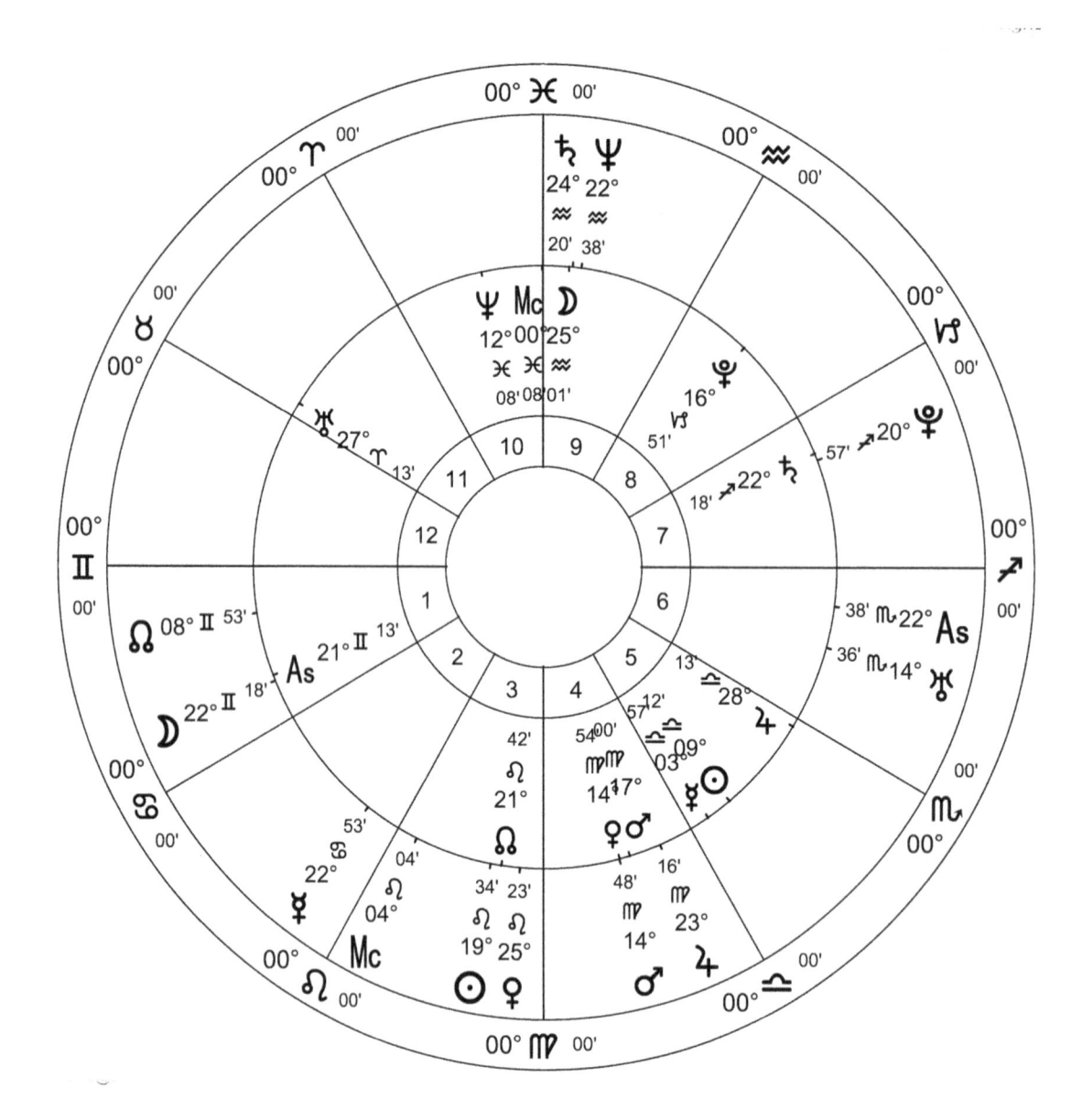

Note that **the Moon/Pluto opposition in the profected chart sits right on top of the Ascendant/Descendant axis at the time of the shooting**.

Also note that the Moon at the time of the shooting is at 25 Aquarius - on the profected Sun/Saturn opposition, which coincides with the natal Moon/Pluto opposition. The oppositions and the angles are activating each other.

Profected Mars and Jupiter are sitting on top of Venus and Mars in Virgo, and all are square to the Ascendant/Descendant axis.

The natal chart, the profected chart, the solar return chart, and the chart of the shooting interact here like five mirrors all reflecting back on each other.

And now we add the directions.

I want to close our study by reviewing the directions in effect at time of the shooting, and look at where they interact with the other charts. The sheer number of tight aspects they make speak for themselves, and are quite overwhelming.

Z (Gemini)Saturn D --> Sun 63.092568 2016.05.12
Z Trine Saturn D --> Sun 63.433971 2016.09.14

The directed Sun is at 24 Gemini, conjunct the Ascendant at the time of the shooting, opposite transiting Saturn, recreating the natal Sun/Saturn opposition while being in the bounds of Saturn.

Z Sun D --> Moon 63.490470 2016.10.05
Z (Aries)Mars D --> Moon 63.999264 2017.04.08

The directed Moon is at 20 Aries, conjunct the natal Sun and opposite natal Saturn and Neptune - again activating the Sun/Saturn opposition, again linking the Sun/Saturn and Moon/Pluto oppositions, while in the bounds of Mars which squares the Moon/Pluto opposition.

Z Trine Venus D --> Saturn 59.720472 2012.12.28
Z (Sagittarius)Mars D --> Saturn 60.409081 2013.09.05/

Directed Saturn is at 25 Sagittarius, conjunct the Descendant and transiting Saturn at the time of the shooting, in the bounds of Mars.

Z (Cancer)Mercury D --> Mars 59.260622 2012.07.13
Z Sextile Mars D --> Mars 61.245482 2014.07.08

Directed Mars is at roughly 17 Cancer, conjunct natal Uranus and near the natal Ascendant, squaring natal Sun and Saturn.

Z (Cancer)Jupiter D --> Jupiter 58.067500 2011.05.04
Z Square Saturn D --> Jupiter 64.125315 2017.05.24

Jupiter is at roughly 24 Cancer, square natal Saturn and Venus, conjunct the Natal Ascendant, squaring natal Sun and Saturn.

Finally, here are the annual directions of the solar return Ascendant right around the time of the October 1 shooting.

Z Opposition Saturn D --> Asc 2017.09.08
Z (Cancer)Mars D --> Asc 2017.09.11
Z Sextile Mercury D --> Asc 2017.09.16
Z (Cancer)Venus D --> Asc 2017.09.19

Z (Cancer)Mercury D --> Asc 2017.09.26
Z Square Jupiter D --> Asc 2017.10.02
Z (Cancer)Jupiter D --> Asc 2017.10.03

The directed Ascendant has moved to Cancer, his natal Ascendant, **squaring the Jupiter opposition to Sun and Uranus in the solar return. This is very near his natal Ascendant and square the Sun/Venus opposition to Neptune and Saturn** that we have noted repeatedly in this analysis.

The only aspects I have noted in this entire study are the major conjunctions, oppositions, and squares.

Remember that the necessary conditions for a major event have to do with fulfilling the promise of the natal chart, and activating major points in that chart and in the event, especially at angles. I find the sheer number of tight, significant and redundant correlations and hard aspects in this particular cluster of charts to be overwhelming. This is the most extreme set of correlations I have ever seen.

This is a very good example of how a major event can show tight correlations between all of the parts of the cycle of the year - the natal chart, the directions, the profection, the solar return, and finally the event itself. All the charts and directions converge in this case. Too well.

This example also points out how it can be well worth checking the directions of significant planets that are activated by the solar return and profections for a year, their bounds and participators, and also their degree position.

We have thoroughly demonstrated one of the main themes of this book, that the bounds are important for the consistently effective use of primary directions, and primary directions are very effective when used in conjunction with the cycle of the year techniques of profections and solar returns.

Napoleon Bonaparte

I want to look at two important years from the life of the legendary political leader Napoleon. We will look at a big year on the way up, when he is appointed Consul for life, and a pivotal year on the way down, the year of the catastrophic invasion of Russia.

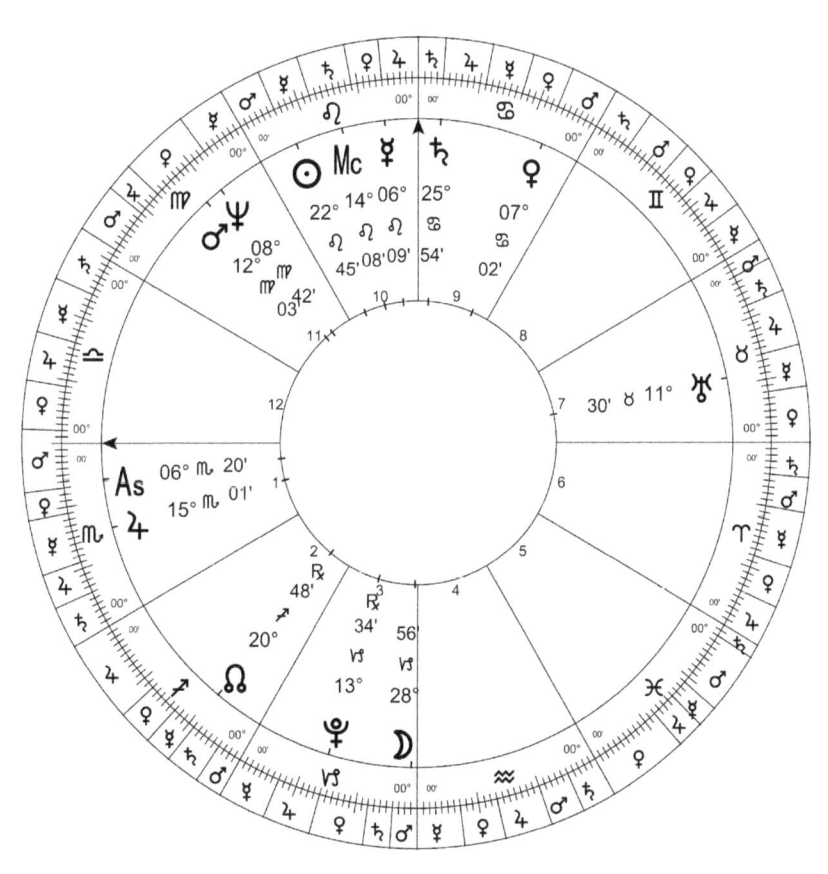

Napoleone di Buonaparte, 15 August 1769, 11:30 AM, Ajaccio, France. Rodden Rating A.

The big planets on the angles set the tone - Sun and Jupiter. Jupiter is on the Ascendant ruled by Mars in a tight applying sextile aspect. Mars, in Virgo, is conjunct Neptune - this suggests illusion, theater, glamour, and also a lack of a sense of limits. In traditional astrology the ruler of the Ascendant represents the person, so Mars is Napoleon himself - Mars conjunct Neptune suggesting a grandiose self-conception. Mars is ruled by Mercury which is prominent in Leo near the Midheaven. Mercury in turn is ruled by the Sun, shining gloriously in Leo near the Midheaven in the tenth house. This whole group of planets suggests that power, glory and reputation are prime motivating values, and Mercury and Neptune in the mix suggests that much of that is done by communication, by persuasion, and by illusion.

The planet in the worst shape is Saturn, in detriment Cancer in the ninth house - remember the association of Saturn in the ninth house with distant lands when we look at the Russian invasion. The tight opposition between Saturn and the Moon is interesting - each planet is in its own detriment, but the two are in mutual reception with each other. Planets in detriment have a restless, unsettled and unbalanced quality.

From what we have seen we should expect that Jupiter and the Sun, along with Mars, should be strong when Napoleon has strong years - and conversely Saturn should be strong in negative years.

Here are the directions for the year 1802, when Napoleon was appointed First Consul of France for life.

Asc - Jupiter(Sag)/Moon
MC - Jupiter(Virgo)/Jupiter
Sun - Mars(Virgo)/Saturn
Moon - Venus(Pisces)/Venus

Both the Ascendant and Midheaven are in Jupiter bounds, and the Midheaven has Jupiter as participator also. The prominent Sun is in the bounds of aggressive, expansive Mars.

Note that both the Sun and the Midheaven have directed into Virgo, the sign where we find natal Mars and Neptune. I am finding that planets directing into a sign where natal planets reside increases the communication and influence of those planets with each other. We will see that again in a later example.

Finally, note that the Moon is now in the bounds of Venus with Venus participator. The directed Moon is in Pisces, opposite the natal Neptune in Virgo and soon applying to an opposition with natal Mars. We mentioned the emptiness and restlessness of that Moon in detriment, and here it is aligning with the Mars/Neptune urge for power and recognition.

This is the profected chart for 1802 in a bi-wheel with the natal.

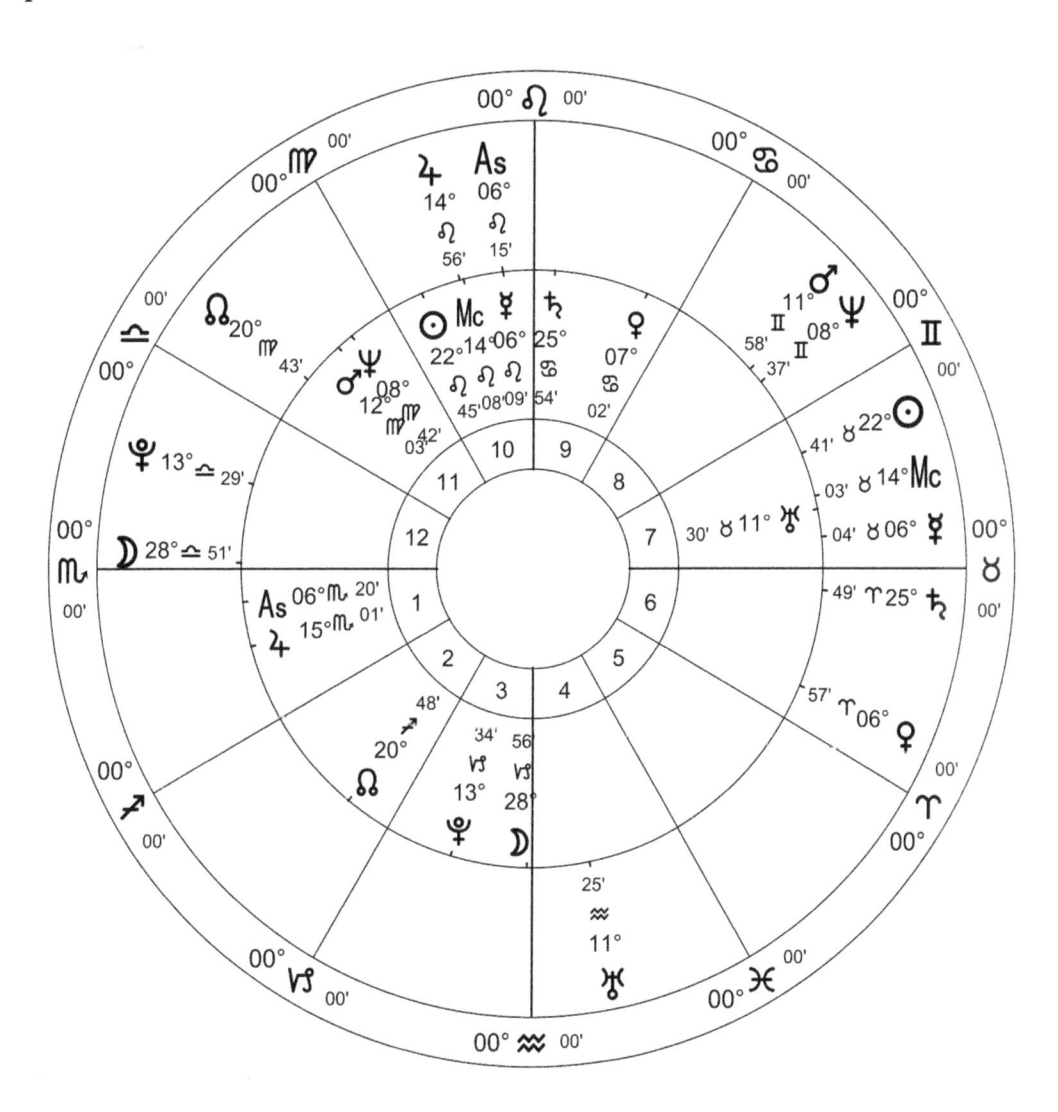

The profected sign is Leo, in the tenth house, and profected Jupiter is dead on his Midheaven - so as we expected, Sun and Jupiter are activated. Also note that the axes activated in the profection are the fixed signs, which is the same as the axes in the natal.

The profected Ascendant up at the top of the chart on the MC speaks of Napoleon being exalted.

This next chart is the solar return for same year.

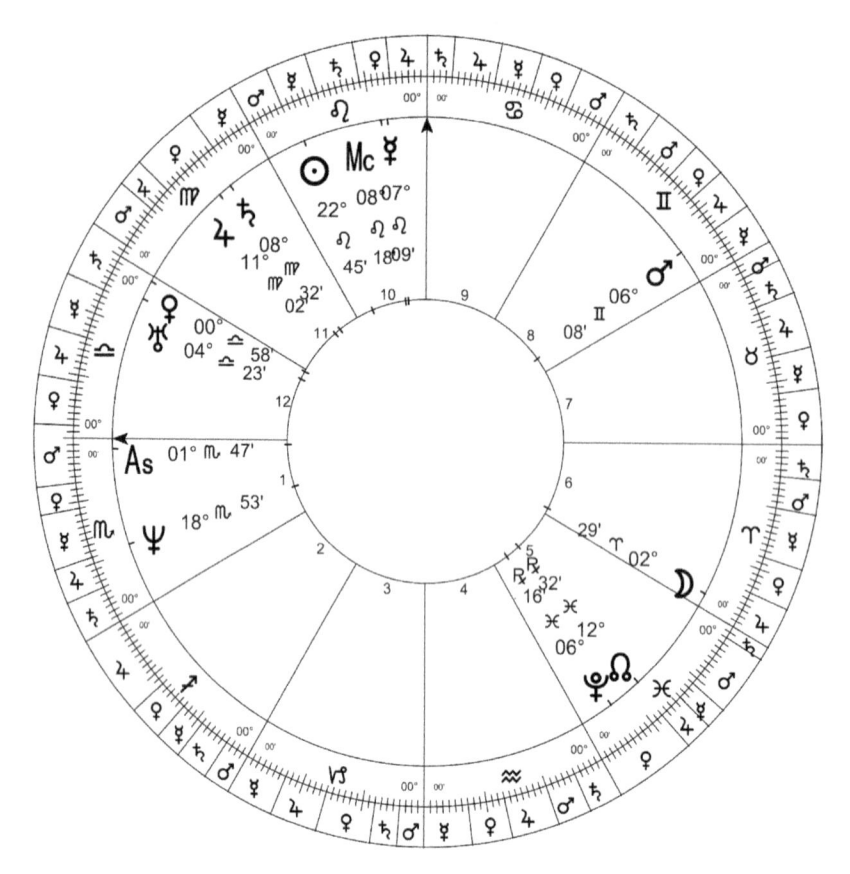

The solar return has the same Ascendant and Midheaven signs as in the natal, each within a 6 degree orb, which is a very strong marker an for important year. That is accentuated by the axes in the profected chart also lining up in fixed signs. LOY Sun is still the Midheaven, and SR Mercury dead on the MC as in the natal.

There are some ominous configurations here - Jupiter is in detriment in Virgo, in a pretty tight separating conjunction from Saturn. Those two planets are sitting on the South Node, which is further challenging and diminishing, and both are square to Mars in Gemini in the eighth, and loosely opposite Pluto on the North Node in Pisces. Yes, this is a year of glory, but there are signs of trouble.

Next is a bi-wheel of the natal and SR, clearly showing the closeness of the angles in the two charts.

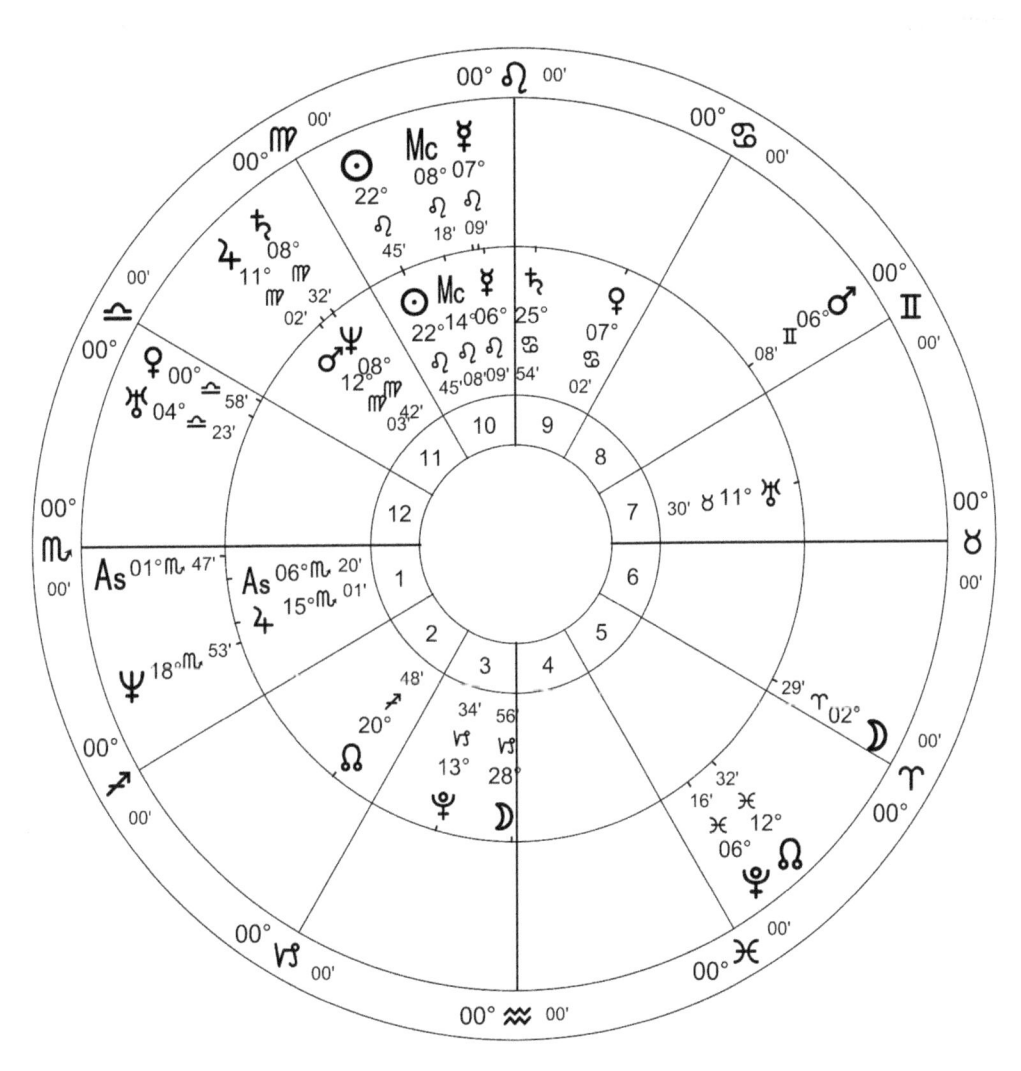

Note that the Jupiter/Saturn conjunction we noted in the SR is sitting on top of the Mars/Neptune conjunction in the natal, and SR Neptune is rising in the natal first house, sitting conjunct SR Jupiter. That makes two prominent Neptune hits, on Jupiter and Mars, planets associated with his Ascendant, hence his self-image and self-worth. The myth of Napoleon is taking shape here - and from what I have read, this was a deliberately cultivated image. In modern terms we would say that Napoleon knew how to play the media of his day to create the kind of image he wanted to project - the glorious, undefeatable Emperor.

As we expected, Jupiter, Mars and Sun are all prominent this year - but not always in helpful ways. There is a lot of illusion, a lot of glamour. The Neptune influence is unsettling and deceptive. Mercury is within a degree of its natal position and more tightly conjunct the SR Midheaven - so again, much of the theme of this year is related to communication, persuasion, perception.

The invasion of Russia was the turning point of overreach that led to his downfall. The Russian invasion began on June 24, 1812, so I am using Napoleon's August 1811 charts.

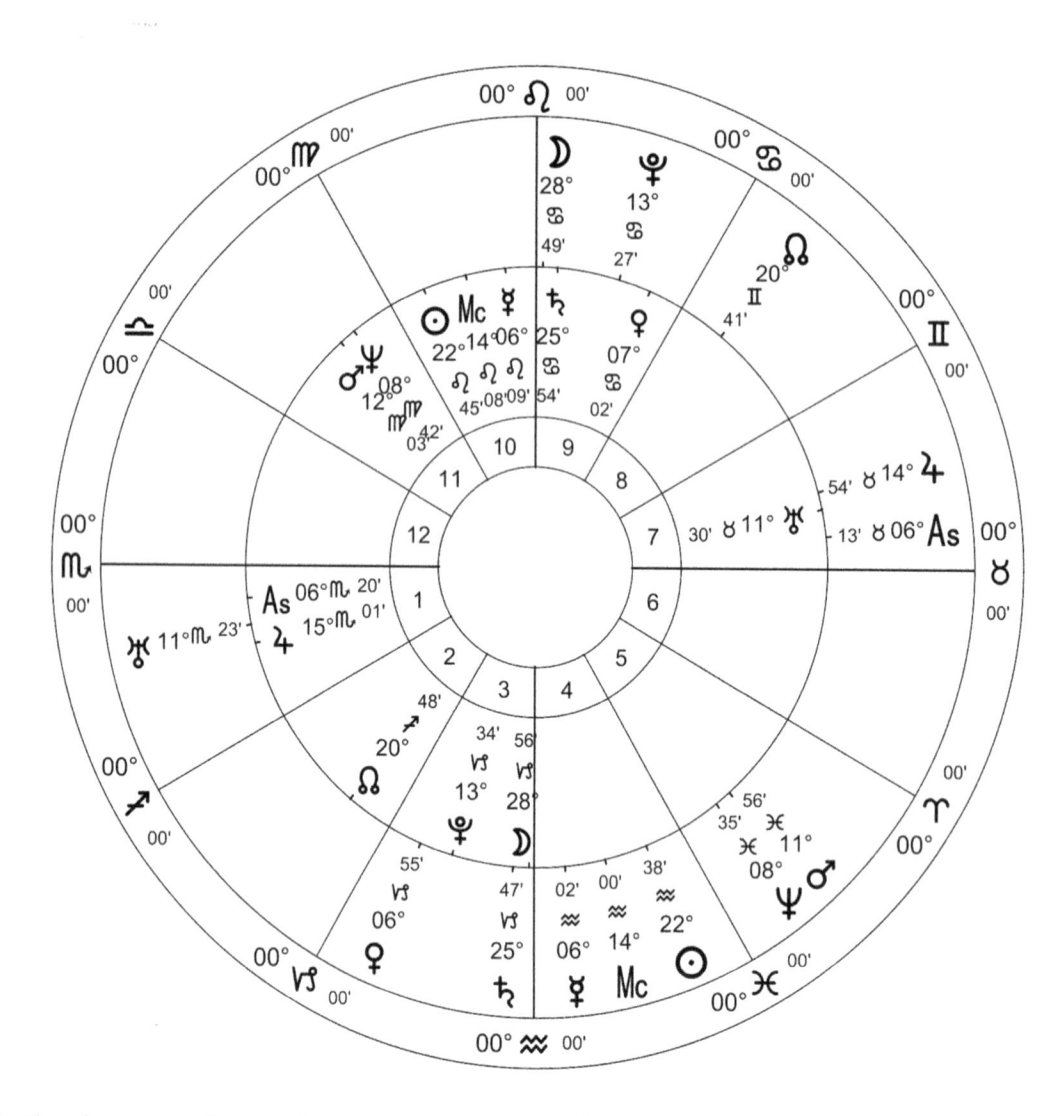

The profection has moved to a 7th house year, a year of open enemies, and the LOY is Venus, ruler of Taurus. Venus is cadent in both the profection and natal charts.

Once again the natal and profected angles line up in fixed signs, but in this chart the profected Ascendant has moved to the seventh house of open enemies and conflict, and the profected Midheaven has moved down into the bottom of the chart, in the fourth house.

You also have that curiosity of profected charts, that in a seventh house year all planets are opposite their natal position. All planets in rulership in the natal are in detriment here, and vice-versa. In this chart that is particularly visible with the Moon Saturn opposition swapping places, so we now have profected Saturn in rulership on top of Moon in detriment, and profected Moon in rulership on top of Saturn in detriment. To my mind that suggests a kind of emotional restlessness and craving for power and exceeding limits, that plays in with the urges for power and glory we see prominently featured in the chart as a whole.

Here are the directions in place for the year of the invasion of Russia.

Asc - Jupiter(Sag)/Mercury
MC - Saturn(Virgo)/Saturn
Sun - Mercury(Libra)/Mercury
Moon - Jupiter(Pisces)/Mars

The big switch in directions is the Midheaven, which has moved into Saturn/Saturn bounds. When Napoleon was appointed Consul for Life in the previous configuration we looked at, the MC was in Jupiter/Jupiter directions. We will see Saturn prominently activated in both profected and SR charts.

The Saturn bounds of Virgo are very late in the sign, so Saturn is coming near leaving the sign and directing into Libra, the sign of his exaltation, and the natal twelfth house of self-undoing. The Midheaven directed into the 12th house in 1813, after the collapse of the Russian invasion and shortly before Prussia invaded France. Paris fell and Napoleon abdicated in 1814.

It is also worth noting that the Sun has just recently directed into Libra, the sign of its fall, and the natal 12th house. The Sun has Mercury for both bound lord and participator.

The directed Ascendant is now in mid Sagittarius, in Jupiter bounds with Mercury as participator.

The directed Moon is in Pisces and has moved into the bounds of expansive Jupiter, and has perfected the opposition to natal Mars.

We will note the positions of these directed points as they interact with the solar return chart for this year. That is next.

This is the solar return for 1811.

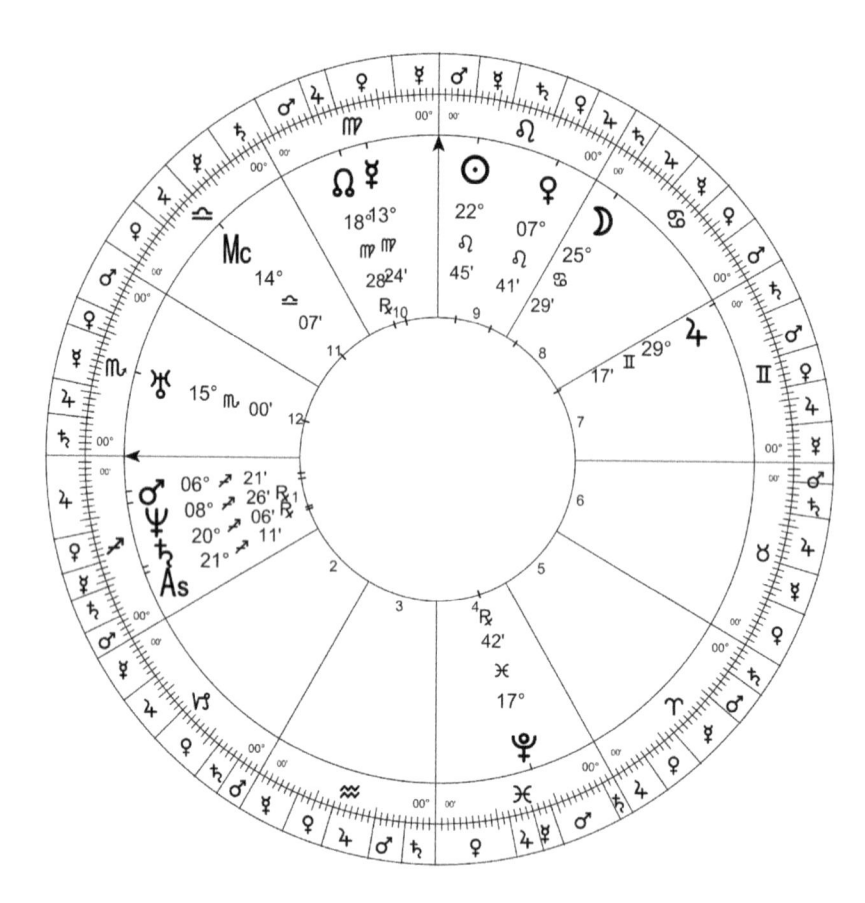

Note the solar return Saturn dead on the Ascendant. There is a Mars/Neptune conjunction in the natal chart, and this SR repeats that Mars/Neptune conjunction again, this time in the first house, above the Ascendant. Those two planets are in an applying trine with LOY Venus which is in the SR ninth, associated with distant lands.

In whole sign houses it often happens that planets in the first house above the Ascendant are visible to people observing the person, but are out of the person's awareness, having a kind of twelfth house quality. Here this shows Napoleon's expansive megalomania invading Russia, visible to everyone but himself.

Looking further at Mars, as it moves it is applying first to Neptune, then to Saturn. First to limitless dreams, then to harsh limitation.

Jupiter, the ruler of the solar return Ascendant, is in detriment in the seventh, in opposition to the difficult first house. Our glorious Sun is now in the ninth house of distant lands.

Looking at the directed planets, the directed Ascendant is sitting in the SR first house near the Mars/Neptune conjunction. The directed Moon is in Pisces in Jupiter bounds, very near SR Pluto in the fourth house, and conjunct the SR South Node. The directed Sun is applying to conjunction to the SR Midheaven.

This next chart shows the natal and solar return in a bi-wheel.

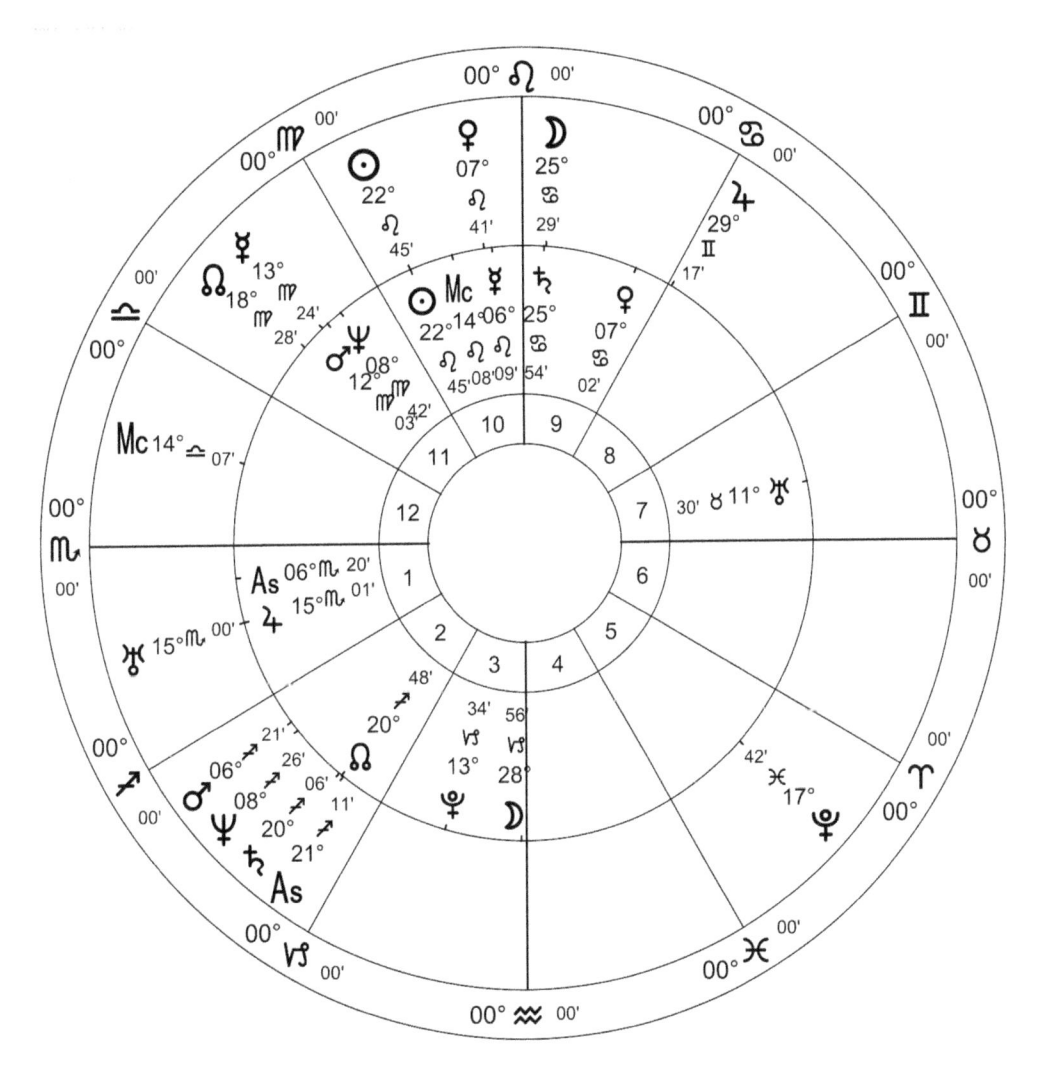

The solar return Moon is triggering natal Saturn, which repeats the Moon/Saturn configuration in the profected chart. In the solar return in the mutable signs there is a T with Mercury, Pluto and Saturn, and Mercury at the point of the T is sitting on top of the natal Mars/Neptune conjunction. Again we see that connection of Mercury with Mars and Neptune. This next is conjecture, but I wonder how much of this Russian invasion was a PR stunt on Napoleon's chart, where he dreamed of presenting such an invincible image that he would encounter little opposition from his awed opponents.

SR Saturn is sitting on the natal North Node which magnifies it. Disruptive SR Uranus is rising, sitting conjunct natal Jupiter. The SR Uranus is also sitting opposite natal Uranus which is in the seventh house. This is an unstable and stressed pair of charts, and Saturn is strongly configured across the two charts.

This wheel flips the two charts and puts the solar return in the center.

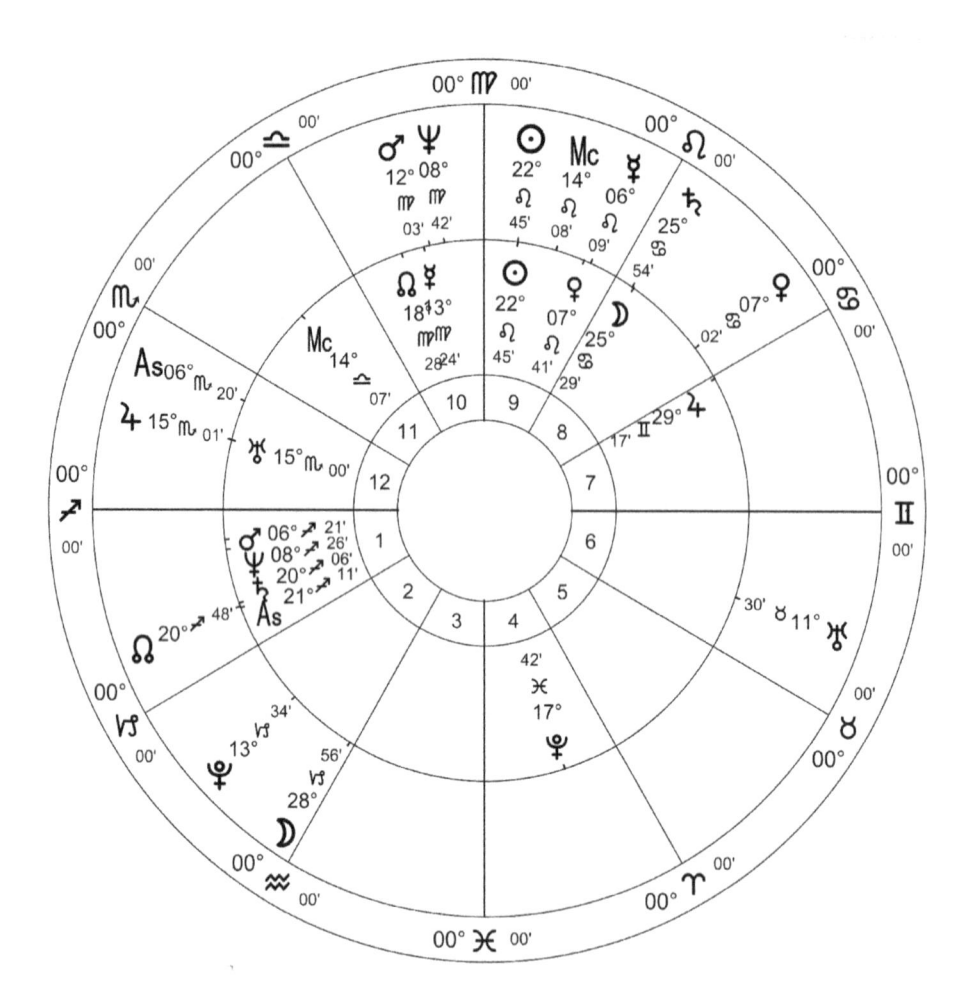

Here the natal North Node sitting on SR Saturn and Ascendant is highlighted. Also, in this view of the chart, the natal Ascendant is sitting in the SR twelfth house of self-undoing. Saturn's position and condition, in natal, directions, profection and solar return, are an important key to making sense of this particular group of charts. We have some of the same megalomaniac expansiveness we see in the natal and in the Consul series of charts - but here Saturn is activated, and the limitations and consequences of the overreach are striking home.

The Russian invasion began June 24, 1812. These are the directions of the SR Ascendant.

Z (Scorpio)Venus D --> Asc 304.460811 1812.06.20
Z Square Venus D --> Asc 305.344837 1812.06.21.

The SR Ascendant is directed to his natal Ascendant sign Scorpio - **in the bounds of Venus and square SR Venus, trine natal Venus - and Venus is Lord of the Year in the profected chart. The invasion happened shortly after the directed SR Ascendant crossed his natal Ascendant.** As in the traditional rules, the significant event is marked by tight aspects by the directed Ascendant to the Lord of the Year. In this case they are aspects to both natal and SR positions, and are in the bounds of the LOY.

The Gods Smile on Me - Charles Obert

1985 was one of the most important years of my life. This is the year I began the love affair with the woman who was to become my second wife. We stayed together for 24 years, until her death in November 2009. (That year was covered in a previous example.)

I call this my Venus year - it will be obvious why when you look at the directions for the year. I am listing the directions for both angles, the Lot of Fortune, and the main planets, since the pattern is so very striking and unusual.

Asc - Venus(Pisces)/Venus
MC - Venus(Sag)/Saturn
Sun - Venus(Taurus)/Moon
Moon - Venus(Virgo)/Venus
LOF - Venus(Libra)/ Venus

Venus - Venus(Aries)/Mercury
Mars - Mercury(Sag)/Venus
Jupiter - Saturn(Taurus)/Venus
Saturn- Jupiter(Scorpio)/Venus
Mercury - Mercury(Taurus)/Moon

Every directed point except for Mercury has Venus influence!

6 of the points are in Venus bounds, including the "Big Five" traditional points - Ascendant, Midheaven, Sun, Moon, and Lot of Fortune. The Ascendant, Moon and Lot of Fortune also have Venus as participator.

This shows the profected chart of the year outside my natal.

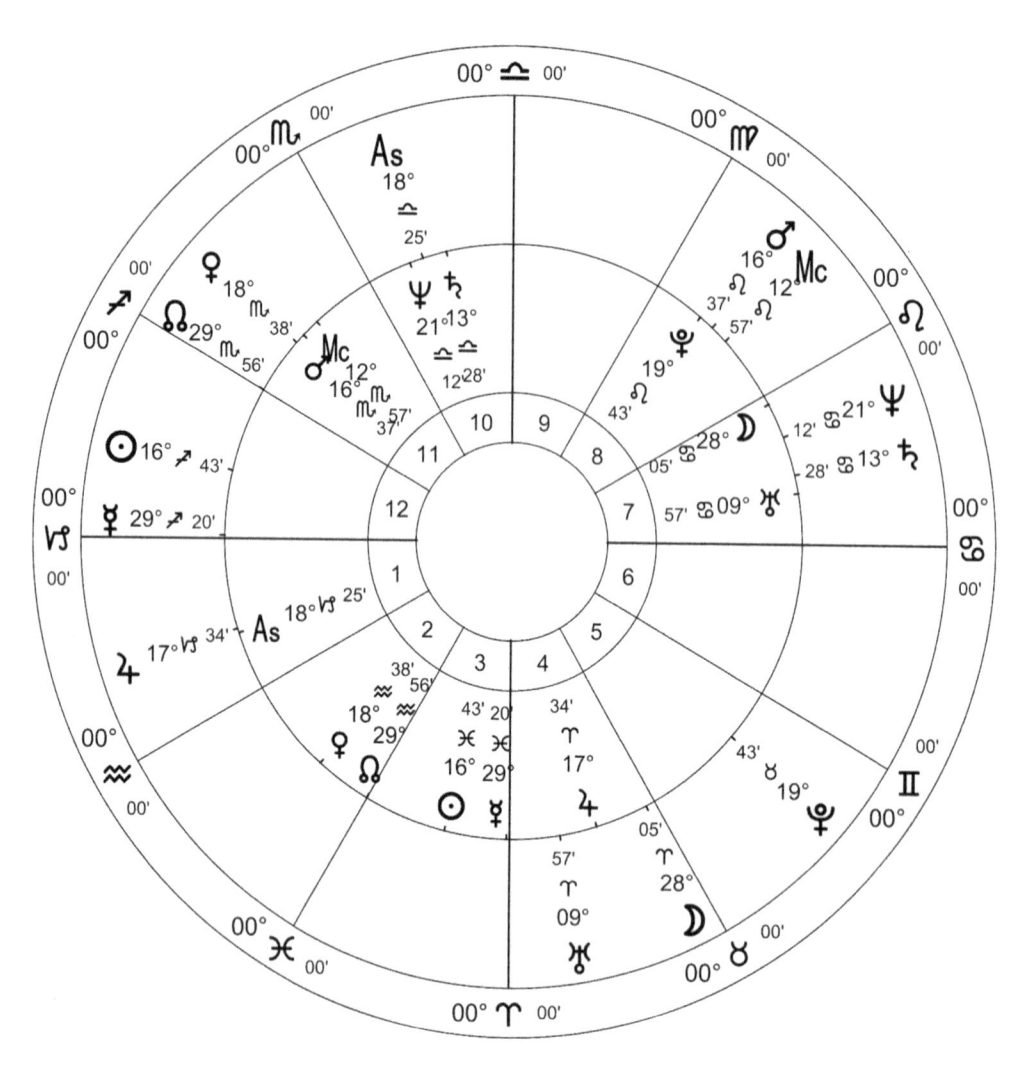

The profected sign of the year is Libra, and **the Lord of the Year is Venus.**

Note that profected Venus is sitting in Scorpio, conjunct natal Mars. We will see that Venus/Mars connection again in following charts. There is another Mars/Venus activation with profected Mars opposite natal Venus.

Saturn and Neptune are both in Libra, so they are activated by the profection. In my natal chart Saturn and Libra are in a close trine relationship and are in mutual reception, so the two planets work well together. Note that profected Saturn is in the seventh house of primary relationship. Given the condition of Saturn exalted in my natal chart this speaks to the longevity of the relationship.

I mentioned that the relationship lasted until Cindy's death 24 years later, so you see the same profected chart that year. The conditions in the solar return were significantly different, as you will see.

This next chart is the solar return for the year.

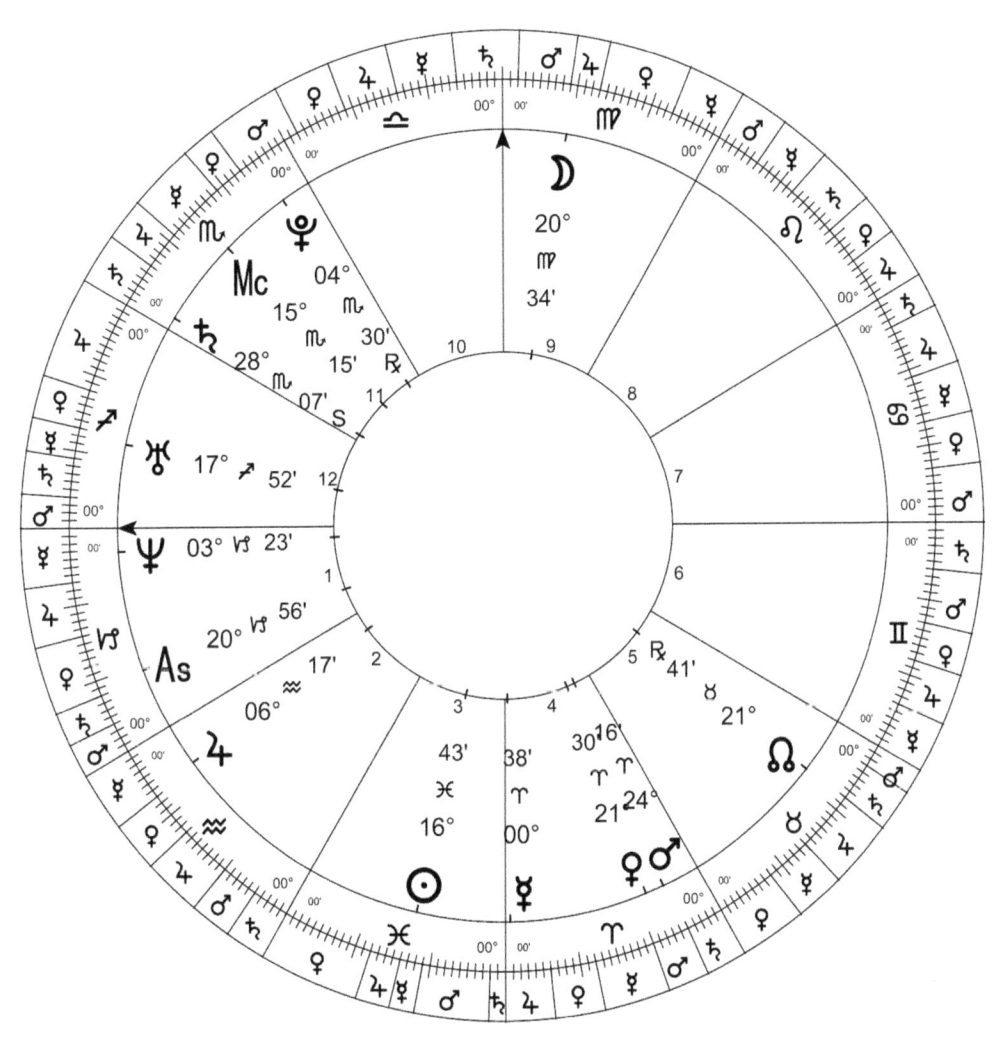

Ascendant 20 Capricorn is within a few degrees of my natal Ascendant, which is a strong marker for a big year. LOY Venus is in detriment in Aries in 4th house (we moved in together), but is applying to conjunction to a very strong Mars in rulership - so they do what Mars and Venus do together in the privacy of the fourth house. This repeats the pair of Mars/Venus connections in the profection.

Another noteworthy aspect is the Sun/Moon opposition, Virgo to Pisces. Sun/Moon connections are often featured in relationships like this. The most common planetary connections to look for in synastry for relationships are Sun to Moon, and Venus to Mars, and this chart has both.

The next chart shows my natal chart in the inner ring with the solar return in the outer.

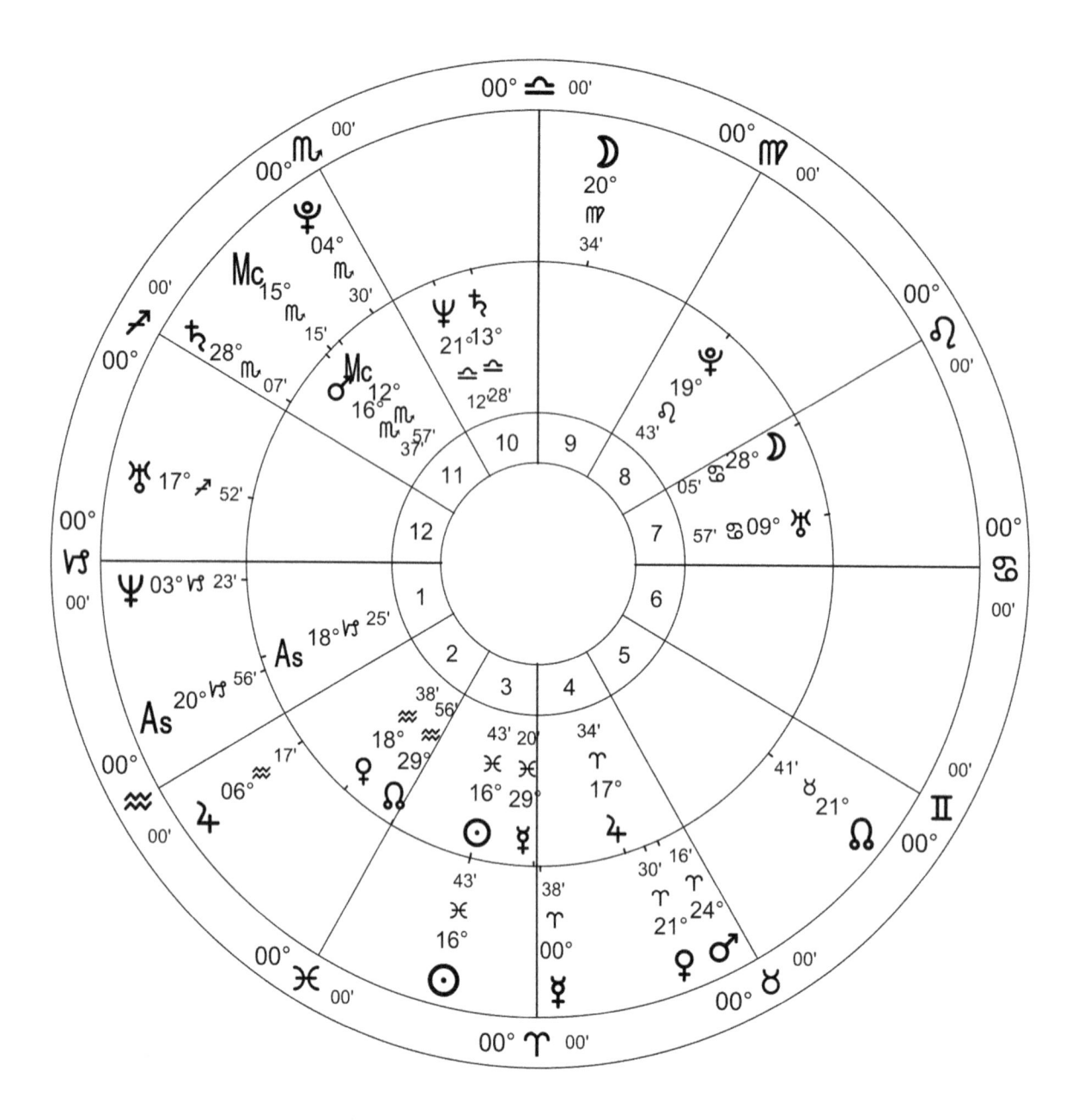

Here the closeness of the two Ascendants by degree is very obvious. With the same Ascendants the house placements are all the same.

Also note that SR Venus is tightly opposite natal Neptune... I suppose you could say there was more than a little Neptunian glamor and romance in this start of our affair - we were indeed star-struck with each other, and Neptune added the rosy glow and the special effects - the whole affair was larger than life, and it felt like living in a Hollywood movie.

Cindy and I began our affair in the spring, shortly after my birthday, and we moved in together later in the year, in November. The yearly directions of the SR Ascendant around the chart in that period are listed here.

(**Libra**)Saturn D --> Asc 227.017125 1985.10.23
Opp Mercury D --> Asc 227.830358 1985.10.24
(Libra)Mercury D --> Asc 234.577874 1985.10.31
Trine Jupiter D --> Asc 1985.10.31
(Libra)Jupiter D --> Asc 1985.11.10
(Libra)Venus D --> Asc 253.539551 1985.11.19

The solar return Ascendant directed to Libra, the profected sign of year, in late October, while we were preparing to move. It is in Jupiter/Jupiter bounds, and Jupiter is in my natal fourth house - very fitting for our moving in together. We celebrated Thanksgiving with the directed Ascendant in the bounds of Venus in her own sign.

We noted that the profection activated my natal Saturn in Libra. We married three years later in 1988, when the profected sign of the year was Capricorn, ruled by Saturn. An action begun in the profected sign where Saturn resides was completed in a sign Saturn rules.

Recall that this is a profected Libra year, as was 2009, the year Cindy died. Saturn and Venus were prominent and important in both of those years, but in profoundly different ways.

Maya Angelou

The first part of this chapter, on Maya Angelou's natal chart, appears in an expanded form in my book, *Using Dignities in Astrology*. I will focus on the parts of the natal chart that apply to an analysis of the solar return chart, profection and directions for her pivotal year 1968.

Maya Angelou is poet, writer, and civil rights activist, and is best known for the first in her extended series of autobiographies, *I Know Why the Caged Bird Sings*.

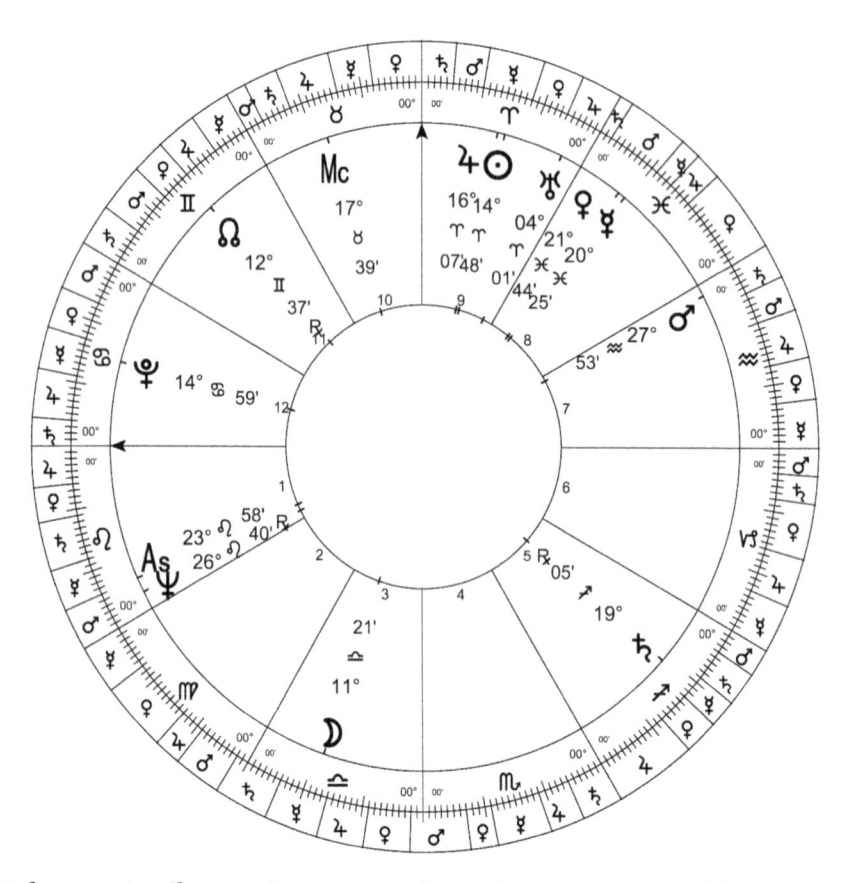

Marguerite Ann Johnson, April 4, 1928, 2:10 PM, St Louis, Missouri. Rodden Rating AA.

The rulers of the Ascendant and Midheaven, Sun and Venus, are both exalted. That is itself a signature for fame. Also, with this very strong Sun exalted, she is as famous as a person as she is for what she wrote or did.

By sign, the Sun is trine the Ascendant, and Venus is sextile the Midheaven. The angular rulers are strong both by dignity and by smooth aspect to the angles.

Sun and Jupiter Together

The center of the chart is the Sun/Jupiter conjunction in the ninth house. It is in Aries, the Sun's exaltation. The ninth house relates to writing, teaching and world travel, and her life abundantly includes all of those. She described herself as a teacher who writes.

Jupiter is approaching conjunction with the Sun. The Sun is exalted in Aries, and Jupiter and the Sun share a minor dignity called triplicity, so the two planets are strong and work well together. With both planets strong, Jupiter combust here can mean that the inner effect of Jupiter is intensified. We see the effects of Jupiter through her solar identity.

The Jupiter/Sun conjunction gave her an unshakable optimism and sense of self-worth, and she was a proponent of the positive thinking and mental healing movement. This conjunction resonates with a positive philosophy that gives power to the mind and to words to influence reality. It also gives her a very strong dedication to her moral ideals, as we saw in the chart of Harry Belafonte. Much of Angelou's work aligns with and supports the civil rights movement, for racial minorities and for women.

Venus and Mercury Together

For Angelou's writing and art, we need to consider the Venus/Mercury conjunction in the eighth house, a house which is considered negative and is related to suffering, to fear and to powerlessness.

Mercury is in detriment and fall, while Venus in exaltation and triplicity, so Venus very clearly predominates here. Her Mercury writing comes completely out of the Venus artistic perception. This is not the objectivity of a scientist, it is deeply emotional and artistic.

Mercury is square Saturn, and Mercury receives Saturn in the minor dignity of bounds, which is related to how she implements her ideas. This shows her life strategy of processing her past, and any suffering she experiences, in terms of her writing. The art of writing is the method she uses to cope with and to create her life. Saturn plus Mercury is also good for discipline, form and hard work in writing.

Mars

Mars is the most difficult planet in Angelou's chart and it is also the most angular planet, being within 3 degrees of the Descendant. Through house rulership Mars is linked to eighth, ninth, third and fourth houses, so we have connections between the suffering caused by Mars and her family and relatives, and how dealing with those affected her philosophy.

Mars is strong by accidental dignity, being angular, direct and fast, but it is peregrine and out of sect, and it is dominated in its dignities by the other malefic, Saturn, which rules over it.

At age 7 on a visit to her mother, Angelou was raped by her mother's boyfriend. She talked about the rape and who did it with her relatives, and a few days later the rapist was killed, probably by one of her uncles. Later in life she related that she stopped speaking because she was convinced her speaking had killed the man who raped her. The entire experience was so traumatic that she was silent for around five years.

Looking at her long period of silence after the rape, note that Mercury is in detriment and fall, in the eighth house of silent suffering. Note also that fall means not being listened to, which could equally well mean, not speaking. That period of verbal silence likely contributed to her particular artistic perception and sensitivity.

We noted that she was convinced that her speaking had killed the man who raped her. This ties in with her lifetime belief in the power of words to directly shape the world. She had a very strong reverence for the power of words, and this experience of the trauma of rape and death is a core experience in giving her that conviction.

Mars in the seventh house is also linked to the instability of her marriage and other relationships with men. Her one child was born from a high school affair, and her early marriage to a Greek sailor fell apart after around three years.

Saturn

The other malefic, Saturn, is in the fifth house in Sagittarius. It has dignity by triplicity but it is also retrograde. Saturn rules the sixth house of illness along with ruling the seventh.

We have noted that she had no good long term marriage relationships. The Lord of the seventh house is in the fifth house. She bore a child while in high school that she raised on her own, and at times this was a great burden for her. Saturn in the fifth house ruling the sixth house is related to her caring for her son's health problems, including nursing him for an extended period after a serious accident.

Along with Mars, We can also link this Saturn in the fifth house ruling the seventh house to the rape experience in her childhood.

On the positive side, this Saturn makes a trine with the Sun/Jupiter conjunction in the 9th house, and both Sun and Jupiter receive Saturn. She was able to take all of her difficulties and misfortune and work with them.

Saturn also provides an important connection between Jupiter and Sun in the ninth house, and Venus and Mercury in the eighth. Jupiter rules Venus and Mercury in Pisces, but there is no direct connection between them since there is no aspect between them. Jupiter is trine Saturn and rules Saturn, and Saturn is square to Venus and Mercury, so the hard creative work of Saturn provides a link between the idealism and moral force of Sun and Jupiter with the artistic sensitivity and creativity of Mercury and Venus. **Keep this connecting function of Saturn in mind.**

Neptune

Note Neptune is the rising planet, conjunct the Ascendant by 3 degrees.

Given what we have said about Maya Angelou being her own created character, this Neptune placement is very apt. The Ascendant and Neptune are in Leo, ruled by the Sun. Much of her public persona was created through her writing. She is her own greatest fictional creation. Neptune on the Ascendant connects to Sun and Jupiter in the ninth house of publishing and writing.

Note that Neptune and the Ascendant make a grand fire trine with the Jupiter - Sun conjunction and with Saturn, linking the first, fifth and ninth houses. This further emphasizes the importance of the pivotal connecting function of Saturn.

This brings us to the year 1968, the focus of our study.

Angelou was close friends with Martin Luther King and worked with him. King had asked Angelou to organize a march, and she had stalled in doing it.

Martin Luther King was assassinated on Maya Angelou's birthday, April 4, 1968, and after that she did not celebrate her birthday, but always sent some kind of remembrance to King's widow.

On the next page is the profected chart for 1968 in a bi-wheel with her natal chart.

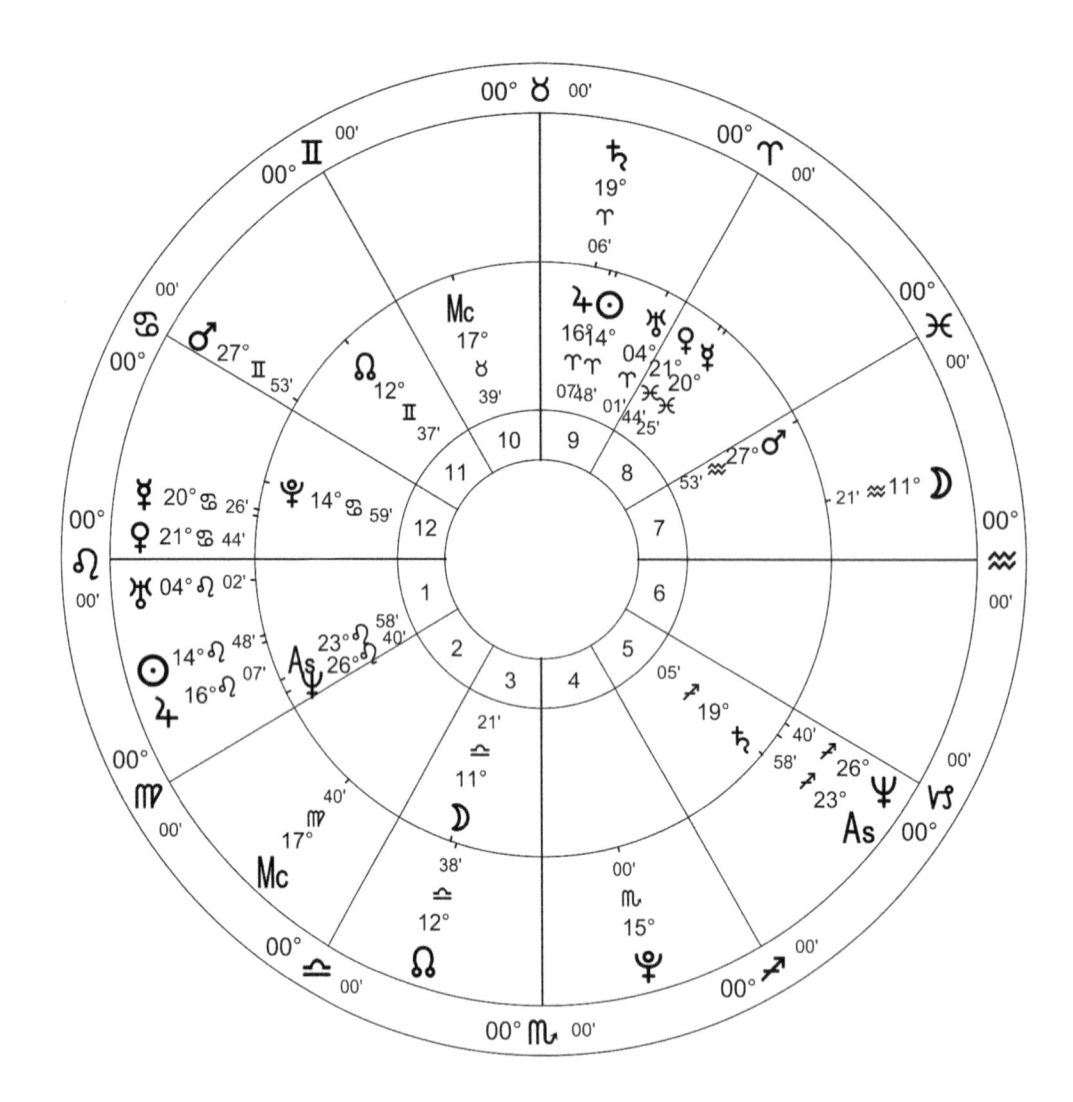

The profected Ascendant is in the 5th house, Sagittarius, ruled by Jupiter, and LOY Jupiter is conjunct the Sun, which is also activated. Very important, note that Saturn is in Sagittarius in this house. Those three planets, Saturn, Sun and Jupiter, will be central to the rest of the symbolism of the year. Jupiter being LOY activates the other house that Jupiter rules - Pisces, the eighth house.

Looking at the rest of the chart, profected Jupiter and Sun are on the Ascendant, profected Saturn is conjunct natal Jupiter and Sun, and profected Ascendant and Neptune are near Saturn. **The grand fire trine has rotated around in the profected chart to align with itself.** That will happen with the profected chart every four years, which is 120 degrees of rotation.

The profected South Node is sitting on the Sun Jupiter conjunction. In traditional astrology the South Node is of the nature of Saturn and is considered to diminish or suck the life out of the points it hits.

Noted that the profected Venus/Mercury conjunction has moved to the twelfth house - the twelfth will feature very prominently in what follows.

This next chart is Maya Angelou's solar return for the day Martin Luther King was shot and killed.

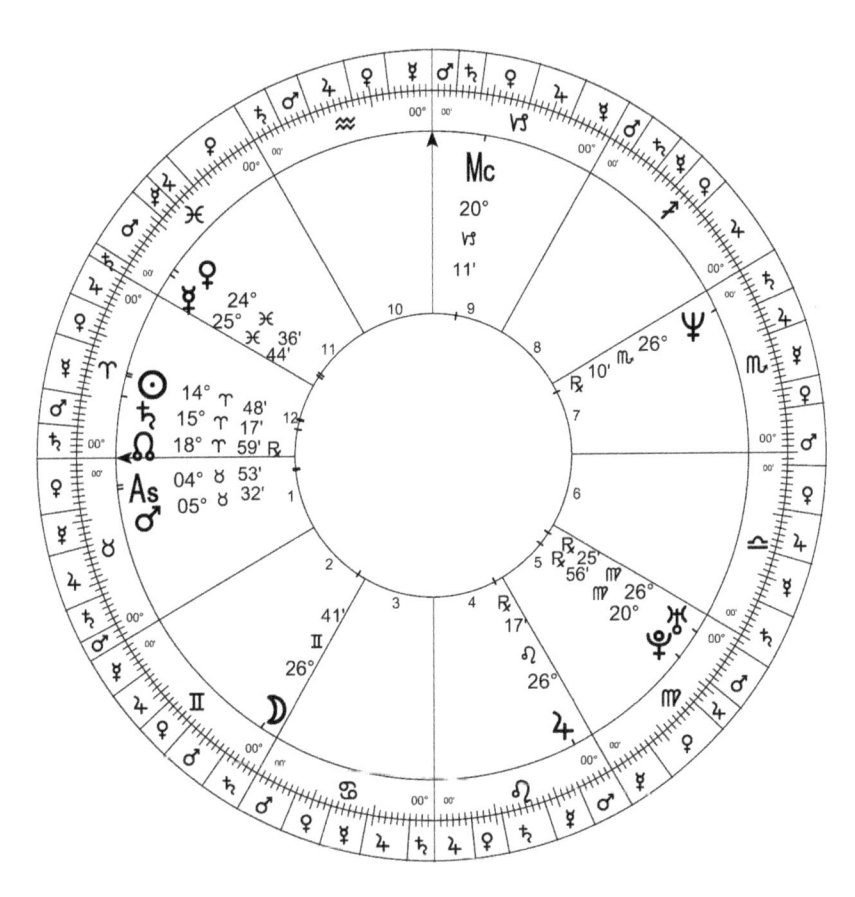

Consider the twelfth house, where the Sun is in Aries applying to a tight conjunction to Saturn. The Sun is exalted, a word that is sometimes translated royalty or king, and Saturn is in fall, meaning casting down or falling from prominence, in the twelfth house of hidden enemies - **the King was cast down by a hidden enemy. The planet Saturn is associated with the metal lead, and King was killed by a lead bullet. The sign Aries is associated with the head and face, and the bullet hit King in the cheek.**

The literalness of the symbolism is chilling.

Angelou spent much of the time after King was shot in a deep depression, staying in her room, not eating, not bathing, not answering the phone. She was cajoled out of this situation by her writer friend James Baldwin, who talked her into going to a party.

It was at this party, in late 1968, that the interchange and challenge from her friends took place that led to her writing her first autobiography, I Know Why the Caged Bird Sings, which was published in 1969 or 1970 - I have seen both dates online. This book was nominated for a National Book Award in 1970, spent a couple of years on best-seller lists, and brought her international recognition and acclaim.

Given that background we can now go more deeply into the chart configuration.

Profected sign of year, Sagittarius, is in the solar return eighth house, associated with death, helplessness and loss. (Recall that we saw an eighth house connection in the profected chart, where

129

that is the other house ruled by LOY Jupiter.) The profected sign of the year is Sagittarius. We saw that Saturn was activated by being in Sagittarius in her natal chart, and have already seen part of the extreme importance of Saturn in the SR.

The malefic Mars, Lord of the solar return twelfth house, is in detriment in Taurus and sitting right on the Ascendant. Mars also rules the seventh house of close partners, and also of open enemies.

Venus and Mercury are conjunct in Pisces in the solar return as in the natal, but in the SR they are in the 11th house of friends, groups and gatherings - this connotes the party she went to where James Baldwin suggested she write the book that became *Caged Bird*. Those two planets are opposite Pluto and Uranus in 5th house (associated with creativity in modern astrology), and square to the Moon in the second, part of a major aspect configuration we will see featured when we look at bi-wheels with the natal chart.

Angelou isolated herself for a long period in order to write the book, and that isolation shows up in the SR chart in a couple of ways. The LOY Jupiter holed up in the fourth house at the bottom of the chart shows the isolation, and also the period of depressed isolation right after the shooting. Isolation also fits the symbolism of the Sun Saturn conjunction in the 12th. It is also mirrored in the profected chart, where we saw profected Venus and Mercury in the 12th house. As we have seen before with significant events, the same quality is mirrored in multiple places.

The combined Sun - Saturn - twelfth house symbolism also fits the title of her book, about a Caged Bird, and it fits the subject matter - both Saturn and the twelfth house are associated with slavery, oppression and limitation, and her book is on her struggle to overcome those. The Sun Saturn configuration will take on more meaning when we link it to her natal chart.

Consider the cover of the book, *I Know Why the Caged Bird Sings* - you need to picture or see it in color to catch the symbolism. **The cover shows the gold Sun emerging from a vivid red background, and in front of them is the silhouette of a bird in flight, in black. Red, gold and black are the colors associated with Aries, the Sun, and Saturn.**

The symbolism of Sun and Saturn in the twelfth house resonates strongly through the events of this year in multiple ways, and the main themes of her life that year are reflected in the solar return.

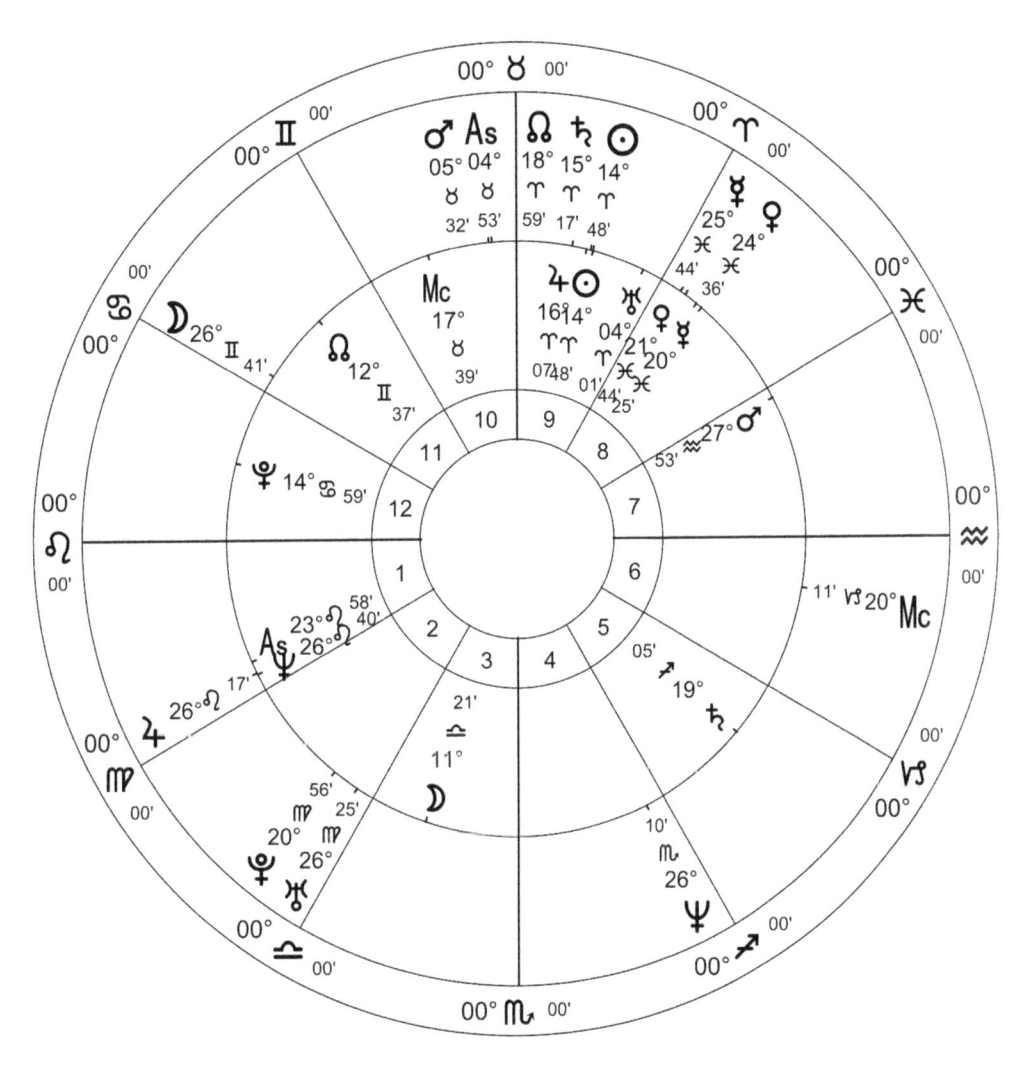

The next chart is a bi-wheel with the natal chart inner, solar return chart around the outside. LOY Jupiter is featured here in multiple ways. Jupiter from the solar return is sitting on the natal Ascendant, conjunct Neptune, repeating the configuration we saw with profected Jupiter on the Ascendant. Natal Jupiter is conjunct SR Saturn in the ninth house. Jupiter sitting on Neptune rising links to her symbolic autobiography - she took the loss and turned it into a book, which was her creation of her life as an autobiographical novel. Jupiter's natal location, conjunct the Sun in the ninth house, speaks of the core of the book being a spiritual affirmation of the worth and integrity of the human spirit to triumph over adversity, and in this chart we see both the adversity and the triumph in extreme form. We have already mentioned SR Saturn sitting right on Jupiter, and Saturn is also applying to a conjunction with SR North Node which magnifies its importance. Transiting north node was sweeping her ninth house Sun Jupiter during the year.

Solar return Venus and Mercury are very close to their natal position. We noted that they had moved from the natal eighth house (death and suffering) to the SR eleventh (the party and her group support from friends) and the same two planets are in the profected twelfth house. The symbolism of all of the houses fits different aspects of her experience this year.

The SR Ascendant is in the tenth natal house, along with SR Mars, which is reflected in this being the year that led to her rise to worldwide fame - and Mars links back to the early event, the rape that is a central, dominating part of the book.

We mentioned the SR T pattern, Venus/Mercury opposite Uranus/Pluto and square the Moon. That pattern is completed and triggered by the natal Saturn in Sagittarius, turning the T into a mutable grand cross, including the important planets Venus and Mercury related to writing, the Moon to the emotional hurt, and Saturn to both the tragedy, and the hard work and discipline that transmuted it into art.

There is another important T configuration in the natal chart, with Pluto in 12th house as focus, square to the Sun/Jupiter opposition to the Moon. This relates to King's death, and to her writing about slavery and oppression. This is completed, or rather triggered, by the SR MC axis hitting the 4th point of the T. Crossing the 2 charts, 2 different T squares are completed, and we have two different grand cross configurations here in the combination of the two charts.

The chart on the top of the next page switches the two wheels, and puts the SR chart in the inner wheel and the natal in the outer.

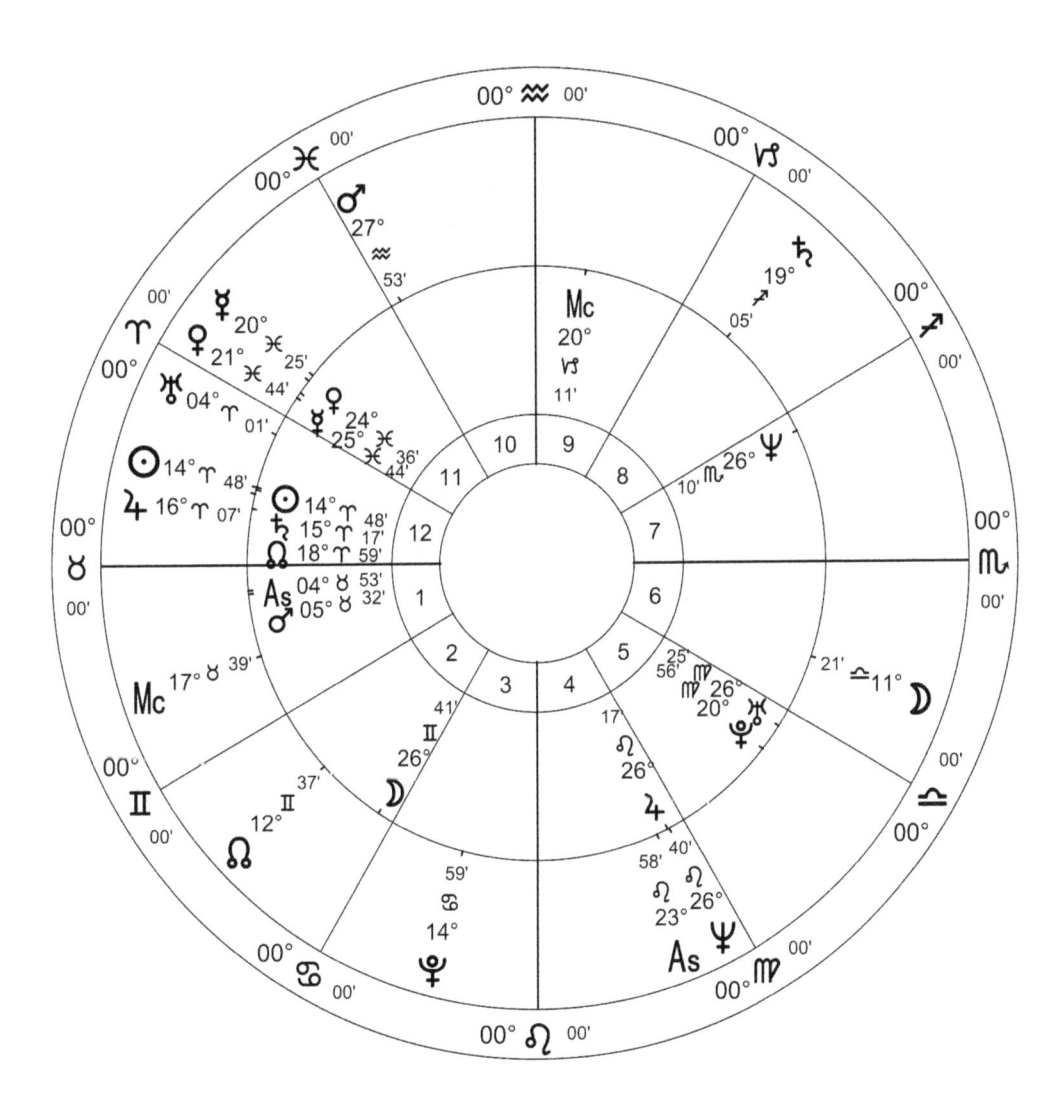

We already mentioned Mercury and Venus in the solar return 11th house. Here we see the link between the between 9th and 12th houses, since the 9th house Jupiter/Sun conjunction has moved to the SR 12th. This shows her spiritual purpose in overcoming slavery, hardship and spiritual oppression with her strong sense of inner worth and purpose. The natal Midheaven is here in the SR first house, related to her coming to extreme public prominence.

Note that the natal grand fire trine now falls in the solar return fourth, eighth and twelfth houses. The natal grand trine in the houses of identity and self-expression, creativity, and spiritual ideals, is linked here with the houses of isolation, death, seclusion and endings.

We have consistently seen how very important the planet Saturn is in this series of charts. It will be interesting to see if there is any connection with Saturn in the primary directions for the year. I ran the directions for both angles and for the important planets Mercury, Venus, Jupiter and Saturn, and this is what I found.

Primary Directions for 1985

Asc - Mars(Virgo)/Venus
MC - Saturn(Gemini)/Venus
Sun - Saturn(Taurus)/Venus
Moon - Mercury(Scorpio)/Mars

Ven - Saturn(Aries)/Saturn
Mer - Saturn(Aries)/Saturn
Jup - Saturn(Taurus)/Venus
Sat - Saturn(Cap)/Venus

The heavy predominance of Saturn is obvious, and it is noteworthy how often Saturn is paired with Venus as partner - the tragedy, the hard work, and the art and poetry.

Here are the directed points placed as symbols around a bi-wheel with the natal inner, SR outer.

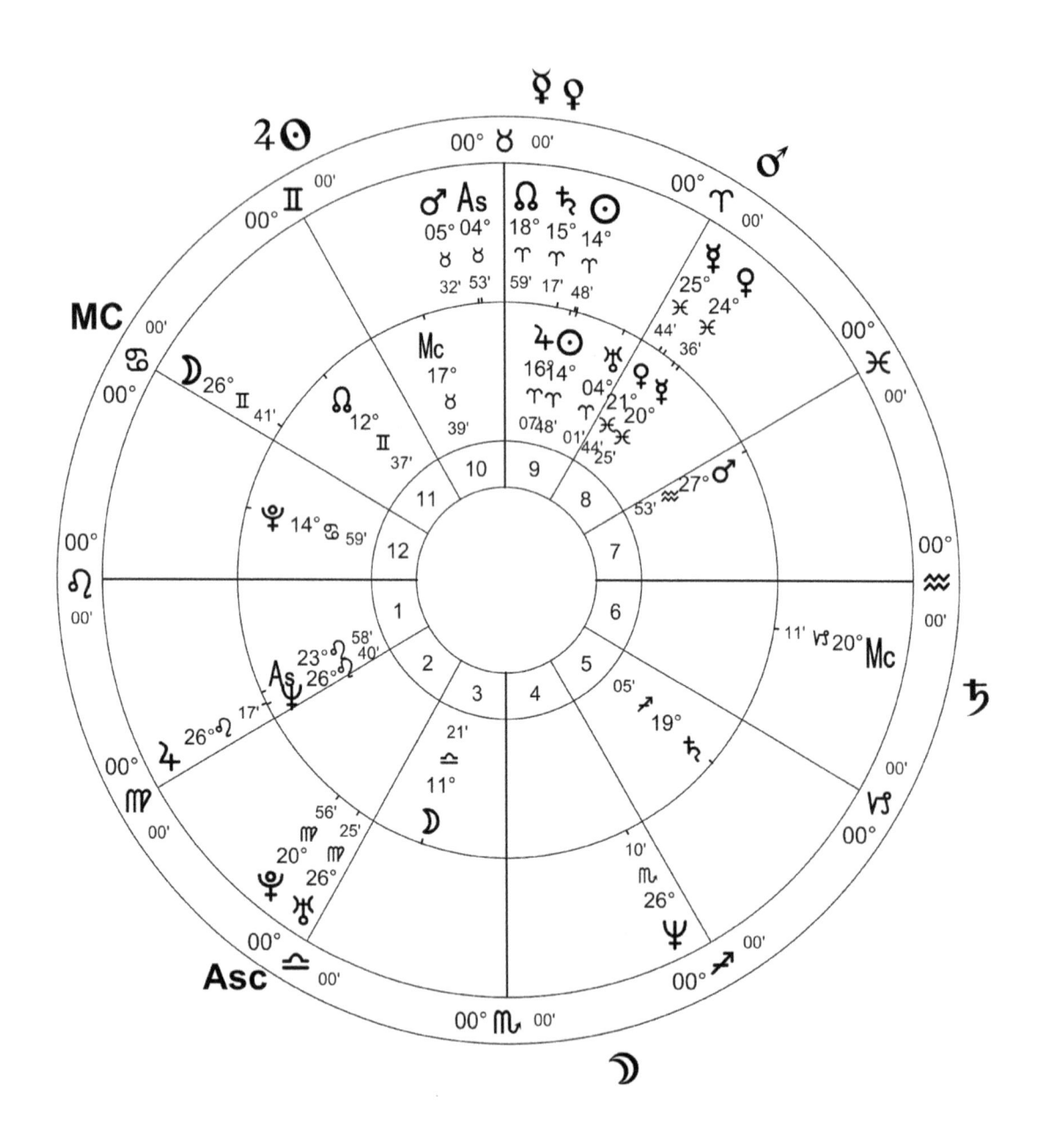

The directions for the Venus/Mercury pair are particularly noteworthy - **Venus and Mercury have directed to Aries and the ninth house, so they are now in the same house as natal Sun and Jupiter. Both directed planets are now trine natal Saturn, so they are poised to work together - and Saturn has Venus as partner planet.**

Note the locations and configurations of these other directed points.

The directed Ascendant is conjunct SR Uranus-Pluto and opposite SR and natal Mercury - Venus.

Directed Saturn is conjunct the SR Midheaven.

Directed Sun and Jupiter are opposite SR Neptune. We saw repeated connections of these three planets in previous charts.

Directed Moon is opposite the natal Midheaven - I associate the Moon down at the bottom of the chart with the isolation and seclusion, and also with her going deeply into her childhood emotional memories, and into her ancestry.

The directed Midheaven is conjunct the SR Moon, and square the two ends of the opposition of Mercury - Venus and Uranus - Pluto.

Every one of these directed planets forms a significant degree aspect to one of the major configurations we discussed.

I want to close this section by comparing two other solar returns. The first is for 1937, the year of the childhood rape incident. The second is for 1970, the year that Caged Bird received a National Book Award nomination and reached worldwide fame.

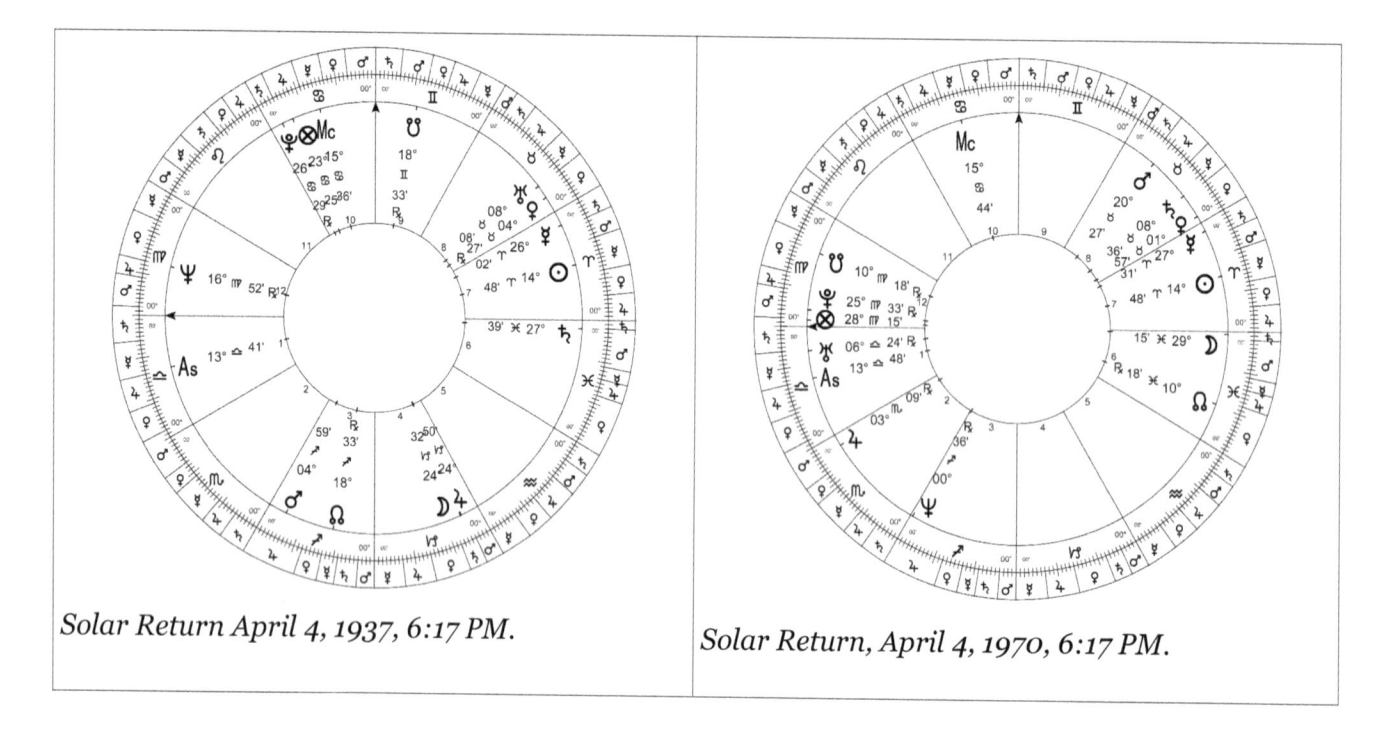

Solar Return April 4, 1937, 6:17 PM.

Solar Return, April 4, 1970, 6:17 PM.

The 1937 chart has Ascendant 13 Libra 41. The 1970 chart has Ascendant 13 Libra 48.

The two Ascendants are conjunct to within seven minutes.

The events of 1937 were re-presented, took on new life, in the book that reached world fame in 1970.

Conclusions and Questions

In this section I want to touch on some general conclusions I have drawn about predictive work. I also want to raise some questions I have about how these techniques, especially primarily directions and the use of the bounds, might be considered in further research.

Prediction Techniques Work Best Responding to Questions

This is an important general conclusion I have reached about astrology in general, and it is especially applicable when dealing with the massive amount of data involved in correlating all these predictive systems. The system works best when the techniques are focused by the use of a specific question, topic or concern that a person brings to the table. General, open-ended readings of the "tell me what will happen" type do not work anywhere near as well as focused readings. The significations of astrology symbolism are broad and multivalent, and they need a question to focus the interpretation.

This focus on topics matches how the chart examples are worked in this book. What I know about a particular period of a person's life in the example gives the focus, and the charts are read from that point of view. That is true when studying the known life of an historical figure, and it is true in an effective reading where the client is deeply involved and provides the area for focus.

Go for the Big Points

When you combine this many charts and systems - natal chart, directions on multiple points, profection and solar return - and then you stir in real time transits and directions for smaller periods, the sheer amount of information and number of combinations is overwhelming. When I am dealing with a set of charts for a reading I first concentrate just on the things that jump out at me, the big correlations - planets right on angles, dignity or debility of LOY, major tight aspect patterns - and I pay special attention whenever I see the same factor or mix of factors coming up repeatedly, across multiple systems. With aspects between charts I mainly use the major hard aspects, conjunction, opposition and square. When I have a specific topic to focus on and have done a general survey I sometimes go into further detail than that, but very often just the big picture points tell the story.

This is why I find it so very useful to have a question or area of concern from the client to have a focus - that helps me figure out what to focus on and what to ignore. I have often had the uncanny experience of feeling like the chart is guiding me to the important points, the ones that apply just at that spot in the reading. You could call that guidance or intuition, but it only works if I have done my homework and am familiar with the overall chart configuration.

Using Direction Through the Bounds

These two points about primary directions are very important and worth re-emphasizing here.

First -

Primary directions are concerned with periods of time rather than specific points or events.

And second -

The bound lords are the most important rulers to consider in primary directions to determine how a specific period of time works out.

The base principle is that the directions through bounds as a set gives the overall tone, themes, and working conditions for a time period. It is a way of taking the annual timing tools of profections and solar returns and giving them a larger framework.

In any given chart, and at any given time, the particular planetary directions that are important will vary. Directing the Ascendant is the most generally useful point, and I use it very regularly in client work - though, as I pointed out, it is not always easy to interpret with celebrity charts where we often do not have the information on the overall meaning of the person's life as it appears to that person.

I now usually look at what I consider the Big Four points - Ascendant, Midheaven, Sun and Moon - and we touched on their general significance in the introductory part of this study. The first two points, Ascendant and Midheaven, are the most consistently meaningful. I also pay attention to stressed directions of the Moon if there are health concerns, or issues with problems like depression.

I am convinced that it is also worth looking at any planets that are particularly highlighted and active in a given year in the solar return and profections, or standout planets in the natal chart like Belafonte's Sun - Jupiter configuration.

In looking at the bound lord and participator active at a given time, It is important to consider each of their conditions and the natal relationship between them to see how the two planets will work together - we saw that in the study of the Las Vegas shooting with the Sun and Saturn. A supportive partner planet can make a big difference in how a bound lord works out, and vice-versa. We also saw that the condition and relationship of the two in the active solar return is also worth considering.

Using the Bounds in Other Contexts

I am increasing convinced of the importance of the not-so-minor dignity of bounds in general. They are the most under-rated and under used of the minor dignities. The bounds are very useful for showing how a planet actually implements or is expressed - not ruling, but implementing - and in that area, they are very important and need much more research. (See my book on *Using Dignities in Traditional Astrology* for further research on the bound.)

Just as the bounds are important in the natal chart, it is worth considering the bounds in other predictive charts, like the solar returns and profections. I have not pursued that in detail, and it is yet another area that needs more research.

It is worth exploring use of the bounds with other timing techniques like secondary progressions. I am particularly intrigued by the notion of looking at the bounds in solar arc directions, which is a kind of modern equivalent to the kinds of things that primary directions do. I know from experience that solar arc directions can be very effective. If I am right, then noting when a planet changes bound lords should be worth noting there also.

Remember that primary directions, profections, secondary progressions, solar arc directions, are all different varieties of **symbolic** movement through time, with a very heavy emphasis on symbolic. Once you grant the validity of symbolic directions in general, there is no a priori reason why the bounds should be significant with this one technique and not with others, or why one particular direction technique is "real" while others are "fantasy".

How Aspects Work

Regarding the use of the partner planet with directions, the working rule is that the last aspecting planet continues to have an effect until the next aspect perfects. I wonder if this should lead us to re-think how aspects work in any context. The usual modern approach seems to be to view an aspect as most important while it is applying and then briefly after it perfects, and then to view it as rapidly dropping off in significance as it separates. The use of the partner in directing the bounds is very, very different. **Modern astrology considers aspects as points in time, traditional astrology considers aspects as periods of time.** Again, this needs more research.

The series of aspects to partners that a directed point makes has parallels to the series of aspects that the Moon makes in the context of interpreting a horary chart. There the last perfected aspect continues to have an effect until the next aspect is made. Perhaps this principle of aspect perfection can be generalized.

Aspects, Periods and Returns

There is a similar difference in thinking about how returns work. Modern astrologers tend to think of a planet's return as it coming to a specific degree, while traditional astrologers think of returns as applying to an entire sign. For example, I consider the period of a Saturn return to apply to the entire time it transits its home sign, a period of around 2-1/2 years. The point of Saturn's return to its degree location is an important point of extra emphasis, but it is best understood within the whole time period.

Bound Lord Changing Signs

Another question is the significance of a directed point changing signs along with bounds. To my knowledge this is not generally noted in the traditional material on directing the bounds, and that is another area that could use further research. I know that noting when a planet changes signs in secondary progressions is a consistently significant marker for starting a new phase. Just as changing bounds could be considered in secondary progressions, changing signs could be considered in directions through the bounds.

Location of Directed Point on Natal and Other Charts

Along with considering the changes of bound lord and partner, it is definitely worth looking at the specific location on the chart that the given point is directed to. We saw this in the examples with Monroe, and with Harry Belafonte, and very, very significantly in the freaky set of correlations with the Las Vegas shooting and Stephen Paddock's charts, and with the Maya Angelou 1968 series.

It is worth drawing in the directed planets on the outside of the wheel around the natal or other chart being considered, the way we used to do with progressions and transits back in the old days before computer programs came up with multi wheel charts.

Directing the Outer Planets

So far, with the very noteworthy exception of Neptune in the Monroe study we looked at, I have done very, very little with including the three modern outer planets in directions, either as points to direct, or as points aspecting the directed point. This is another area for further inquiry. By definition the outer planets cannot be bound lords, and I seriously doubt whether they should be considered as candidates for partners, but directing the outer planets themselves is an open area.

The modern version of the Morinus program includes the modern planets. The traditional version does not. I have both versions, but I use the traditional version almost exclusively.

To clarify my own take on the three modern planets - I do use the outer planets in my chart interpretation, as in the examples here, but I do not consider them to have any dignity or sign rulership, and thus they are not candidates for being time lords in directions, profections, or solar revolutions.

Profecting the Entire Chart

In this book I have focused on the main use of profections, which is to determine the profected sign of the year and the Lord of the Year, which will be the main focus in the context of solar returns.

In some of the examples I have considered the meaning of the profected chart of a whole. There is historical precedent for this - Valens profects points other than the Ascendant, and William Lilly profects all of the points in the chart, and his example interpretations he is clearly looking at the profected chart as a whole. I have pushed the technique a bit further here in considering the profection as an entire valid chart in its own right, and my findings so far support its significance. This is another area that needs further exploration.

Combining the Cycle of the Year with Secondary Progressions

In my personal astrology practice I use these techniques as the center of my predictive work. I also combine them with the use of secondary progressions. I find those to be consistently useful, especially progressed lunar phases, and planets either stationing or changing signs. There is precedent for using secondary progressions in Valens, but they were not as consistently used in the general tradition until relatively recently.

Secondary Progressions as a Time Lord System

Given the nature of symbolic directions, and that primary directions and profections are time lord systems, it makes sense to re-think secondary progressions in a similar manner. Modern astrology tends to look at progressions in the same way as transits, with aspects approaching exact, perfecting and then separating. When I use progressions I pay most attention to how they affect periods of time. For example, the Sun changing signs marks a distinct change in tone and emphasis that is in effect for around thirty years. It is worth taking the sign change, and interpreting it in terms of a change in the time lord over the Sun for the new sign - where is the ruler, what condition is it in, and so on.

The Cycle of the Year and Modern Astrology

Do these traditional techniques also work in the context of a modern astrology approach? Yes, emphatically so.

There are some important dimensions of traditional predictive technique that greatly enrich modern astrology, especially the concepts of time lords and periods rather than points of time.

Going the other way, some of the psychological developments of modern astrology have validity and shed further light on some of the traditional techniques. For example, I am convinced that the bound lord partner has an inner, psychological dimension along with its traditional meaning of referring to other people or groups that affect that point. The different approaches are complementary and can benefit from being used together.

I hope that I have introduced you to some useful techniques to deepen and enrich your astrology predictive practice, and some new ways of thinking about how astrology works.

Enjoy.

Where to Go from Here

This section lists further resources for further pursuing the topics covered in this book.

For a general introduction to traditional astrology and to using dignities to evaluate a chart, I recommend my first two books. These three books together are intended as a series.

Charles Obert, **Introduction to Traditional Natal Astrology**. Almuten Press, 2015.

_____ , **Using Dignities In Astrology**. Almuten Press, 2018.

I regularly teach classes at Kepler College on this predictive technique and on using dignities - you can find out about them at their site, **https://keplercollege.org/**.

This is a conversation I had with Chris Brennan about Essential Dignities on his astrology podcast - **http://theastrologypodcast.com/2018/05/10/essential-dignities-and-debilities-with-charles-obert/**

I highly recommend the Seven Stars Astrology website, **http://www.sevenstarsastrology.com/**. This site has many outstanding articles and presentations on traditional astrology topics, including excellent material on profections, revolutions, and directions.

For more advanced information on Solar Revolutions and on Directions, explore the work of Ben Dykes. His audio programs and books are available at his website, **https://bendykes.com**. The following four audio programs are recommended.

- **FAA 2010 Introduction to Solar Revolutions**
- **Primary Directions Without Tears**
- **Workshop: Distributions Through the Bounds**
- **Workshop: Elements of Solar Revolutions**
- See also this translation by Ben Dykes: **Persian Nativities 3: On Solar Revolutions: Abu Mashar's On the Revolutions of the Years of Nativities**. Cazimi Press, 2010. This book is the fullest presentation of the Cycle of the Year that I am aware of.

The standard book on Primary Directions is by Martin Gansten - **Primary Directions: Astrology's Old Master Technique**, Wessex Astrologer, 2009.

For profections in particular, and Hellenistic astrology in general, the work of Chris Brennan is noteworthy. Chris goes much further into the use of profections by themselves as a predictive tool.

- Chris has a two hour podcast on Profections available for free here -

http://theastrologypodcast.com/2018/04/26/annual-profections-a-basic-time-lord-technique/

- Chris has a very thorough online course on Hellenistic Astrology -

https://courses.theastrologyschool.com/courses/hellenistic-astrology-course

- The module on Profections from that course is also available separately -

https://courses.theastrologyschool.com/courses/annual-profections-timing-technique-class

- Chris Brennan also wrote the book, **Hellenistic Astrology: The Study of Fate and Fortune**. Amor Fati Press, 2017.

Tables of Essential Dignities

Sign	Ruler	Detriment	Exaltation	Fall	Triplicity Day	Triplicity Night	Triplicity Partner	Face 0-9	Face 10-19	Face 20-29
♈	♂	♀	☉	♄	☉	♃	♄	♂	☉	♀
♉	♀	♂	☽		♀	☽	♂	☿	☽	♄
♊	☿	♃			♄	☿	♃	♃	♂	☉
♋	☽	♄	♃	♂	♀	♂	☽	♀	☿	☽
♌	☉	♄			☉	♃	♄	♄	♃	♂
♍	☿	♃	☿	♀	♀	☽	♂	☉	♀	☿
♎	♀	♂	♄	☉	♄	☿	♃	☽	♄	♃
♏	♂	♀		☽	♀	♂	☽	♂	☉	♀
♐	♃	☿			☉	♃	♄	☿	☽	♄
♑	♄	☽	♂	♃	♀	☽	♂	♃	♂	☉
♒	♄	☉			♄	☿	♃	♀	☿	☽
♓	♃	☿	♀	☿	♀	♂	☽	♄	♃	♂

Bounds or Terms

♈	0	♃	6	♀	12	☿	20	♂	25	♄
♉	0	♀	8	☿	14	♃	22	♄	27	♂
♊	0	☿	6	♃	12	♀	17	♂	24	♄
♋	0	♂	7	♀	13	☿	18	♃	26	♄
♌	0	♃	6	♀	11	♄	18	☿	24	♂
♍	0	☿	7	♀	17	♃	21	♂	28	♄
♎	0	♄	6	☿	14	♃	21	♀	28	♂
♏	0	♂	7	♀	11	☿	19	♃	24	♄
♐	0	♃	12	♀	17	☿	21	♄	26	♂
♑	0	☿	7	♃	14	♀	22	♄	26	♂
♒	0	☿	7	♀	13	♃	20	♂	25	♄
♓	0	♀	12	♃	16	☿	19	♂	28	♄

The degree in the term table is the degree that bound starts. For instance, Venus term in Aries begins at 6 degrees.

Using the Morinus Astrology Program

There are two versions of Morinus, modern and traditional. The modern version, includes the 3 outer planets, and the traditional version does not.

I highly suggest starting with the traditional version. The modern version adds lines in directions for the Descendant whenever the Ascendant is chosen, and that can be confusing until you know how to weed it out. Also, the traditional method of using directions does not include the outer planets, and the outer planets are not considered as partner or participating planets.

This is the link to get the traditional version.

 - https://sites.google.com/site/tradmorinus/morinus (for Windows - download MorinusWin.zip - the link is at the bottom of the page.)

Put the file where you want the program and unzip the file. The program, morinus.exe, is in the folder and is ready to run.

For instructions on setting up and using Morinus on a Mac, see the following sites:
- https://code.google.com/archive/p/morinus-astro/
- http://astro-morinus.blogspot.com/
- https://kb.wisc.edu/helpdesk/page.php?id=25443

To set up the minor dignities correctly, go to the Options menu to Minor Dignities, and make sure Triplicity is set to Dorothean, bound to Egyptian, and Face to Chaldean. In the Options menu, for Primary Keys, I have been using Ptolemy static key with good results.

Also in the Options Menus, go to Appearance 1, and turn on the check box to display the ring with the Terms (same as bounds). You can check Face if you use all of the essential dignities and want to see those in a ring. This is also the place where you can choose to see your charts either in color or in black and white. If you are going to be printing images, I find that black and white prints much more clearly.

1) Enter your chart data - here is a snapshot of the data entry screen for a natal chart. Enter the exact latitude and longitude for the location, and set the correct time zone offset in the second column. A time zone West of Greenwich is minus, East of Greenwich is plus. You can use a chart from the free site astro.com, or from another astrology program to get the necessary latitude, longitude and time zone data to enter.

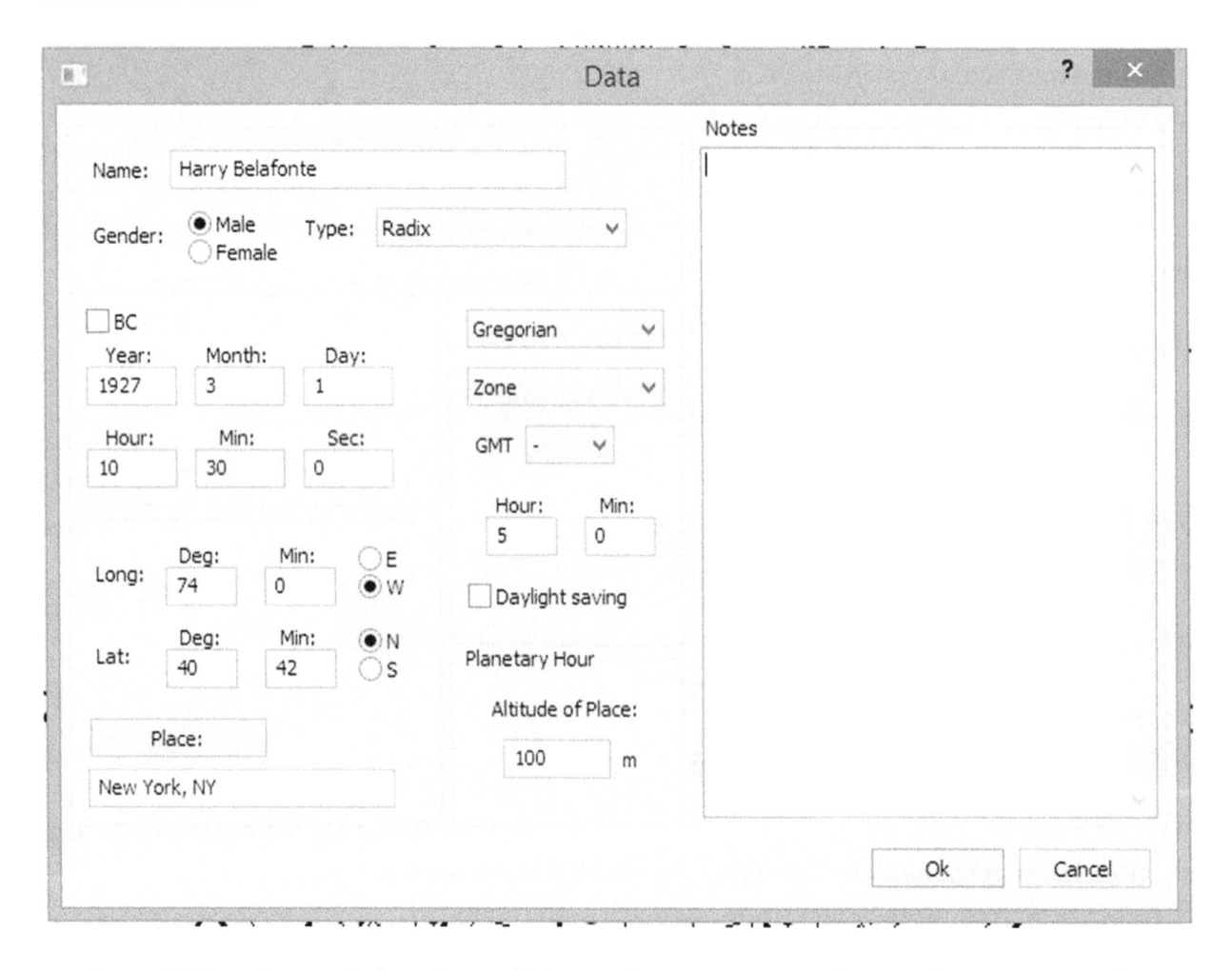

Name:	Harry Belafonte
Gender:	● Male ○ Female
Type:	Radix
BC:	☐
Year:	1927
Month:	3
Day:	1
Hour:	10
Min:	30
Sec:	0
Calendar:	Gregorian
Time:	Zone
GMT:	-
GMT Hour:	5
GMT Min:	0
Daylight saving:	☐
Long Deg:	74
Long Min:	0
Direction:	● W ○ E
Lat Deg:	40
Lat Min:	42
Direction:	● N ○ S
Altitude of Place:	100 m
Place:	New York, NY

In the middle column, below the pull-down that says Gregorian, make sure your choose *Zone* for almost all modern charts, which use standard time zones. For birth data prior to the use of time zones, choose *Local Mean* here.

Belafonte was born in New York City which is Eastern Standard Time, 5 hours earlier than Greenwich time. For this chart GMT is marked as minus 5 hours. If Daylight Savings time applies, you can use the standard 5 hour time zone offset and check the Daylight Savings box, or you can leave Daylight Savings unchecked and adjust the time zone offset to 4 hours.

Here is Belafonte's birth chart image from Morinus. The bounds are the irregularly sized areas near the outside of the ring. The Ascendant, marked as a left arrow, is currently in the bounds of Jupiter. Moving counter-clockwise, the next bound after that is Venus, then Mars, and so on. The dignity of face is shown in the ring inside the bounds, in which the signs are divided into three sections of ten degrees each.

In the chart pictured below the Midheaven is in Aquarius, in the bounds of Jupiter and the face of Mercury.

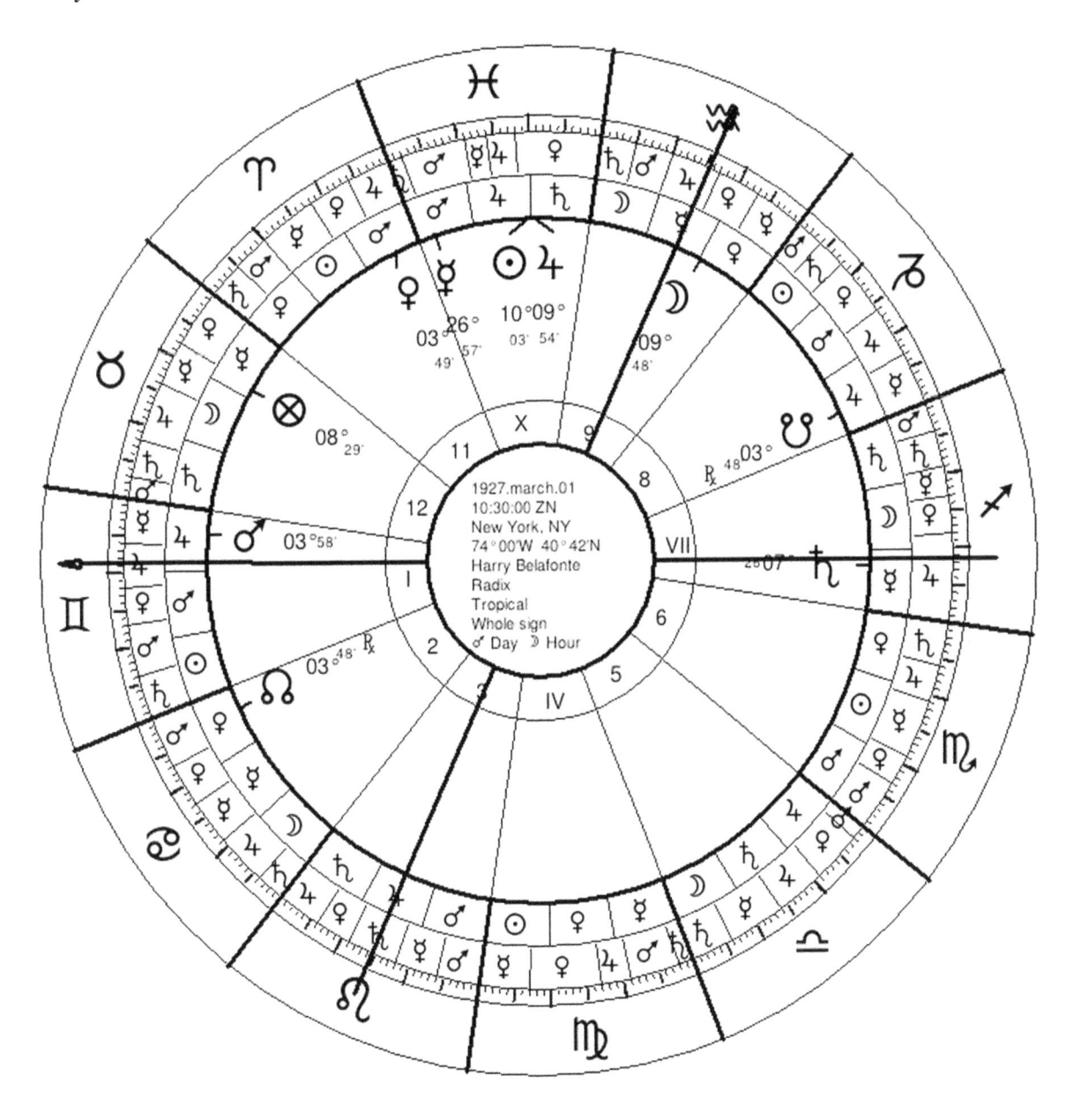

Primary Directions

Go to the Options menu and choose Primary Directions. Set them up as shown here.

149

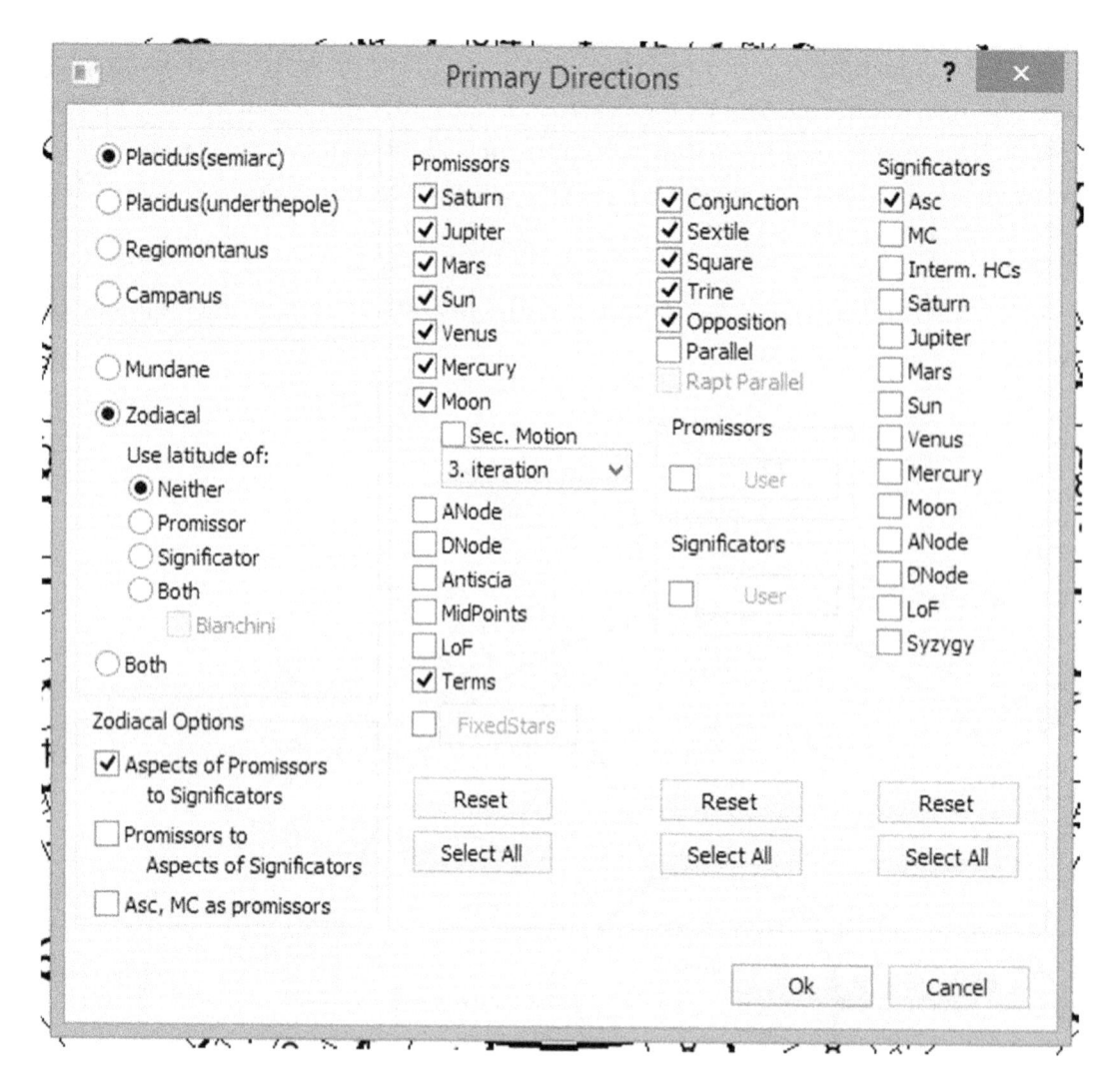

Set the left column up as shown - Placidus(semiarc), Zodiacal using latitude of neither, and at bottom, aspects of Promissors to Significators

In the second column, under Promissors, select all the planets, and also select bounds (listed as Terms, the other name for this dignity) in the second column. Note that you can also do directions to the lunar nodes or antiscia points. Finally, and most important, select Terms.

In the third column select all aspects except Parallel. The traditional version of Morinus has only the major Ptolemaic aspects.

The right column is where you check the point or points you wish to direct. In this example the Ascendant is checked in the right column as the only significator - I suggest you start there. This right column is the only one you need to adjust going forward.

When you run the primary directions from the Tables menu, the program has you choose 25 year blocks of time. Or, if you just choose a range of 1 to 100, you can get the entire set of distributions for a lifetime in a single listing. If you right-click on the resulting listing, it can be saved as a bitmap or as plain text.

The default is to choose only direct, following the movement of the zodiac through the day. You also have the option of doing converse directions, which rotates the wheel in the opposite direction.

Here is an image of the directions for the most active period of Belafonte's professional life as a singer. In the first column, the glyph of a sign is shown each time the Ascendant moves into a different bound. The other line items show an aspect symbol each time the Ascendant makes a Ptolemaic aspect to a planet. The D with the arrow in the second column means these are Direct - there is another style of directions called Converse which moves in the opposite direction. The third column shows the directed point (in this case the Ascendant), the fourth column shows the number of degrees of arc the point has moved from the natal chart, and the final column shows the date this direction corresponds to.

Refer back to the wheel of the chart while you read this listing, and pick out the bounds and aspects. That will help you understand the listing.

♋ ♂	D →	Asc	21.156	1948.04.26	On April 26, 1948 the distribution entered the bounds of Mars, in the sign Cancer. In July 1952 the Ascendant made a square aspect to Venus, which became the partner planet. in February 1956 the Ascendant moved into the bounds of Venus, with Venus still the partner planet. In July 1959 the Ascendant made a trine aspect to Jupiter, which then became the partner.
□ ♀	D →	Asc	25.386	1952.07.19	
♋ ♀	D →	Asc	28.982	1956.02.23	
△ ♃	D →	Asc	32.343	1959.07.05	
△ ☉	D →	Asc	32.514	1959.09.05	
♋ ☿	D →	Asc	35.976	1963.02.20	
♋ ♃	D →	Asc	43.19	1970.05.09	
♋ ♄	D →	Asc	51.825	1978.12.27	
△ ☿	D →	Asc	53.018	1980.03.07	
♌ ♃	D →	Asc	56.838	1984.01.01	

Here is the text file showing the same information as in the above screen snap for the first four lines. (The "Z" stands for Zodiacal directions. - there is another form of directions called Mundane.)

Z (Cancer)Mars D --> Asc 21.156134 1948.04.26   Z (Cancer)Venus D --> Asc 28.982617 1956.02.23
Z Square Venus D --> Asc 25.386705 1952.07.19   Z Trine Jupiter D --> Asc 32.343921 1959.07.05

All lines with a sign name in parentheses indicate moving into a bound. All other lines indicate an aspect or conjunction, which means the partner planet changing at that point.

The Cycle of the Year with Morinus - Profections and Revolutions

Once you have a natal chart loaded and calculated, Morinus also does a very nice job creating charts for revolutions - for solar, or any other planet - and profections. Both can be accessed from the Charts menu.

Instructions for Running a Solar Return

On the menu, go to Charts -> Revolutions - this opens a dialog box for you to enter the date. The one little quirk to be careful of here is that the program gives you a starting date the day AFTER the birth date, searching forward in time from there. I usually put it a day or two prior to the birthday for the year you want.

Expand the image. You can right click on the image to save it as a file - it is a good idea to make the image large on the screen to get a larger saved image.

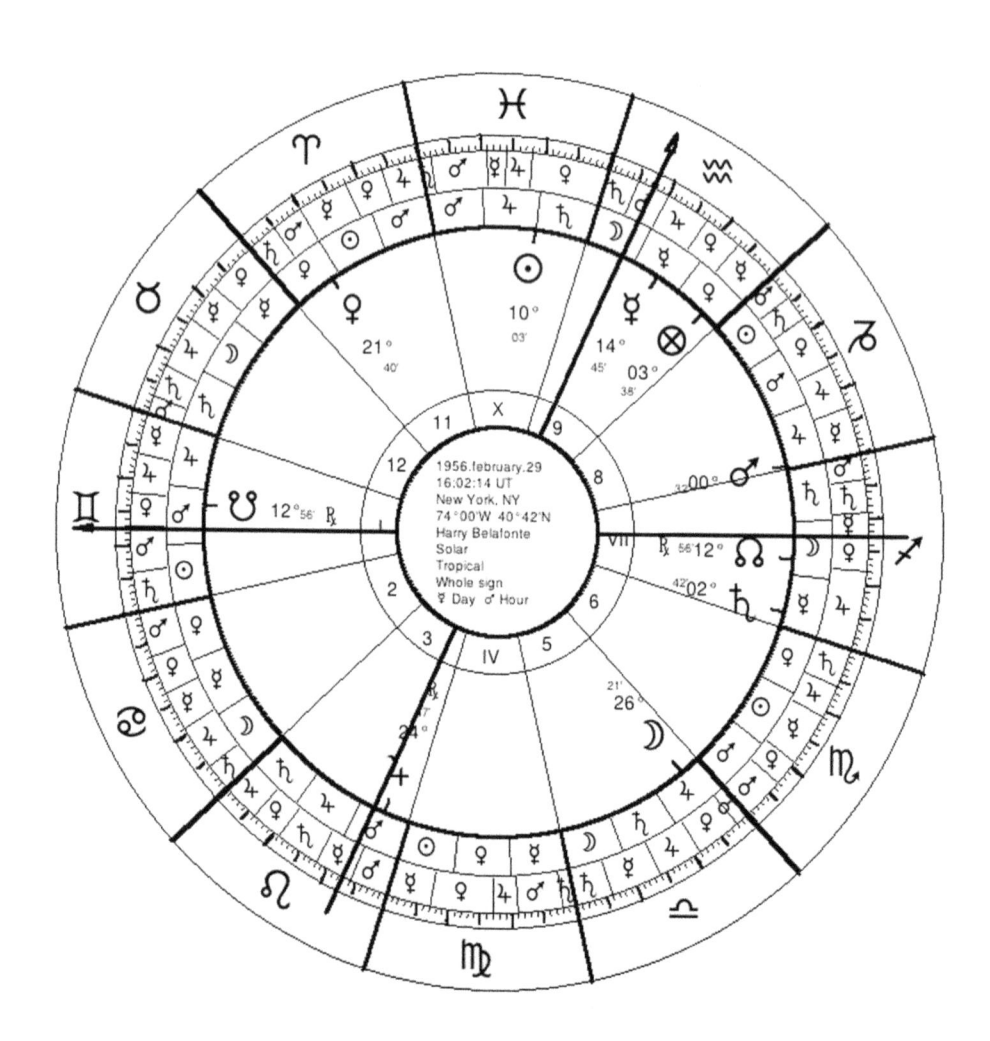

Right click on the chart, and choose Window -> Comparison, and you will see a bi-wheel. This gives the natal chart in the inner ring, and the planets of the Solar Return in the outer ring, as shown below.

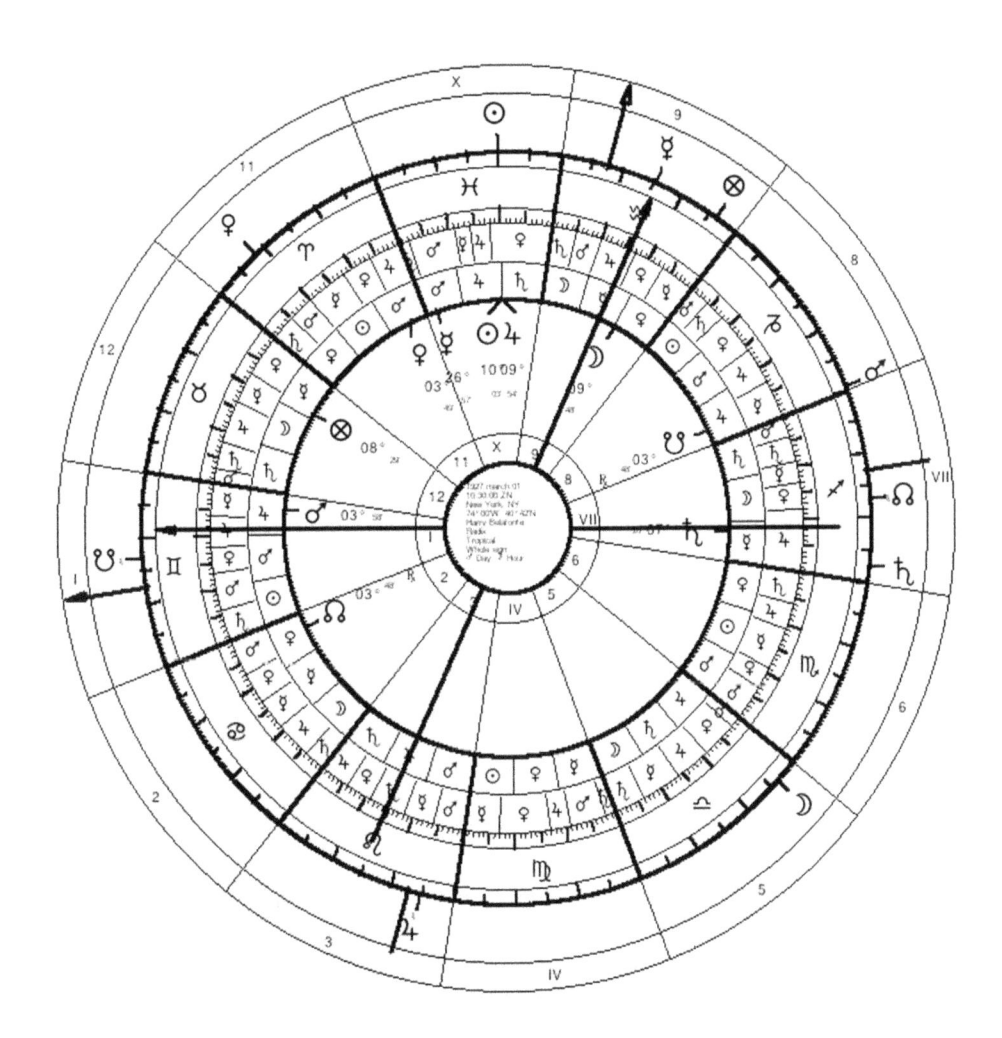

Directing a point around the Solar Return chart over a year.

Right click on the solar return chart and choose, Directions-> direct. This gives a listing of the chosen directed point around the solar return for the year. The format is the same as for the regular direction through the bounds, but the point moves the entire 360 degrees of the circle in the course of the year. It is the annual equivalent of the lifetime directions. Below is a sample - the solar return Ascendant starts in Mars bounds on March 1, moves to a sextile of Venus March 5, enters Saturn bounds on March 7, and so on.

Z Sextile Venus D --> Asc 4.312176 1956.03.05
Z (Gemini)Saturn D --> Asc 6.709430 1956.03.07
Z Sextile Jupiter D --> Asc 7.539264 1956.03.08
Z Trine Moon D --> Asc 9.173594 1956.03.09
Z (Cancer)Mars D --> Asc 13.095236 1956.03.13

Instructions for Running Profections

Go the Charts menu and select Profections. Choose the birth date for the year you want.

Along with the chart, you will see a little control panel pop-up, pictured below, that lets you advance the profection a year, a month, or a day at a time. This makes it easy to run profections for a series of years.

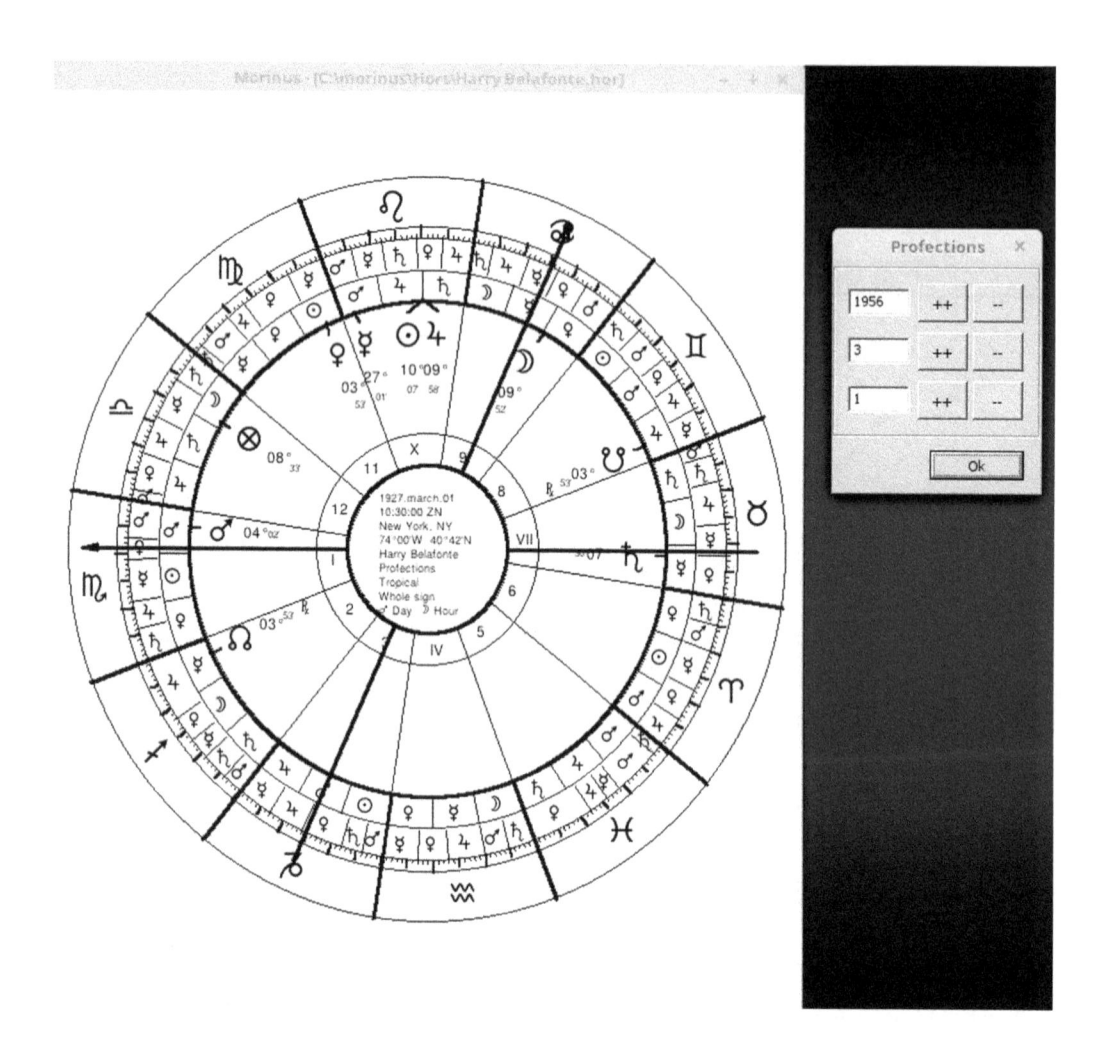

As with the solar return, you can right click on the wheel and choose window->comparison to get a bi-wheel with the natal in the center and profection around the outer edge. That image is not shown here since it has the same format as the solar return comparison wheel.

If you want to quickly check profections for a series of dates, go to the Tables menu and choose profections. You get a table like the following, that shows profections for the main 5 points for a series of years in groups of 12.

Mouse left click on the age cell to activate the Monthly Profections

Age	Date	Asc	MC	☉	☽	⊗
0	1927.03.01.	8°44'57" ♊	14°28'12" ♒	10°03'22" ♓	9°48'05" ♒	8°29'41" ♉
1	1928.03.01.	8°44'57" ♋	14°28'12" ♓	10°03'22" ♈	9°48'05" ♓	8°29'41" ♊
2	1929.03.01.	8°44'57" ♌	14°28'12" ♈	10°03'22" ♉	9°48'05" ♈	8°29'41" ♋
3	1930.03.01.	8°44'57" ♍	14°28'12" ♉	10°03'22" ♊	9°48'05" ♉	8°29'41" ♌
4	1931.03.01.	8°44'57" ♎	14°28'12" ♊	10°03'22" ♋	9°48'05" ♊	8°29'41" ♍
5	1932.03.01.	8°44'57" ♏	14°28'12" ♋	10°03'22" ♌	9°48'05" ♋	8°29'41" ♎
6	1933.03.01.	8°44'57" ♐	14°28'12" ♌	10°03'22" ♍	9°48'05" ♌	8°29'41" ♏
7	1934.03.01.	8°44'57" ♑	14°28'12" ♍	10°03'22" ♎	9°48'05" ♍	8°29'41" ♐
8	1935.03.01.	8°44'57" ♒	14°28'12" ♎	10°03'22" ♏	9°48'05" ♎	8°29'41" ♑
9	1936.03.01.	8°44'57" ♓	14°28'12" ♏	10°03'22" ♐	9°48'05" ♏	8°29'41" ♒
10	1937.03.01.	8°44'57" ♈	14°28'12" ♐	10°03'22" ♑	9°48'05" ♐	8°29'41" ♓
11	1938.03.01.	8°44'57" ♉	14°28'12" ♑	10°03'22" ♒	9°48'05" ♑	8°29'41" ♈

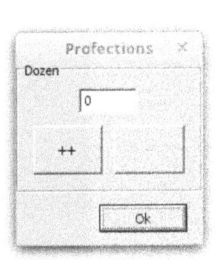

The ++ button in the little window on the right lets you move forward in blocks of 12 years at a time. This shows simply how profections work.

There is a further level of profections, that I do not cover in this book, that takes a single year and moves the profected sign around the wheel at the rate of one sign per month. With the above table, clicking on an age in the left column shows you the dates of the monthly profections.